THE LIGHT'S ON
AT SIGNPOST

THE FLASHMAN PAPERS
(IN CHRONOLOGICAL ORDER)

FLASHMAN
(Britain, India, and Afghanistan, 1839–42)

ROYAL FLASH
(England 1842–43, Germany 1847–48)

FLASHMAN'S LADY
(England, Borneo, and Madagascar, 1842–45)

FLASHMAN AND THE MOUNTAIN OF LIGHT
(Indian Punjab 1845–46)

FLASH FOR FREEDOM!
(England, West Africa, U.S.A. 1848–49)

FLASHMAN AND THE REDSKINS
(U.S.A. 1849–50 and 1875–76)

FLASHMAN AT THE CHARGE
(England, Crimea, and Central Asia, 1854–55)

FLASHMAN IN THE GREAT GAME
(Scotland, India, 1856–58)

FLASHMAN AND THE ANGEL OF THE LORD
(India, South Africa, U.S.A., 1858–59)

FLASHMAN AND THE DRAGON
(China, 1860)

Also by George MacDonald Fraser

MR AMERICAN
THE PYRATES
THE CANDLEMASS ROAD
BLACK AJAX

SHORT STORIES

THE GENERAL DANCED AT DAWN
McAUSLAN IN THE ROUGH
THE SHEIKH AND THE DUSTBIN

HISTORY

THE STEEL BONNETS:
*The Story of the Anglo-Scottish
Border Reivers*

AUTOBIOGRAPHY

QUARTERED SAFE OUT HERE
THE HOLLYWOOD HISTORY OF THE WORLD

THE LIGHT'S ON
AT SIGNPOST

GEORGE MacDONALD FRASER

HarperCollins*Publishers*

HarperCollins*Publishers*
77–85 Fulham Palace Road,
Hammersmith, London w6 8jb

www.**fire**and**water**.com

This paperback edition 2003

1 3 5 7 9 8 6 4 2

First published in Great Britain by
HarperCollins*Publishers* 2002

Copyright © George MacDonald Fraser 2002

George MacDonald Fraser asserts the moral right to
be identified as the author of this work

ISBN 0 00 713647 1

Set in PostScript Linotype Minion with ITC Garamond
and Castellar MT display by
Rowland Phototypesetting Ltd,
Bury St Edmunds, Suffolk

Printed in Great Britain by
Clays Ltd, St Ives plc

CONTENTS

LIST OF ILLUSTRATIONS   viii
PREFACE   xi
FOREWORD   xiii

SHOOTING SCRIPT 1
"One for All, and All for Fun"   1

ANGRY OLD MAN 1
Fourth Afghan   17

INTERLUDE
Law for Sale?   24

SHOOTING SCRIPT 2
With the Tudors in Hungary   26

ANGRY OLD MAN 2
The Westminster Farce   44

INTERLUDE
Orcs and Goblins   53

SHOOTING SCRIPT 3
*Gene Hackman Should Have
Blown up Vesuvius*   55

ANGRY OLD MAN 3
The Europe Fiasco   66

INTERLUDE
Act of Settlement   80

SHOOTING SCRIPT 4
"Not a Bad Bismarck, Was I?"   81

v

ANGRY OLD MAN 4
The Day of the Pygmies   88

INTERLUDE
A Writer, a Soldier,
a Comedian, a Football Hero,
a Beverly Hillbilly   94

ANGRY OLD MAN 5
The Truth that Dare not
Speak its Name   104

INTERLUDE
To Scotland, with Love   120

SHOOTING SCRIPT 5
"Phlam with Cheese" for the Stars   130

ANGRY OLD MAN 6
Crime and Punishment   142

INTERLUDE
No One Did it Better   157

SHOOTING SCRIPT 6
"Thirty Years in Hollywood
and You can still Learn
Something New"   160

INTERLUDE
Pictures of Russia   176

ANGRY OLD MAN 7
The Defeat of the British Army   180

INTERLUDE
Special Relationship   194

SHOOTING SCRIPT 7
Everywhere but Hong Kong   198

ANGRY OLD MAN 8
How to Encourage Race Hatred   213

INTERLUDE
Not According to Lady Bracknell   233

SHOOTING SCRIPT 8
"You Want to Put Bond in a
Gorilla Suit?"   234

ANGRY OLD MAN 9
Dumbing Down, Down, Down . . .   247

INTERLUDE
The Perfect Premier   263

SHOOTING SCRIPT 9
"Forget Fellini!"   264

ANGRY OLD MAN 10
This Unsporting Life   272

SHOOTING SCRIPT 10
The Ones that Got Away   278

FOR THE RECORD   287

CONCLUSION   313
INDEX   319

LIST OF ILLUSTRATIONS

On location in Spain for *The Return of the Musketeers*. (**Entertainment/ Timothy Burrill Productions/Fildebroc-Cine5/Iberoamericana. Produced by Pierre Spengler. Directed by Richard Lester**)

The leading players in *The Prince and the Pauper*. (**International Film Production/Ilya and Alexander Salkind. Produced by Pierre Spengler. Directed by Richard Fleischer**)

A trio of brilliant directors: Richard Lester; Richard Fleischer. (**Photo: BFI Collections**); Guy Hamilton (**Photo: The Kobal Collection/United Artists**)

Two faces of Steve McQueen. As Hilts in *The Great Escape*. (**UA/Mirisch/ Alpha. Produced and directed by John Sturges. Photo: The Kobal Collection/Mirisch/United Artists**). As Stockmann in (Ibsen's *An Enemy of the People*. (**First Artists. Produced and directed by George Schaefer. Photo: The Kobal Collection/Solar/1st Artists**)

"The Coleys", Ethel and John Colman Smith

"Beery", Walter Barradell-Smith

Kath and GMF as reporters in Regina, Saskatchewan, 1949

Malcolm McDowell, Britt Ekland, Oliver Reed, Henry Cooper and Alan Bates in *Royal Flash*. (**TCF/Two Roads. Produced by David V. Picker and Denis O'Dell. Directed by Richard Lester**)

The members of *Force Ten from Navarone*. (**Columbia/AIP/Guy Hamilton. Produced by Oliver A. Unger. Photo: BFI Collections**)

Burt Lancaster with Nick Cravat in *The Crimson Pirate*. (**Warner/Norma. Produced by Harold Hecht. Directed by Robert Siodmak. Photo: BFI Collections**)

Brigitte Nielsen and Arnold Schwarzenegger in *Red Sonja*. (**MGM-UA/

Thorn EMI. Produced by Christian Ferry. Directed by Richard Fleischer. Photo: BFI Collections)

Roger Moore in clown makeup in *Octopussy*. (Eon/Danjaq. Produced by Albert R. Broccoli. Directed by John Glen. Photo: BFI Collections)

Roger Moore making the presentation to Cubby Broccoli at the Academy Awards (Associated Press)

What all the wise men promised has not happened, and what all the damned fools said would happen has come to pass.　　　　　LORD MELBOURNE

It is most expedient for the preservation of the state that the rights of sovereignty should never be granted out to a subject, still less to a foreigner, for to do so is to provide a stepping-stone whereby the grantee becomes himself the sovereign.

JEAN BODIN, *Six Books of the Commonwealth*, 1576

Any writer or journalist who wants to retain his integrity finds himself thwarted by the general drift of society rather than by active persecution.　　　　　GEORGE ORWELL

Oh, I'll keep it to myself – until the water reaches my lower lip, and then I'm going to mention it to somebody!

Jack Lemmon as Professor Fate in
The Great Race, screenplay by Arthur Ross

When this book was published in hard covers last year, I was not surprised that almost all the reviews in the British press were unfavourable. I had expected that my old-fashioned views would get a fairly hostile reception, but the bitterness of some notices did astonish me; I hadn't realised how offensive plain truth can be to the politically correct, how enraged they can be by its mere expression, and how deeply they detest the values and standards respected fifty years ago, and which dinosaurs of my generation still believe in, God help us.

That belief was evident in readers' reactions to the book, which were the exact opposite of critical opinion. I've never received such wholehearted and generous support; for the first time in thirty years as a professional writer I had to fall back on the form letter, a printed card thanking readers for writing, apologising because I couldn't reply personally to them all. (In a footnote to the book I had given warning that this might happen, but in came the approving tide nonetheless.)

Most of the letters came from the older generation, but by no means all. I was made aware that among the middle-aged and people in their twenties and thirties there is a groundswell of anger and deeply-felt frustration at the damage done to Britain by so-called reformers and dishonest politicians who hardly bother to conceal their contempt for the public's wishes. And that is why I am writing this preface, to assure all those who have agreed, by and large, with the views expressed in this book, that they are not alone in some reactionary minority, as plainly many thought they were. A general reluctance to speak out for what they believed to be right, a fear of being thought out of step with politically correct fashion, has led many people to think that they were voices muttering to themselves in the wilderness.

Well, you are not. There are more of you out there than you realise – very many more, perhaps even a majority.

That's all. I just wanted you to know. I should add only that although events have marched quickly during the past year, I have left the original text unaltered except for one or two minor literary corrections. The world is not all that different, and my views have not changed. Indeed, the gratifying support (and the virulence of opposition) have only confirmed them.

G. M. F.

FOREWORD

On the Isle of Man, where I am lucky enough to live, we have a saying: "The light's on at Signpost". I'll explain it presently; sufficient for the moment to say that it's a catchphrase about the island's famous TT (Tourist Trophy) race, the blue riband of world motor-cycling, and the nearest thing to the Roman circus since the hermit Telemachus got the shutters put up at the Colosseum. Riders come from the ends of the earth every June to compete on the thirty-seven-mile course, hurtling their machines over mountain, through town and village, round hairpin bends, along narrow, twisting stone-walled roads where the slightest misjudgment means death at 150 m.p.h., and on straights where they dice for position with each other and the Grim Reaper.

Inevitably there are deaths. Never a year passes but the TT or its companion races claim their victims, but still they keep coming, for it is the ultimate test of the road racer's skill and daring, and the man who wins it, be he an Italian six-times victor with a mighty organisation behind him, or a humble garage mechanic, has nothing more to prove. He is the best in the world, and needs his head examined. But there it is: the TT will last as long as there are crazy men on machines – Germans, Italians, Irish, Swedes, Japanese, and every variety of Briton, including of course the Manx themselves.

That the race was world famous I had always known, but I was astonished when the late Steve McQueen, of Hollywood fame, who had never been to the island, talked of the TT course with the familiarity of old acquaintance. He was motor-cycle daft, to be sure, and even kept a bike, an old Indian, in the living-room of his penthouse in the Beverly Wilshire Hotel, and at some time, somehow, he had plainly informed himself about the course and its more celebrated features and hazards – the Verandah, Ramsey hairpin, Creg-ny-Baa, the Highlander where the bikes touch 190 m.p.h., and the rest – and I was properly impressed. He must come to the island, I said, and ride the course for himself: thirty-seven miles in less than twenty minutes.

He considered this in that calculating blue-eyed silence which captivated audiences round the world, smiled his famous tight-lipped smile, and shook his head. "I'm forty-eight, remember. You can drive me round."

I never had the chance. The light was already on for him at Signpost – and it is time to explain the saying. The TT is six circuits of the course, and each time a rider passes Signpost Corner, about a mile from the end of the circuit, a light flashes on at his slot on the grand-stand scoreboard, to let spectators know he has almost finished a lap; when it lights up on his last lap, they know he is nearly home, the end is in sight, as it was for McQueen that afternoon when I said good-bye to him in Beverly Hills. Not long after, he was dead, and the movie in which he was to star, and which I had written, was never made. But whenever I hear that saying, which the Manx, with their Viking sense of humour, apply to life as well as to the TT, I think of him, chewing tobacco and spitting neatly into a china mug, making notes in his small, precise writing as we went through the script.

But that's by the way for the moment, and I have dropped McQueen's name at this point because I know that nothing grips the public, reading or viewing, like a film star – and we shall meet him again, and many others, later on. And another reason for introducing that fine Manx saying is that it applies to me, too; at seventy-seven, my light is on at Signpost – mind you, I hope to take my time over the last mile, metaphorically pushing my bike like those riders who run out of fuel within sight of the finish.

So I'm turning aside from the stories with which I've been earning a living for more than thirty years, to tell something of my own. In itself it may not interest more than a few people (those kind readers of my books and viewers of my screenplays who have written to me, perhaps), but apart from telling a bit of my own tale there is something else I want to do, not just for myself, but for all those others whose lights are on at Signpost, that huge majority of a generation who think as I do, but whose voices, on the rare occasions when they are raised, are lost in the clamour of the new millennium.

We are the old people (not the senior citizens or the timeously challenged, but the old people), and if I am accused of lunatic delusions of grandeur for presuming to speak for a generation, I can only retort that someone's got to, because nobody has yet, not in full, and if we're not careful we'll all have gone down the pipe without today's generation (or any other) getting a chance not just to hear our point of view, but perhaps to understand how and why we came to hold it. (Very well, *my* point of view, but I know that countless older people, and not a few younger ones, share it, for whenever I've had the chance to express it, in has come the tide of letters*, their purport being: Thank God somebody's said it at last!)

It's not a view that will find much favour with what are called the chattering classes, or the politically correct, or the self-appointed leaders of fashionable opinion, or so-called progressives, or liberals in general. (Actually, I'm a liberal myself, as well as a reactionary. I'm often surprised at just how liberal I can be; I'll have to watch it.) It is a view that would have seemed perfectly normal and middle-of-the-road in my childhood, which makes it anathema today, when mis-called "Victorian values" are derided, and the permissive society has turned a scornful back on so many things that my generation respected and even venerated.

Such elderly hand-wringing is not new. Old folk in every genera-

---

* I am taking this opportunity to thank any readers who may be kind enough to write to me about this book, whether in approval or deep damnation, because I doubt if I'll have the energy to reply to their letters. I'm not being churlish, but life's too short, honestly, and the postage costs a fortune.

tion since the Stone Age have seen huge changes, for better or worse, but none in Britain has seen the country so altered, so turned upside down, as we children born in the twenty years between the great world wars. In our adult lives Britain's entire national spirit, its philosophy, its values and standards, have changed beyond belief, and probably no country on earth has experienced such a revolution in thought and outlook and behaviour in so short a space. Other lands have known what might seem to be greater upheavals, the result of wars and revolutions and invasions, but these do not compare with the experience of a country which passes in less than a lifetime from being the mightiest empire in history, governing a quarter of mankind, to being a feeble little offshore island whose so-called leaders have lost the will and the courage, indeed the ability, to govern at all.

This is not a lament for past imperial glory, although I can regret its inevitable passing, nor is it the raging of a die-hard Conservative. I loathe all political parties, which I regard as inventions of the devil, and if I inclined to vote Tory thirty years ago it was out of no admiration for them but simply to keep the incompetent wreckers out. We have no real political parties in the Isle of Man, thank heaven. Having had a parliament from a time when Westminster was a mere geographical swamp and had not yet become a moral one, we know what democracy is, which unfortunates in mainland Britain and the United States most certainly do not. It follows that we regard Westminster and Washington politics with revulsion and contempt.

But I am deeply concerned for the United Kingdom and its future. I can view the Signpost light with fair equanimity, I've looked death in the eye before, and now I have only a past, a little future, and no great care on my own account. But England and Scotland are my countries still, they are the lands where my children and grandchildren live, and I care most damnably about what lies ahead for them.

I look at the old country as it was in my youth, and as it is

xvi

today, and frankly, to use a fine Scots word, I'm scunnered. I don't despair altogether, because I have studied enough history to know that nothing is forever, but I and my generation have to shake our heads in disbelief, ask ourselves how it happened, and wonder if it can ever be repaired.

Who would have believed, fifty years ago, that by the end of the century it would have been deemed permissible, by the BBC of all people, to call the Queen "a bitch", or that the foulest language and vilest pornography would be commonplace on television, or that we would have a government legislating to break up the United Kingdom, barely bothering to conceal their republican bent, guilty of atrocious war crimes, rashly declaring war on Muslim terrorism which did not threaten us, while crawling abjectly to the IRA and even assisting it by releasing murderers from prison, making a criminal out of an honest shopkeeper because he sold in pounds and ounces, and jailing for life a decent householder who dared to defend his home by shooting a burglar, refusing to take any effective action against violent crime, encouraging sexual perversion by lowering the age of consent and drug abuse by relaxing the law on cannabis, legislating for women to serve in the front line (while the gallant warriors of Westminster sit snug and safe), showing themselves dead to any notion of patriotism and even discouraging the use of the word "British", falling over themselves to destroy our institutions simply because they are frightened of offending hostile aliens, seeking to deny the right of habeas corpus, pandering to the bigotry of black racists and encouraging racial strife by their timid stupidity, letting foreign interests wreck our farming and fishing industries, and allowing the children of those wonderful people who gave us Belsen and Dachau a vital say in making our law and undermining our constitution . . .

That's what we fought two world wars for? What millions of precious British lives were lost for? That's a land fit for heroes and their families?

This, of course, can all be patronisingly dismissed as the raving of a blimpish Right-wing* dinosaur. Not denied, though, because it is all patently true, and therefore poison to the politically correct. The very core of their philosophy is a refusal to accept truth, to look it squarely in the face, unpalatable as it may be. Political correctness is about denial, usually in the weasel circumlocutory jargon which distorts and evades and seldom stands up to honest analysis.

You conclude that I do not care for political correctness, but before they bury me under a tide of enlightened derision, there is a question which even a Liberal Democrat or *Guardian* reader might care to consider. It is this: why do I, and millions of my contemporaries, think the way we do? It doesn't profit us. If all the wrongs that I have listed were righted tomorrow, it would bring us no material advantage, put nothing in our pockets, serve no ulterior purpose. Setting aside our care for our descendants, we are as disinterested as it is possible for people to be: we don't seek election, or power, or wealth, we have no great personal ambitions left to realise or any compulsion to trample on our fellows' fingers in a mad scramble up the ladder. For we are yesterday's people, the over-the-hill gang, the light is really blazing for us at Signpost, and we seek no more than what we believe to be our country's good.

Perhaps we have it closer to heart than younger folk do. Perhaps we value Britain more because we had to fight for it tooth and nail, and saved it and the world from evil and slavery and a new Dark Age, whereas later generations have had it handed to them on a plate, welfare-insulated and (sorry to have to say it) rather spoiled

---

* Just for interest, there is a mistaken belief that the terms Left and Right in politics originated in the French National Assembly during the Revolution. In fact, Edward Gibbon, writing before the Revolution, used the words to indicate the radical and conservative sides in Church politics, as the following quotation from his *Decline and Fall* makes clear: "The bishops . . . were attached to the faith of Cyril, but in the face of the synod, in the heat of the battle, the leaders . . . passed from the right to the left wing, and decided the victory by this seasonable desertion."

and not knowing how well off they are. But whatever of that, please believe that our motives are respectable, and our convictions honestly held. We are not without understanding; we know, from hard experience, that every generation thinks itself the repository of all wisdom, and imagines that the progress of mankind is one of continuous improvement, and that whatever may be wrong with today, things are still a hell of a lot better than they were.

They are not. They are worse, and like to get worse still. Some things, indeed, are wonderfully better: the new miracles of surgery (which have kept me alive who would otherwise have handed in my dinner-pail), public attitudes to the disabled, the health and wellbeing of children (how wonderful they look), intelligent concern for the environment (hideous word, but necessary), the massive strides in science and technology (though I hate to think what Thomas Carlyle would have made of the internet and the mobile phone). Yes, there are material blessings and benefits innumerable which were unknown in our youth.

But much has deteriorated. To one of my generation, who remembers pre-war, war-time, and post-war (as most of the present population and their governors do not) and who has travelled widely and now lives, in a real sense, overseas, the United Kingdom begins to look more and more like a Third World country, shabby, littered, ugly, running down, without purpose or direction, misruled by a typical Third World government, corrupt, incompetent and undemocratic. My generation has seen the decay of ordinary morality, standards of decency, sportsmanship, politeness, respect for the law, the law itself, family values, politics and education and religion, the very character of the British – oh, how blimpish this must sound to modern ears, how out of date, how blind to the "need for change" in the new millennium!

Well, perhaps it is. We elderly pessimists may be wrong. God knows, if we had a pound for every mistake we've made, you could keep the pension. But, if we are old, we are experienced, we have been about, and seen things, and perhaps learned lessons that our juniors do not know ... yet. In comparing past and present we have an advantage denied the young: we were there *then*, and we are here *now*.

Certainly we tend to be resistant to change, on the whole, but that is because we have learned the hard way that change for its own sake is not a good idea,* and that if something works more or less satisfactorily, it is best not to alter it without long and careful thought. Above all, we have learned Cromwell's wisdom:

"In the bowels of Christ, think it possible you may be mistaken."

Oh, we were young once, and just as cocksure and clueless as younger people today – but we were luckier then than they are now because the means of self-destruction in our time were much more limited, and we laboured under fewer disadvantages.

It follows that I am sorry for the present generation, with their permissive society, their anything-goes philosophy, and their generally laid-back, in-yer-face attitude (sorry, attichood). They regard themselves as a completely liberated society, when the fact is that they are less free than any generation before them since the Middle Ages. Indeed, there may never have been such an enslaved generation, in thrall to hang-ups, taboos, restrictions, and oppressions unknown to their ancestors. (To say nothing of being neck-deep in debt, thanks to a money-lenders' economy.)

They won't believe, of course, that they don't know what freedom is, and that we were freer by far fifty years ago – yes, with conscription, censorship, direction of labour, rationing, and shortages of practically everything that nowadays is regarded as essential to enjoyment, we still had a liberty beyond modern understanding. How so? Because we had other freedoms, the really important ones, that are denied the youth of today.

We could say what we liked; they can't. We were not subject to

---

* To quote the wise old judge: "Reform? Reform? Are things not bad enough as they are?"

the aggressive pressure of special-interest minority groups; they are. We had no worries about race or sexual orientation; they have (boy, do they ever!) We could, and did, differ from fashionable opinion with impunity, and would have laughed political correctness to scorn (had our society been weak and stupid enough to let it exist); they daren't. We had available to us an education system, public and private, which was the envy of the world; we had little reason to fear being mugged or raped (killed in war, maybe, but that was an acceptable hazard); our children could play in street and country in safety; we had not been brainwashed into displays of bogus grief in the face of tragedy, or into a compensation culture that insists on scapegoats and huge pay-outs for non-existent wrongs; we had few problems with bullies because society knew how to deal with bullying, and was not afraid to punish it in ways which would send today's progressives into hysterics; we did not know the stifling tyranny of a liberal establishment determined to impose its views, and more and more beginning to resemble Orwell's Ministry of Truth.

And we didn't know what an Ecstasy tablet was. God, we were lucky. But above all, perhaps, we knew who we were, and we lived in the knowledge that certain values and standards held true, and that our country, with all its faults and need for reforms, was sound at heart.

Not any more, and we wonder where it went wrong. Speaking from a fairish knowledge of British history and governance, I find it difficult to identify a time when the country was as badly governed as it has been in the last fifty years. I know about Addington and the Cabal and Aberdeen and North but they really look a pretty decent and competent lot when compared with the trash that has infested Westminster since 1945. Of course there have been honourable exceptions; I speak of the generality, and I am almost as disenchanted with Conservative as I am with Labour. Between them they have produced the two worst Prime Ministers in our history (and

xxi

what bad luck it has been that they have both fallen within the last thirty years). They are, of course, Heath and Blair. The harm that these two have done to Britain is incalculable, and almost certainly irreparable.

Whether the public can be blamed for letting them pursue their ruinous policies is debatable; short of assassination there is little that people can do when their political masters have forgotten the true meaning of the democracy of which they are forever prating, are determined to have their way at all costs, and hold public opinion in contempt.

Does it matter whether today's and future generations know what the overwhelming majority of their parents and grandparents believed and valued? Probably not; it is a fact of life that after a certain age no one is taken seriously, and an era in which the official wisdom is that history is bunk is not going to pay much heed to a reactionary eccentric like me. But I've written it anyway, for the reason that I've written all my books: simply because I want to. It's the best of reasons. Dr Johnson, who said many wise things, could talk tripe with the best of them on occasion, as when he said that no man but a blockhead ever wrote except for money.

What follows is not one long die-hard bellyache, however. It contains some autobiography of one who has been a newspaperman, soldier, encyclopedia salesman (briefly), novelist, and historian, and because, as I said earlier, I know the fascination the film world exerts, my reminiscences of almost thirty years, on and off, as a writer in the movie business. These last will not be sensational or denigratory; I liked, almost without exception, the great ones of the cinema whom I met and worked with, actors, actresses, directors, producers, moguls, and that great legion of technicians, experts, and fixers without whom films wouldn't get made.

But if I have no exposés, no juicy scandals, it may be that film buffs will still find some interest in Rex Harrison's enthusiasm for lemonade, Arnold Schwarzenegger's technique with head-waiters,

Federico Fellini's inability to master his office burglar alarm, Burt Lancaster's knack of losing car keys (and his possible descent from John of Gaunt), Guy Hamilton's system for assessing the rough-cut of a picture, Alex Salkind's consideration of Muhammad Ali for the role of Superman (it's a fact, I was there), and Oliver Reed's unique method of crossing the Danube – as well as his thoughts on Steve McQueen, and vice versa.

And other phenomena and personalities. Looking back on Holly-wood, Pinewood, Cinecittà, and various other studios and locations from Culver City to the mountaintops of Yugoslavia, I find some of it hard to believe, but I wouldn't have missed it for anything.

That, then, is the purport of this book, some of which was written as long as twenty-odd years ago, and has been waiting until I had time to finish it and arrange it in some sort of order; it's fairly random and haphazard, but at least it's true. It won't please every-one, I know, but those of ultra-liberal views can console themselves with the thought that my kind won't be around much longer, and then they can get on with wrecking civilisation in peace; in the meantime (assuming they've read this far) they should stick this volume back on the bookshop shelves and turn to recipes about aubergines or shrub cultivation or political memoirs.

For the rest of you, I hope I strike a chord, and that you find the movie stuff as much fun as I did.

SHOOTING SCRIPT 1

"One For All, and All for Fun"

MY CAR, an ageing Vauxhall Cresta, broke down within a few yards of the Sizzler Restaurant, Onchan, Isle of Man, where Richard Lester and I had been discussing my possible participation in a new film version of *The Three Musketeers*, which left us facing a walk of about a mile along Douglas Promenade to his hotel. No way to treat an eminent film director, and I wondered if he might be offended to the extent of getting another writer – I didn't know him in those days, or realise that to a man who'd made two movies with the Beatles, a mile walk along a surf-lashed coast in the middle of the night in late December was a mere bagatelle.

All I could suggest was that we push the rotten vehicle to the top of a nearby slope, and then leap in, free-wheeling downhill to a point reasonably close to his destination; he sportingly agreed, we heaved and strained and sprang aboard at the psychological moment, coasting down and fetching up, with Richard sitting patiently and me crying: "Roll, you bastard!" not far from home.

That was when I asked him (eager to know if he was still talking to me): "How d'you want the Musketeers – straight, or sent up?" I knew his reputation for offbeat comedy, and was by no means sure that I could give him what he wanted. He responded with perhaps the nicest reply a screenwriter ever received: "I want it written by the man who wrote *Flashman*."

I didn't know, then, just how astonishingly lucky I was. It was the week between Christmas and New Year, 1972, I had three novels, a history, and a short-story collection to my name, but my only experience of film writing was a script which I'd done from my short stories at the request of a rather eccentric Scots-American entrepreneur; like so many projects, it had died some distance short of pre-production.

Then Lester's offer came out of the blue. I knew him not only by reputation but because he had been engaged to direct a movie of my first novel, *Flashman*, but that, too, had been stillborn. I hadn't been involved in the script, so Lester's fastening on me, on the strength of my fiction alone, to write what promised to be a mammoth star-studded blockbuster, was a considerable leap of faith. I thought he was crazy; when I think of the chance he was taking, I still do, but I thank God he took it.

He flew across to the Isle of Man, we talked for about four hours, and while I can't remember anything of our discussion, I know that one thing, the vital thing, became clear: we were on the same wavelength, and that, from a writer's point of view, is something beyond price.

My first thought on meeting him was "Pied Piper", for he was tall and slim and restless and mercurial and

his sharp eyes twinkled
like a candle flame where salt is sprinkled.

I was to discover in the ensuing weeks that he thought like lightning, always questing for the joke, jumping from idea to idea at speed, imagining, improvising, full of enthusiasm, listening eagerly; eventually it would become like a game of ping-pong in which we batted notions to and fro, many of them well over the top – but it's a great truth of the film business that if you never go over the top you never get anywhere.

There are limits, of course. The original notion of a remake of the Musketeers had come, I believe, from Ilya Salkind, son of the great Alex, and one of the shrewdest ideas men in the business; he later came up with Superman, and frankly, if Ilya suggested a movie based on the Book of Job I'd think hard about it. Whether it was he who floated the notion of the Beatles as Dumas's band of adventurers, I can't say, but I imagine that was how Lester, as the Beatles' director, had come to be involved in the project. Fortunately (at least from my point of view) the casting of John, George, Paul, and Ringo went no further, and Lester was commissioned to come up with a more orthodox version.

At all events, he left me on the Isle of Man with a remit like a pipe-dream: one of the great classic adventures to adapt into four hours of film, the assurance that it was going to be a big-budget spectacular, a free hand to write as I wanted, and one hint about the quality of cast he was looking for: he wanted Richard Chamberlain for Aramis. That told me a lot; in most Musketeer movies the trio tend to blend into each other, three jolly swordsmen all for one and one for all, but Richard had hit on a man who was ideal for Dumas's priestly killer, cold, urbane, supercilious, and cruel. In doing the script I wrote little separate character studies for the actors, and I remember describing Aramis as quite the least likeable of the Musketeers.

The first half of the script, up to the Intermission, took me three weeks; Richard was enthusiastic, and then we went into heavy sessions in his office at Twickenham Studios, changing, editing, discarding, re-casting, and going through that long, painful and ultimately rewarding process which eventually transforms the first draft into the finished article. (But always, said Billy Wilder, keep that original draft by you, because you're sure as hell going to go back to it.)

There were occasions when our drama became a crisis: at one stage another writer, a household name, was asked to rewrite an early scene, but to my delight Lester flung it into the bin. Again, when my suggestions seemed to be falling on stony ground, I lost patience and offered to quit, at which he sighed and said: "You're being hysterical, George, in your own quiet way." Looking back, I'd say he was the ideal director for a novice screenwriter to work with, always encouraging, always optimistic, convincing me that I, and only I, could do his script for him.

We gradually developed a close harmony, with a kind of short-hand in which one had to speak only a few words for the other to latch on and elaborate; some scenes we had to discuss in detail, others hardly needed more than a few words. It's a strange process of cross-fertilisation, and I can only describe it by examples.

Dick wanted the Musketeers to be rather less stainless than they are usually portrayed; could they be seen stealing, say, in some novel way which would take the hard edge off the crime, perhaps diverting wine along a gutter by some ingenious device? I suggested a tavern fight in which their brawling would hide the fact that they were lifting all the food in sight – that was enough; we kicked around various ways of pinching comestibles, I sketched the scene out in script form, and Dick arranged and choreographed the whole thing as only he could.

The same thing happened when we were looking for a new way to stage a sword fight which would give opportunity for some knockabout action; I suggested staging it on a frozen pond, and Dick gave what I can only call a hungry grin and said: "Say no more!" And beyond writing a line or two for Porthos to bellow, and devising a piece of sadism for Aramis, I didn't need to.

It was fascinating, in writing a scene, to see what he would do with it. I had a perfectly tranquil meeting between the Queen of France and Buckingham which, for sheer novelty's sake, I set in the palace laundry – Lester doesn't miss chances like that, and concluded the lovers' meeting with the most colossal turn-up among the soap suds between the Musketeers and the palace guards. I had what I thought was another cute idea, with the King and Cardinal Richelieu eating canapés from a line of gold plates; pull back, and lo! each plate is on the head of a dwarf. A nice little visual effect, which Dick embellished by having the little buggers *talking*.

My technique then, and I followed it in later films, was to describe every shot in detail, the idea being to let the director and actors know exactly how I saw the thing. If they liked it, fine; if they didn't, it could be done another way. Some directors regard this as an intrusion on their territory; the best ones, the Lesters and the Fleischers and the Hamiltons, are all for it, because as experienced professionals they are always open to suggestions – which is not to say that they will always follow them. They have forgotten more about composition and camera angles and various kinds of shot than I will ever know, but there's no harm in giving them your ideas.

It could be very rewarding with Lester, because when the movie was shot and I saw the rough-cut, I realised a strange thing – he and I had very much the same visual sense, in that we saw things the same way. Time after time I would have envisaged a scene in my head – and there it was on the screen, "realised", as the French say, by Lester. One instance sticks in my mind: when D'Artagnan arrives at the Hotel Treville and becomes embroiled with one Musketeer after another, the overall scene is one of tremendous bustle and activity, with people jostling and hurrying and a fine confusion reigning. Dick approved my final draft (probably my fifth or sixth) and then suddenly asked: "What does it look like?" Off the top of my head I said: "Like a Breughel painted by Rembrandt." He smiled, nodded, said nothing – and shot it gloriously.

I can't be sure how long it took before the four-hour script was finished, but I know that Kathy and I were on holiday in Borneo in March, and Dick was phoning via Australia about something or other – I rather think it was to do with the scene in which the Musketeers rescue Christopher Lee from a firing squad commanded by Bob Todd, but I'm not sure. By that time the casting was coming together, and I was going about in a state of euphoric disbelief that I had written a movie for Heston, Dunaway, Welch, Reed, Finlay, Chamberlain, Lee, York, and a supporting cast which included the likes of Roy Kinnear, Geraldine Chaplin, Simon Ward, and Spike Milligan. (Someone remarked to me that I had managed to get Spike into bed with Raquel Welch, to which Spike retorted: "It's in the script, mate, not in my contract.")

I was at home working on a novel while Dick shot the picture, mostly in Spain, and did it in some incredibly short time – I'm not sure how long, but I know that as the weeks went by and his schedule shortened he was going at high speed, for he told me afterwards that with the second half he was "shooting the script", which I took to mean that he was not hanging about worrying about different ways of doing things.

The rough-cut of the first half was shown at Twickenham Studios on a bleak morning of early autumn, and I found myself sitting in the front row of the little viewing theatre with Michel Legrand, who was to do the music, while Dick and Ilya and Pierre Spengler, that prince of executive producers, sat behind. Michel had the devil of a cold, and made frequent forays into his attaché case, which contained, as he explained to me apologetically, "les medications".

He was plainly feeling awful, poor soul, and from time to time would give a deep groan, which was disconcerting at first because I wasn't sure whether it arose from his condition or what he was seeing on the screen. It didn't worry me long; I got lost in the magic.

Seeing a film that you've written is a weird experience, and one of the most thrilling I know. I'd hate to have to choose between it and holding the first copy of your first novel in your hand. I think the film probably has it by a nose – there they are, up there, the biggest names in the business, speaking the lines you've written, enacting the scenes you've constructed, and doing it far, far better than you'd imagined it could be done. You sit lost in admiration of Olly Reed's first glowering look and rasping opening line, of

Faye Dunaway's gorgeous languor, of Christopher Lee's splendid nonchalance, and of Michael York's bumbling heroics . . . and that's only the start. Forgive me if I warm still at the thought of them, and of the superb director who made it all happen.

You can even forgive the occasional lines changed or added during shooting, or the recast scenes, or the total surprise of something you just don't recognise, like the laundry fight, or those voice-over ad-libs which Dick so dearly loves (talking dwarves yet!) – if it's for the good of the movie, your only regret is that you didn't think of it yourself. From what I've heard, I've been lucky in having my stuff left pretty well alone, especially in the Musketeer movies; before that first screening Dick told me: "It's 85–90 per cent you," which in view of some of the horror stories about writers finding themselves entirely rewritten, was vastly reassuring.

I learned for the first time that morning that we might have not one movie with an intermission, but two separate films. My contract, when I came to look at it (I didn't sign until the job was half-done, which happens more often than you'd imagine, or used to) specified a film "or films". I had written the thing as one complete picture with an interval, and the entire script was there, all four hours of it, before shooting began.

I emphasise this because all kinds of garbled rumours get about in the film industry, and one of these was enshrined in Alex Salkind's obituary in a quality newspaper in 1997. It said, without qualification, that

> *halfway through the filming, Salkind realised that the director Richard Lester had shot twice as much film as he needed. Without telling the actors, he asked the writer George Mac-Donald Fraser to string together the spare scenes, with a few new ones thrown in, and so make a sequel.*

Twaddle. Likewise tripe. As I said in a letter to the editor, I never discussed the screenplay with Alex at all, and certainly never strung together "spare scenes with a few new ones thrown in, to make a sequel." The decision to split the picture into two, *The Three Musketeers* and *The Four Musketeers* (or, as they became known to the production team, the M3 and M4) was taken long after the script had been written, and for all I know, possibly after the whole thing was shot.

That not all the actors knew about this I didn't discover until the Paris premiere, which began with a dinner for the company at Fouquet's and concluded in the small hours with a deafening concert in what appeared to be the cellar of some ancient Parisian structure (the Hotel de Ville, I think). Charlton Heston knew, for when we discussed it before the dinner he shrugged philosophically and remarked: "Two for the price of one." Roy Kinnear did not, for Kathy and I shared a table with him and his wife, and Roy, a hearty trencherman, said earnestly that we had best get something inside us, as the film lasted four hours.

I assured him that only the first half was being shown, and he shook his head in admiration and said: "They don't care, do they?"

Alex's obituary was marginally nearer the truth when it said that a host of law suits had been brought against him by the actors, but that he had easily been able to settle out of the films' profits. In fact, I was told that only four of the cast complained, and that a settlement was reached; if there were more than four, then I was misinformed.

What was never in doubt was that the profits would be substantial. We knew we had a hit when the Paris audience gave a great roar of delight as the end titles came up with a caption reading: "Soon – The Four Musketeers" over a montage of shots from the second half, and they realised that they were going to get a sequel, the same show all over again, only different – which is what the ideal sequel should be. *Time* magazine called the M3 "a truly terrific movie", and this was confirmed when it was chosen as the Royal Command Film, with the Queen Mother attending the London premiere.

Kathy and I must have arrived early, for the only people in the reception room were Spike and Mrs Milligan, he visibly chafing at the wait ahead. "This," he cried, "is living! Let's go to Kettner's." We didn't, and presently he cheered up and was soon autographing waiters' jackets, to their immense delight. We stood in a great horseshoe to be presented to the Queen Mother, and the show was stolen spectacularly by Raquel Welch. I had met her for the first time at a press reception in the morning, and had been taken aback to be confronted by a small lady neatly attired in a sensible skirt and jacket and flat shoes, her hair severely dressed, who conversed soberly about the script; for the premiere she was transformed in a gown that appeared to have been sprayed on her, last in the presentation line and performing the most astonishing curtsey in the history of obeisance, sinking all the way down to floor level before the Queen Mother, and up again in one graceful movement. How that dress stood the strain, only her couturier knows.

It was a night to remember, but as usual my memories are fleeting: dancing with Kathy to the music of Joe Loss and almost colliding with Les Dawson; Milligan singing "Viva España!" Christopher Lee complacently indicating a rave review in one of the papers; Michael York smiling contentedly and pushing his hair back in a characteristic gesture; having dinner at a table with Frank Finlay, Mr and Mrs Simon Ward (whose London garden had been invaded by foxes), and Mrs Bertha Salkind, Alex's wife. You will gather that I have an erratic memory, and am incurably star struck, and always will be. Who isn't?

A year later the M4 did good box-office, but less than the M3, and the pundits were correspondingly less enthusiastic. It was certainly a darker film than the M3, largely because I had stuck to Dumas in Milady's murder of D'Artagnan's mistress, and the subsequent execution of Milady at the hands of the Musketeers. The sight of Faye Dunaway in a nun's habit strangling Raquel Welch with a rosary was strong stuff after the knockabout cheerfulness of the first film; so was her beheading, and whereas in the M3 the fights had been mostly light-hearted affairs, the final duel of the M4, fought in a church, and ending with Michael York transfixing Christopher Lee against a Bible open on a lectern, was stark and grim beyond the norm for a swashbuckler.

For what it's worth, I still like it better than the M3, because I do love to jolt an audience, or a reader, and the direction was Dick at his inspired best – I did not take seriously his remark after we'd watched the rough-cut on the little Moviola machine at Twickenham: "One of these days you're going to have to tell me what this film is about." He knew, all right, but it wasn't a conventional costume melodrama by any means. I value it for Oliver Reed's superb Athos, and the splendid playing of Faye Dunaway against him and Heston and Michael Gothard – the sequence in which Michael is turned from Milady's Puritan jailer into her lover is one of the best in the two pictures; it did in a few minutes what took Dumas a few chapters, thanks to the expertise of Faye and Michael and Dick. But they were all terrific, and as I once wrote in another book, no screenwriter was ever so fortunate, or more grateful.

One interesting exercise arose from the splitting of the production into two films: I had to write a prologue to the M4, for the benefit of anyone who hadn't seen the M3. This was done by having a Musketeer voice the prologue over clips from the end of the first film, and worked very well. What intrigued me was that I had to do *two* prologues, worded slightly differently, one spoken by Porthos (Frank Finlay) for British audiences, the other by Aramis (Richard Chamberlain) for the American market. Don't ask me why this was necessary, or why it was thought advisable to have Jean-Pierre Cassel's excellent King Louis dubbed by another actor. There is much about the movie business that I still don't understand – and that includes such controversial things as percentages which you think are going to accrue, but don't. I'm not complaining; I was incredibly lucky to be asked to write the M3 and the M4, and I'd have done them for nothing. Well, almost nothing.

Time magazine, like the other journals, was less rhapsodic about the M4, but still complimentary, reflecting that it would be nice to see D'Artagnan and Co. "just one more time." I thought privately that two Musketeer movies were about as much as the market would bear at the moment, but that it would be fun to do *Twenty Years After*, Dumas's sequel to the first book, one of these days – perhaps twenty years after. In fact, it was only fifteen years later that Pierre Spengler, who had been executive in charge of production on the first two films, suggested that we get together again and continue the saga with the Musketeers coming out of retirement to rescue King Charles I from Cromwell's executioners and face the wrath of Milady's vengeful offspring.

In the intervening years I had worked with Dick on *Royal Flash*, with Pierre on *Superman*, and with both on various other projects which (like so many productions) hadn't got the length of photography. I was elated at the thought of reprising all the fun of the first movies, and the three of us had the kind of good script meetings that you get only with old friends.

There were two hurdles to get over at the start, the first being that this was Pierre's production, the Salkinds weren't involved, and we weren't going to be able to use any footage from the M3 and M4, which would have been useful for scene-setting, though not vital. I fell back on the old stand-by beloved by scriptwriters and directors in pre-war days: an extended caption on the screen giving the historical background, which is never a happy device, plus a voice-over commentary from Michael York, which helped considerably.

The other problem was a blessing in disguise. Dumas having inconsiderately disposed of heroine and villainess in the first book, there is a decided shortage of interesting femininity in *Twenty Years After*. I solved this by turning Milady's avenging son into a daughter, a blonde and beautiful seductress who would also be a dab hand with rapiers, explosives, and miniature crossbows. That done, Dumas's main plot was straightforward, and needed only the usual cutting and embroidery.

It was fascinating to see the original cast in musketeer uniform again. Oliver Reed and Frank Finlay were showing grey, but Chamberlain was Chamberlain still, and Michael York looked so ridiculously young that a rumour arose suggesting that somewhere in an attic there was a Dorian Grey portrait of him showing the ageing process. Roy Kinnear was as portly a Planchet as ever, Christopher Lee stalked the screen as a formidable Rochefort, and Jean-Pierre Cassel ranted splendidly as Cyrano de Bergerac (with his own voice this time).

In addition to the old hands, Pierre had assembled a first-rate cast of newcomers to the musketeer canon: Bill Paterson was a fine lookalike King Charles and Alan Howard an imposing Cromwell, Kim Cattrall sneered and swaggered it up a storm as the lovely villainess, Philippe Noiret was an urbane, devious Cardinal Mazarin, and C. Thomas Howell a properly stiff-necked and explosive son of Athos. Bill Hobbs was again the fight arranger, and the production wouldn't have been complete without Eddie Fowlie in charge of props. This was the team that set off for Spain with such high hopes.

It is an excellent rule, and one which I've tried to follow with only moderate success, that the farther a scriptwriter can stay away from the actual shooting, the better. For one thing, they'll just make you work; for another, you have to restrain a mad impulse to get into the act and show them how it should be done. Fortunately, I've always been able to master it, and watch the proceedings deadpan – so much so that Lester was once heard to exclaim: "Look at him, standing there in his steel-rimmed spectacles – he's hating it!" In fact, I wasn't; it's just my normal expression.

However, I broke my rule this time. I wanted to watch the old gang at work again, and also to see one particular scene being shot. King Charles I, like most of the Stuarts, was a golfer, and I'd decided it would be nice to see him slashing away in the rough, and wrote a scene to that effect. Dick had the inspired idea of getting Billy Connolly to play the caddy, and the result was quite my favourite sequence in the movie – so, naturally, most of it ended up on the cutting-room floor; there's a malign destiny that causes that sort of thing to happen. But at least I saw it, and have the whole thing on tape.

I flew home again full of optimism. It was a happy shoot, they were plainly enjoying it, and everything was looking good.

Then the blow fell. Pierre phoned me at home one night, and I remember exactly what he said: "Our old friend Roy Kinnear passed away today." I couldn't believe it; when I'd last seen Roy he'd been in splendid form, lying contentedly under a Spanish oak making remarks as Oliver Reed and Bill Paterson rehearsed a scene; now suddenly that jolly, witty, lively man whom everyone had loved, was dead, literally in the prime of life.

It had been a ghastly accident, a fall from a horse in which he suffered internal injuries which proved fatal. It put the production into shock from which it never recovered.

My first reaction was the human one: shocked misery. My second was the professional: what happens to the picture? How much of Roy's part is in the can? Can the remainder be fixed somehow? Pierre answered these questions: the production would continue, and I was needed immediately in Spain to doctor the script; would I fly out next morning?*

In this kind of crisis there's only one thing to do: get on with

---

* Inevitably there was a third reaction, but not until much later, when I found myself wondering if the scene in which Roy had been killed (a link in which he and the Musketeers had to ride through an archway) had been strictly necessary. Could I have omitted it from the script, or done it a different way? Yes, probably; on the other hand, it had been a perfectly proper scene to write, and the script called for it. Heart-searchings of the "if only" kind are pointless – which doesn't stop them from crossing your mind, of course.

it. Shooting had been suspended for one day, then it continued while I scrounged a typewriter and paper and a copy of the script and retired first to a corner of the production office and then to a trailer beside the outdoor set where I could get at Dick or Pierre or whoever else I might want to consult. Then I read through to see what remained to do.

It could have been worse. Roy's final scene, fortunately, was done – the grand finale, in which virtually the whole cast rode past in parade. Most of the other scenes could be fixed by using Roy's double, judiciously shot, and voicing over his lines. "We might get Rory Bremner," said Dick. I don't know if he did, but whoever voiced in the lines did a perfect impersonation.

One scene looked impossible – the meeting between Planchet and D'Artagnan near the start of the film, which was absolutely necessary, and just too long to be played with the double's back to camera. But, think hard enough and it comes: Planchet was in flight from an angry pursuer when he encountered D'Artagnan, who was having his boots polished in the street – so let D'Artagnan hide him under a cloak and use him as a foot-rest while the polishing continues, the pursuer is foiled, and D'Artagnan and the concealed Planchet can exchange their chat in peace. It worked, I typed it up, and spent the rest of the day talking with Christopher Lee on the battlements of the castle where the daring escape of the Duc de Somewhere-which-escapes-me was taking place.

Christopher was in full seventeenth-century fig, rapier, eye-patch, and all, and in no time a crowd of tourists, and sightseers who had come to watch the shooting, were clustering around to stare at him. It struck me then (and still does) that this man was the ultimate film star; he must have made more pictures than John Wayne, even, and the whole world knows him. Beauties and matinee idols may come and go unrecognised, but Christopher Lee is familiar from Indian village to Eskimo igloo, an instant magnet to admiring fans, and it couldn't happen to a nicer man. When a Spanish lady approached and asked timidly if she might have a picture taken with him, he consented at once, and was immediately surrounded by her family, all beaming for the camera, with Christopher towering over them.

"I never know quite what to do on occasions like this," he said, while the lady sidled closer, preening. Tactful Fraser suggested he bite her on the neck, at which he sighed heavily and said: "Don't you start – I gave that up long ago." Which was true. The camera clicked, he swept the delighted senora a bow, and off they all went, fans for life.

Guy Hamilton told me a story which illustrates the kind of admiration which Christopher attracts. Guy was directing him in the Bond movie, *The Man with the Golden Gun*, and the set was visited by Muhammad Ali, professing himself a devoted Lee fan, and requesting an audience. They were introduced, Ali assuring Christopher that he was his favourite movie star, and then he had added: "And I'm gonna dedicate my next fight to you, too!"

This was taken as an extravagant compliment, no more – but sure enough, when Ali won his next fight (I've an idea it was the Rumble in the Jungle) and the ring was awash with fans, handlers, and journalists, the champion fought his way to the nearest TV camera and roared into the lens: "I won that fight for Christopher Lee!" Which, as Guy remarked, was not only a tribute to Christopher, but proved Ali a man of his word.

I didn't stay in Spain, since my job was done, and despite the professionalism with which everyone carried on, you could feel the cloud over the proceedings. My next contact with the film was a press screening in Salford for French journalists (so help me, it's true), and then there was the London premiere, attended by the Duke and Duchess of York, and the reviews, which were pretty unanimously unfavourable.

I wasn't surprised. Roy's death had overshadowed the making of the picture, and the aftermath of recrimination and litigation was no encouragement to the viewing public. But there were other reasons why the film wasn't a success. Dick had fallen seriously ill before shooting began, and while he made an excellent recovery, the pre-production had been affected, not least because he and I had not been able to go over the script as meticulously as we'd done with the earlier films, and I'm sure the picture suffered in consequence; we never got our usual happy ping-pong of ideas. Talking it over years later we agreed that we could have done better – with hindsight, I should have strengthened Christopher Lee's part and put more venom into his father–daughter relationship with Kim Cattrall; that would have worked well. And there were other areas I could have improved, too.

Yet I wonder if the concept itself wasn't the chief flaw. Do people want to see heroes grown old? One can be sentimental about come-backs, but they're seldom joyous affairs; the contrast with the youth-ful zest of the past is all too evident, and it could not be said of the third movie, as it was of the M3 and the M4, that they were "one for all, and all for fun."

Well, you can't win 'em all, and it's enough to have done what I believe we did, and make the definitive version of Dumas's story with the first two pictures. I'm probably biased, but they seem to me to be the last of the swashbucklers in the old Fairbanks–Flynn tradition, and I'd sooner have my credit on them than on *Citizen Kane*.

Fourth Afghan

THE ATTACK ON THE WORLD TRADE CENTER on September 11 was a hideous atrocity, but once the first stunned horror had receded, I confess I was puzzled, dismayed, and at last appalled by some of the reactions to it. These have been discussed and analysed ad nauseam over the past months, and many of the points I made and the questions I raised in a public address *before* the Fourth Afghan War had been declared, somewhat rashly, by Mr Bush, have since come to be taken for granted, although they were far from being accepted at the time. My views may still be out of step with majority opinion, but since I'm writing for a personal record I don't hesitate to repeat them, somewhat at random, as they struck me at the time, and still do.

Was I alone, shortly after the tragedy, in finding something tasteless about a *three*-minute silence which seemed to imply that the victims of a mere terrorist crime, however horrific, were worth more respect and mourning than the dead of two world wars? A trivial point, no doubt, yet it offended me almost as much as the hypocrisy of Bush and Blair in their refusal to explain why the Taliban, for shielding Bin Laden, could be treated as an enemy and targeted with the utmost ferocity, while the Irish Republic, which has given refuge and sympathy to the IRA, could not. We know why, of course: Bush presumably wants to get re-elected some day, and Blair wouldn't dream of disturbing his ill-named peace process, but the fact remains that the intent of those maniacs who flew the aircraft into the twin towers was no more evil than the intent of the heroes who planted the bombs at Enniskillen and Omagh and tried to butcher the British Government at Brighton. Only the scale of atrocity was different, and scale matters nothing to the dead.

I am not suggesting that Dublin should have been treated like Kabul, merely noting the double standard, which has its roots partly in naked racism – just like the dropping on Japan of the atomic bombs, weapons which by no stretch of the imagination could have been used on Berlin or Vienna.

I was certainly not alone in noting that while a generation of terrorism in Britain (a terrorism largely financed from the United States which expected our help last September), and other terror-isms in Spain and Ceylon and elsewhere, barely merited a mention in the American press, it was a very different story when the US was hit by terrorism – suddenly it was an attack on the whole world, on freedom, on "demaahcracy", etc., etc., and everyone was expected to fall in loyally behind American leadership.

It was not, of course, an attack on the world, or on anyone except America, and whatever the wisdom of Mr Bush's war, Britain should have had no part in it. It was simply no affair of ours; we had not been attacked, nor was there any likelihood of an attack until Blair, with extraordinary impudence and stupidity, thrust us willy-nilly into the firing-line, with the patently irrational claim that action was less dangerous than inaction. The propaganda that it was everyone's fight, trumpeted in Washington and echoed in London, was a necessary lie to coerce Europeans, especially the British, into America's quarrel – and to give Blair the chance to strut the world stage in a parody of statesmanship, bask in ludicrous comparisons with Churchill while acting as Bush's gofer, and dis-tract attention from the mess New Labour had made at home.

Why Blair rushed with such indecent haste to stand shoulder to shoulder with America may be obvious; what was incredible was that a spineless Parliament let him get away with it, abusing his position and betraying his trust by railroading us into armed conflict without seeking a mandate from the nation's elected representatives. What, one may ask, is Parliament for?

Wrong though he was, it was not surprising that Blair's rash and unconstitutional behaviour was widely if thoughtlessly approved. The British are a loyal, belligerent, and rather sentimental people, and it was pointed out that America was a staunch friend and ally who had stood by us in the Second World War, so were we not bound to support her now? By all means, and it would have been right and proper to stand by America in 2001 exactly as she stood by us from 1939 to 1942: with moral support, intelligence assistance, boundless good will, and all the material aid we could muster – at a price – but stopping short of joining the fight. God knows the threat to the world now does not compare to that posed by Hitler in 1940; talk of how "the world changed forever" on September 11 is so much twaddle, and Bush's bone-headed claim that whoever was not with America was against her was simply contemptible, as though he had the right to deny the option of neutrality to anyone who chose it.

The dictatorial dragooning of my country into war seemed to me to be quite as important as the moral question of blitzing hapless Afghans; British constitutional liberties were my first concern, not the follies and heedless brutalities of America's present leaders. I might deplore the apparent mistreatment of prisoners of war and the continued killing of Afghan civilians by unnecessary bombing, but I consoled myself that this lapse from the standards of civilised behaviour was a temporary thing resulting from the unprecedented shock of September 11, when it was brought home to the American people that their country was no longer the impregnable fortress of their imagination. They were stunned, and infuriated into an understandable thirst for revenge – never mind silly excuses about self-defence, they wanted to "kick ass", and since Bin Laden's was not available, and the world's greatest superpower was incapable of finding and seizing him, which would have been the sensible and proper course, the bemused Bush had to find another ass to kick, and homed in on Afghanistan's Taliban government with demented slogans about crusades and just causes.

Meanwhile Blair was alarming Britons with deranged rhetoric about British leadership, and "sorting out" various parts of Africa, and generally creating a new heaven and a new earth, in a speech reminiscent of Palmerston's fictitious comic address to the Improvement Club.* This, when everyone knew that Britain hadn't the muscle for even another Falklands campaign.

Now, after all this – my disgust and anger at the risking of British lives in Bush's war; my indignation that millions urgently needed at home should be squandered in rebuilding the country which America had devastated; my conviction that the end being sought in Afghanistan (whatever it was) did not justify the means; my despair at the sheer ignorance of Islam displayed by Western leaders;† my doubt whether disposing of the Taliban and Bin Laden would advance the campaign against terrorism very far; my fear that America's blind belligerence might really let the terrorist genie out of the bottle; my impatience at their inability to understand (not just in Washington but in Little Rock and Shaker Heights) that by ill-treating captives and committing the crowning folly of photographing their cruelty for all the world to see,‡ they were creating a public relations disaster, reinforcing their enemies' hatred,

---

* Lord Palmerston's address to the Reform Club on March 7, 1854, on the eve of the Crimean War, was memorably lampooned in *Punch*.
† And sections of the Western media, like the American news magazine which under the heading WHY THEY HATE AMERICA, told its readers that "Bin Laden's fanatics are the offspring of failed societies", adding that "We stand for freedom and they hate it. We are rich and they envy us. We are strong and they resent this." God help us.
‡ Mr Rumsfeld's contention that the Afghan captives were not prisoners of war prompted an interesting question: would he define the civilian farmers of Lexington and Concord who fired the first shots in the American Revolution as "unlawful combatants", and would he have regarded as "appropriate" the hooding, blindfolding, caging, and sensory deprivation of any taken prisoner?

and setting an example for other ruthless regimes to follow; my total lack of confidence in the leadership of the US and Britain – after all this, it will surely be concluded that I am disloyal, unpatriotic, and above all anti-American, and deserving of the wrath and scorn (often quite venomous) poured on any who dare to oppose or even to criticise Anglo-American policies. Some writers in the British press whom I normally respect waxed almost hysterical about this, damning me and my like as doves if not traitors, and crying a rousing "Gung-ho!" from their armchairs.

Well, I am not anti-American. I'm pro-American to my backbone, and I share their grief and rage at the horror of Manhattan – but I am not prepared to stand shoulder to shoulder with them or anyone else unconditionally, I am not prepared to accept their leadership when they are manifestly unfit to provide it, I am not prepared (unlike Blair) to put our soldiers' precious lives at Bush's disposal, and most of all, I am not prepared to regard US policies and decisions as infallible and beyond criticism. In spite of Bush's inanities, it is possible to be a true friend without giving slavish allegiance, to recognise that the special relationship is not a bed of roses, to be eternally grateful for support in the Falklands while not forgetting Eisenhower's despicable stab in the back at the time of Suez, and to reserve the right to disagree. It's called democracy, but truthfully I would not expect either Bush or Blair to have much notion of it; they've shown none so far.

But nobody seemed to mind that; both men stood high in the opinion polls, and there was general support for Bush's war, except among a small minority who included seventeen very old men with whom I attended a reunion shortly after the crisis began: we were the remnants of the 9th Battalion Border Regiment, part of the 17th Indian Division, the "Black Cats", who fought through the Burma war, spearheaded the last great drive south behind the enemy lines and, in General Slim's words, tore the Japanese Army apart. If there were seventeen good men and ready soldiers in Britain, with nothing to learn about what are called the horrors of war, and never a moment's hesitation in going to battle in a good cause, those were they. Without exception they were against an Afghan war – not only because as one elderly Cumbrian said: "They'll 'ev a bloody rough shift if they ga intil Afghanistan", but because like all old soldiers who have been there and done it, they were pacifists to a man, knowing the wisdom of patience and diplomacy and only fighting when no other honourable course is open. It would have taken a very big man, a real leader, to stay America's hand after September 11, resist the perfectly natural demand of his countrymen for vengeance, and look for a peaceful way.

Also, those seventeen old trained killers (for that is what they once were) felt a distaste at the prospect of the world's most powerful superpower bombing one of the most primitive nations on earth into a bloody rubble; perhaps some of them remembered that the grandfathers of those Pathans and Baluch and Afghans of the Taliban had been comrades in XIVth Army.

I heard one reflecting caustically – and no doubt unfairly – that it struck a jarring note when a prime minister cocooned by the tightest security with armed police and bodyguards, talked of soldiers laying their lives on the line; that is a view straight from the slit-trench, and I was reminded of Dennis Wheatley's "Pills of Honour" – the suicide pills to be taken by any Cabinet declaring war and so inevitably sending others to certain death. Not an option that would appeal to politicians. One would have to go back to Regulus for that kind of honour.

Of course time may prove me absolutely wrong. Perhaps posterity will acclaim Bush's and Blair's behaviour as courageous and statesmanlike. But I doubt it, just as I doubt (whatever the course of events in Afghanistan, whatever terrorist leaders are killed or captured, whatever so-called government exists in Kabul) whether it will be possible to talk of victory until the Palestine question, which is at the heart of the matter, has been resolved. Everyone knows that this is crucial, and that while it remains unsettled, terrorism will continue. Western leaders talk of an indefinite campaign which, although they can never admit it, is an admission that terrorism can't be beaten. It always wins, as we have seen in Northern Ireland and elsewhere, and in the end it has to be looked at across a table, with talk of jihads and just causes forgotten, and reality faced by both sides. Easier said than done, but that's the truth of it, and perhaps when the guns of Gaza and the West Bank are silent, as they have seldom been since I heard them as a young subaltern more than fifty years ago, it will be possible to say that the world has changed indeed.

Law for Sale?

NEVER MIND PEERAGES, can law-making be bought? If an animal rights organisation were to contribute to a governing party's funds, would this assist the passage of a bill against parrot-kicking or butterfly-baiting or some similar blood sport? And if the Fruit of the Month Society made a similar donation, would this win government support for lowering the age of consent for homo-sexuals? I ask these questions in all innocence, and am ready to be told that it is disgraceful even to mention them – which usually means that the question has hit uncomfortably close to home.

On this head, I was an interested observer of the campaign to ban fox-hunting, deer-hunting, coursing, etc., and found myself wondering whether the proposed bill was the result of judicious investment or just mental derangement. I have never hunted, and never would, but I have a foolishly sentimental affection for it which comes of reading Surtees and Trollope and singing at school hearty songs like "Drink, Puppy, Drink", and "A-Hunting We Will Go", and of course "John Peel", and I should be sorry to learn that they were no longer sung in this politically correct age.

This is very wrong of me, but there it is. I haven't shot an animal since I was nine, when I nailed a rabbit and promptly burst into tears. And once I had my copy ruthlessly spiked when I was sent to write an article celebrating the Waterloo Cup, and turned in a passionate denunciation of coursing.

So I understand the position of the anti-blood-sports people (and would gladly shoot those of them who commit evil acts of terrorism, but that's not germane to the argument). I'm neutral to the extent that I don't give a dam about the morality of hunting, but as a country lover I have to defend rural traditions and the right of people to make a living from them. But my real interest, I confess, would be to watch the attempted enforcement of a hunting ban, something which I suspect the banners haven't really thought about. I'm not sure how the police are going to proceed against law-breaking huntsmen – when they assemble, when they set off, when they first get on the trail of a fox, or when they kill it? Assuming they do. I would truly enjoy the sight of PC Plod in pursuit of the Blencathra, running up and down the fells crying: "Stop, in the name of Blair!"

I mustn't be cynical, or wonder why the government debated fox-hunting while the countryside was dying from foot and mouth disease; whom the gods would destroy they first make mad. But I would like to know why the ban-the-hunt brigade don't demand the outlawing of angling, which is horribly cruel, consisting as it does of the slow torturing to death of a fish with a barbed hook in its jaws. Could it be that while they inveigh against people who chase foxes and deer and blow the hell out of grouse and pheasants, on the erroneous assumption that they are all "toffs" and fair game, the antis are scared to tackle the anglers, vast numbers of whom are working-class? Of course it is. They know, too, that a bill against angling wouldn't stand a chance – but being men and women of stainless principle, shouldn't they *try* for one, or at least state boldly where they stand? Or don't they care about fish?

SHOOTING SCRIPT 2

With the Tudors in Hungary

*S*ENSIBLE PEOPLE *do their memoirs by taking daily notes, like Alec Guinness and Alan Clark, which gives the published work an immediacy and excitement lacking in those recollections which begin: "It was in the summer of 1977 . . ." Being idle, and having no great ambition, until quite recently, to write my autobiography, I haven't taken daily notes, but on one occasion I did write up my doings on a weekly basis. That was during the making of* The Prince and the Pauper, *and for the sake of variety, and because it contains trivia which may be of interest, I am including that account as I wrote it, with only a little editing. Since I didn't start my note-taking until some time into the production, I shall have to set the scene with a brief introduction. So . . . it was in the summer of 1977 that Alex Salkind invited me to do a screenplay of Mark Twain's novel, to be directed by Richard Fleischer. A screenplay had already been done, and I was to adjust, or, if necessary, do a complete rewrite. I read it, and decided to start from scratch.*

Accordingly I flew to Paris and met Fleischer, and so began a most happy collaboration with one who was to become my closest friend in the movie business – indeed, Kathy and I have no closer friends anywhere outside our family than Dick and his delightful wife Mickey. We see them only at long intervals, but they have been great fun in London, Los Angeles, the Riviera, Spain, Budapest, Rome, Dublin, and elsewhere, and as David Balfour said of Alan Breck, they can burn down my barn any time.

Dick, whose father, Max Fleischer, was one of the great animators and the creator of Popeye, is a pro from way back, one of the masters of Hollywood's golden age and a meticulous artist of immense versatility. You name it, Fleischer has directed it, from newsreels to such celebrated films noirs as The Narrow Margin; *massive spectaculars including* The Vikings, Barabbas, 20,000 Leagues Under the Sea, and Tora! Tora! Tora!; *musical comedy* (Dr Dolittle), *science fiction* (Fantastic Voyage), *fantasy* (Conan the Destroyer *and* Red Sonja) *and a host of outstanding films which defy classification, among them* Soylent Green, 10 Rillington Place *and* The Boston Strangler. *I've been lucky enough to write for him on three productions, and can only echo what Cary Grant said of Hitchcock: "I whistled all the way to work."*

We agreed that Prince and Pauper *would need a complete rewrite, talked it over with Alex Salkind and Pierre Spengler, and that was that. I flew home, discarded the original screenplay, and did a new version of Twain's charming story (he saw it in fairly dark terms, but I liked it for its excitement, humour, and ingenuity). It's an historical fantasy based on the premise that the boy prince, Edward, heir to Henry VIII, and his double, a young thief named Tom, changed places and found themselves having bewildering adventures in their unaccustomed roles. It had been an Errol Flynn swashbuckler forty years earlier, with the title roles being played by twins; Salkind and Fleischer were to give it blockbuster treatment with a cast which would eventually include Oliver Reed, Charlton Heston, and Raquel Welch (all Musketeer veterans), as well as George C. Scott, Rex Harrison, Ernest Borgnine, and David Hemmings, with young Mark Lester, the angelic hero of* Oliver!, *in the two lead parts – a huge challenge for an actor of eighteen, since it is really four parts, the Prince, the Pauper, the Prince-as-Pauper, and the Pauper-as-Prince.*

I did the first draft, following Twain as closely as possible, and Fleischer liked it. Kathy and I flew to Hollywood, where Dick and I went over the script, and agreed revisions. I flew home and did them,

Dick approved . . . and now I break into my notes, written at the time, when I was waiting for the production to get under way . . .

Fleischer phones, with the splendid news that Rex Harrison is to play the Duke of Norfolk – can I beef up his part? You bet I can.

Down to Penshurst Place, Kent, for the first day's shooting. Ancient house, beautiful grounds, Olde England to the life, with Fleischer setting up his stuff with Jack Cardiff, and yeoman warders lying on the grass looking harmless. Why don't they get great big burly thugs for these parts nowadays? This lot of minions wouldn't frighten anyone. Where are you Harry Cording, Ray Teal, Dennis Wyndham, et al. . . . ?

Through a Tudor arch strides Henry VIII – Heston, in full fig, looking terrific in the true sense of the word, extending a regal hand for Fleischer to kiss (he doesn't).

I'd met Heston in Paris in the production office at the Georges V before the M3 premiere – he had heard me give my name at the desk, and loomed up beside me saying: "I'm Charlton Heston." Taken all unawares at the sudden appearance of a living legend, I had been startled into saying: "By God, so you are!", at which he had taken no offence, handing me a whisky and starting to talk Scottish history (he is part Fraser and immensely proud of it – aren't we all?) He had also confessed to a wish to play Flashman at Little Big Horn, an episode I had yet to write.

F. and H. go into a huddle over the script, and call me in. H. suggests rewording one of my lines to read: "You failed me in Scotland, Norfolk, and you know it well." It sounds a wee bit corny to me, but I'm not fussy – maybe he knows better what will *sound* right. I stick my heels in on another point, the line where Henry says he's been on the throne five and thirty years. H points out, correctly, that at the time Henry had been on the throne thirty-seven years; I plead poetic licence, claiming that five and thirty sounds better, and he yields. He looks horribly like Henry VIII, which is disturbing when you're sitting on a garden bench with him arguing about what he should say, and expecting to be consigned to the Tower at any moment.

Meet Mark Lester, a tall, ethereal-looking, nervous lad who smokes Marlboro as if they were going to stop making them. He writhes convincingly in a muddy flower-bed while Heston stands on him, and Graham Stark, in jester's motley, flings himself prone, crying "Break away, old Hal!" in a variety of accents. Rex Harrison stands by registering polite concern.

Time out, and Graham Stark is busy snapping away with his camera, something which he does, he tells me, on all his films – his collection should be worth a fortune one of these days. He is telling me what I suspect will be a scandalous story about Michael Curtiz, when Rex Harrison, who has been rehearsing with Heston and Harry Andrews, strolls over – and who can stroll like him? – and murmurs to me that now that Henry's line to Norfolk has been changed, he feels that he'd like something stronger to say in reply. Could I possibly . . . ? Sensing a slight needle here, I do a quick think, and give him a line off the top of my head which pleases him inordinately. I'd say it was passable, no more, but he writes it carefully into his script (left-handed), crinkling happily and repeating it with obvious enjoyment. When they come to rehearse the scene again, he drawls it out, Heston's head jerks up in what may be well-acted royal displeasure or sudden suspicion that he is being upstaged (either way, it's a perfect reaction), and Harrison opens his mouth and laughs silently.

The word is that he is notoriously a bastard to work with, and I have heard horror stories about his temperament, but I can only

29

say he seems extremely easy and reasonable to me – of course, I don't have to photograph, produce, direct, record, attire, or act with him, and in my experience actors tend to be more friendly with writers than with anyone else, possibly because they have to depend on them. I'd given him a line, and he'd been happy with it; when I ask him if he has any thoughts about the rest of his part he leafs through the script and delights me by giving a sudden guffaw and exclaiming: "I like this!" It proves to be an exchange between him and Hertford (Harry Andrews) who has been sent to arrest him.

Hertford: In the king's name!
Norfolk (pretending to be taken unawares): Henry, I believe.

It looks nothing on the page; as said by Harrison, with his perfect timing and expression of feigned surprise, it worked beautifully.

We talk about Arthur Barbosa,* and I ask Harrison if he saw *French Without Tears* on TV last night. He frowns and says he did, recalling his own appearance in the original play forty years ago. "I don't know – these chaps nowadays, they seem so bloody *young.*" Sigh. "I suppose we were bloody young, too." He reminisces affectionately about Roland Culver, Guy Middleton, and Trevor Howard; in the background Henry VIII is hauling an enormous mattress onto the grass and collapsing on it, robes, staff, and all.

Lemonade is served from a large urn; Harrison, whom one naturally associates with wines of rare vintage, looks doubtful, but exclaims after an appraising sip, "Not bad, really." He tries for a refill, but the tap yields nothing, so between us we up-end the urn to get the dregs and manage to extract two paper cups-full. Harrison sighs contentedly, savouring the bouquet, and wonders when lunch is.

---

* The talented artist who painted jackets for all the Flashman novels, using himself as a model. For *Flashman at the Charge*, where our hero was seen in fur hat brandishing a sabre, Arthur had got his wife to photograph him flourishing a walking-stick with a tea-cosy on his head. He and Rex Harrison were lifelong friends, both being Liverpudlians and fellow-students.

A buffet has been set up in a tent, and Fleischer, Heston, Harrison, Stark, Mark Lester, and I help ourselves, Heston unbelievable without his robe; he is clad in long johns with an artificial potbelly strapped on. Graham Stark is worried about his lines: is his accent right, is he doing them well? I assure him that not since Barrymore's Hamlet . . . and he cheers up sufficiently to ask Fleischer if his Shropshire accent is acceptable (I gather he has been researching Will Somers, Henry VIII's jester). Fleischer, who wouldn't know a Shropshire accent from Cantonese, says so long as he's comprehensible, that's fine. Mark Lester's nervousness is wearing off.

After lunch discuss children with Heston, and the question of which other monarchs he might possibly play. Since he is a dead ringer for Edward I – bone structure, height, and presence – I suggest that he'd make a fine Hammer of the Scots, but have a feeling he'd rather play Robert the Bruce.

Meet Harry Andrews, whose father, it transpires, was from Scotland, and who glows when I praise his performance as a Scots RSM in *The Red Beret*. Watch him and Julian Orchard shooting with Heston and Harrison. Fascinated by Fleischer's directing technique: after one rehearsal he says quietly: "You're trying too hard, Chuck." Heston nods gravely and moderates his style. "Very good, Chuck; that's it." Fleischer is very neat and precise as he moves quietly round the set, relaxed, amiable, and taking every opportunity to praise, especially young Mark. "That's good, Mark, that's very good."

As the afternoon wears on and the shadows cast by the sun change, Jack Cardiff makes mysterious adjustments to his equipment so that no passage of time will be visible in a scene lasting no more than a minute or so. This is a vastly more technical business than I had realised.

Heston has got shot of his make-up and is pacing in a track-suit, looking like a decathlon winner. He is one year older than I am,

God help us. We adjourn to a Tudor archway, through which young Mark has to be pursued by angry citizens. Endless rehearsals, as Mark practises barging into people, but the star of the show is a stout extra, whose job it is to be jostled and register astonishment. As the rehearsals progress, he expands his moment of mild surprise into something resembling Tod Slaughter going into overdrive in *Murder in the Red Barn*, with clutching of brows, staggering, rolling of eyes and cries of "What the hell?" Mark runs himself silly, Fleischer advises patiently, Nigel Wooll (assistant director), keeps crying, with eternal optimism: "All right, here we go, this time. Quiet, please, everyone, here we go . . . oh, quiet, for God's sake!" Finally we do go, Mark hurtles past the stout extra who is going to win a supporting Oscar or die in the attempt, and B. H. Barry, the sword expert, tells me how he is working out the fight sequences, giving a different theme to each one.

Part of the production was to take place in Hungary, which necessitated two visits.

To Budapest to go location-hunting with Fleischer, Spengler, and crew members. Our principal quest is for a church interior which can pass for Westminster Abbey in the coronation scene – not easy, since Hungarian churches have a rather Byzantine look, being decorated with splendid colours over walls and ceiling. Eddie Fowlie stands in one vast cathedral nave surveying the rainbow riot which covers the echoing interior, and remarks: "We could spray this lot with plastic, easy. Peel it off after, no bother." There is no end to the enterprise of the British film technician, but I doubt if the local Dean and Chapter would take kindly to having their church repainted, even temporarily.

Scour the countryside for anything, architectural or natural, which might bear a resemblance to sixteenth-century England, and are rewarded in Sopron, a town up near the Czech border, which has some Tudorish-looking streets and frontages. Further exploration of the area is called off when we find ourselves being sternly regarded over the hedge by Czech frontier guards armed with tommy-guns. The team go back to Budapest, while I am driven to Vienna to catch a plane home, waiting patiently at the Austro-Hungarian border crossing while the guards take my passport away for three-quarters of an hour. Later, when I mention this to Nigel Wooll and speculate on what takes them such an unconscionably long time to deal with passports, he says: "I think they just read them."

This sounds plausible; I suppose time hangs heavy at East European frontier posts.

Stay one night in Vienna, and am disappointed to see that the Danube is not in the least blue, but insanitary grey.

Back to Budapest, with Kathy, to see some shooting and do possible rewrites. Fleischer tells us over lunch that they have had considerable trouble with Olly Reed. It seems he got into a fight and finished up in a police cell; talk of deportation, but he was released on a promise of good behaviour. Then he had annoyed Fleischer by making a nuisance of himself at Mark Lester's eighteenth birthday party, and had provoked a new crisis by breaking the nose of a rugby-playing friend. The Gellert Hotel, on the Buda side of the Danube, refused to have him back, so he is now in our hotel, the Intercontinental, which is on the Pest bank. Apparently he changed hotels not by taking a taxi across one of the bridges, but by wading and swimming the river in the middle of the night, arriving in the Intercontinental lobby clad only in mud and waterweed. It says much for his persuasive powers that the management allowed him to stay instead of throwing him back. Possibly they were impressed by his line that his behaviour was nothing out of the way, and in England no one would have thought twice about it.

The Salkinds throw a big party for the unit in the Intercontinental ballroom. Kathy looks smashing in green silk, and I feel terribly conventional in my best suit among all these glamorous bohemians, but feel better when Oliver arrives in what is plainly *his* best suit, blue serge with waistcoat and club tie (black with thin orange stripes; who's that?) He is only slightly canned, accompanied by his wife and daughter, and carrying a bunch of bulrushes – possibly a souvenir of his Danube crossing – which he distributes ("reeds", get it?) Raquel Welch receives one graciously (so much for the tales that she and Oliver don't get on; mind you, I can't see them as close friends). As before, she struck me as being a nice, sensible woman, by no means a sex goddess. She is tired, after a day of interviews, and demands wearily: what do the press *want* of her? She doesn't like being photographed or questioned on set, which is hardly surprising, and obviously believes (not without justice, I dare say) that the newspapers hope to be able to report her as difficult and temperamental.

Mark Lester is a nice lad, prattling to us about his part (both of them) and assuring Kathy that the film will have to be the next Royal Command production. He is only slightly tight, which for an eighteen-year-old is pretty creditable in the circumstances; his parents have been out once, for a week, and I wonder who keeps an eye on him. To my surprise he has about fifteen films behind him; another overnight sensation.

Kathy, as usual with her reporter's instinct, has found the most interesting person at the party – a delightful, very old lady who speaks only French and turns out to be Pierre Spengler's grand-mother. We converse with difficulty, but gather that in her opinion Pierre does all the work ("*beaucoup de travail*") which I think is probably true on the production side. She cannot take alcohol or chocolate, but she and Kathy share a plate of ice cream.

Fleischer introduces Lalla Ward (Princess Elizabeth) and Felicity Dean, a stunningly pretty blonde who is Mark's sweetheart on screen; you could, as Dick says, eat her with a spoon. She confides to Kathy that she is still too young to get into RADA, and I think this may be her first part.

To the Hungarofilm studio to see rushes. The film looks beautiful, and the thrill of hearing George C. Scott speak my lines is delightful. Some of them he has decided to chant, which is appropriate to his part, the "Ruffler", a monk-turned-bandit, and it works perfectly. I have nothing but admiration for Anthony Quinn and James Coburn, both of whom were mentioned as possible Rufflers, but I wouldn't swap Scott for anyone. Heston, as Henry VIII, is better than I've ever seen him, Borgnine and Harrison are excellent, Lalla Ward gets every inch out of her raging scene as Young Bess, and there's a nice little love-scene between Mark and Felicity Dean (that boy's heart is in his work, no error; he doesn't need a spoon). Olly is A1 as always, and I'm told steals the movie. It could be a smasher, but I'll have to see it all.

Dinner with Fleischer at the 100 Years, to the deafening accompaniment of a gypsy violinist, whom I summoned accidentally while trying to get a waiter; thereafter he haunts us all bloody night. I complete my Edgar Kennedy act by grabbing for the bill ahead of Fleischer, and succeed in scooping up the check belonging to the next table. Fleischer wants another fight, this time in Westminster Abbey; no problem for me, but they'll have to rebuild Westminster. However, Alex Salkind wants to keep the action going, and says spare no expense. They also want little end-pieces to be voiced over by Harrison, which I'll attend to.

I mention tactfully to Pierre that since I'm having to do extra work, perhaps he should call my agent ... he agrees. (I knew if I came to Hungary I'd finish up working.) Kathy suggests I get a typewriter from the hotel, but remembering the difficulty I had getting one in Hollywood, I suspect I'll end up writing in longhand. But lo, when we try the concierge he produces typewriter, paper, and all the fixings; so much for capitalism's supposed superior efficiency. I do the scene and end-pieces, and we go shopping – pictures, ash-trays, embroidered cloths which we find in the apartment of an old German woman; likewise wooden cooking spoons of a style and shape no longer to be found in the West. Kathy gets me a lovely glass and silver swan whose wings fold over a mustard-pot; he is Ferenc, and will live on my desk.

Car to Sopron, where Olly sits smoking in the stocks waiting to be flogged, while Raquel Welch and David Hemmings, on horseback, rehearse with Olly cueing them. All do well, although she doesn't look at her best; I gather her father died recently and she has had distressing problems with hospital authorities.

Lunch with Kathy, Fleischer and Jack Cardiff. Chicken, caviare, cheese, grapes, peaches, vacuum flask of coffee which comes out stone cold, and wasps everywhere. Jack and Dick laugh at the tail-pieces and approve the new Abbey fight scene; Pierre objects that they can't re-dress the warehouse as Westminster because the owners have got 70 tons of cotton and 56 tons of beetroot which must be stored. Well, that's show business.

Back to the stocks, where Hungarian extras dressed as Tudor peasants stand sipping from Coke bottles while Nigel Wooll, ever the optimist, shouts: "Quiet, please! Okay, everyone, here we go! Start pelting!" A technician translates for the benefit of the mob, who hurl eggs, vegetables, etc. enthusiastically at the stocks-bound Olly. He bears it patiently, wincing nicely when they rehearse the flogging with a velvet whip, while Mark, protesting violently, is dragged away by constables. Small crisis when flogger hits Olly before Fleischer has given the signal, and is severely rebuked. Meanwhile Mark is being pursued by wasps, and vanishes, flapping and cursing.

To burn the witch or not? Much debate. I'm all for dropping it – if we want a U certificate and a Royal Command we'll have to. Fleischer happy to ditch it, fair enough.

B. H. Barry, the fight arranger, suggests a Mel Brooksish touch for the Abbey fight: Olly seizing Raquel, menacing her with dagger to hold guards at bay. I shoot it down gently, and cheer him up by telling him that two-handed swords are to be used in the scene, which delights him, and he is soon lost in two-handed sword dreams.

Kathy and I take Fleischer and Cardiff to dinner, meeting Olly on the way. He is fresh after his ordeal, and when someone remarks that a scene which took me a moment's typing gave him several long hours in the sun, trussed up, belaboured, and plastered with filth, he says happily: "Bing sings."*

Discussion at dinner about a remarkable piece of photography achieved by Cardiff, in a scene in which Mark, as the Prince, is seen walking completely round Mark as the Pauper. I've never seen anything like it, and when I ask how it was done I'm informed that when Sabu was asked by what miracle of special effects he had been showing flying on a genie's back in *The Thief of Baghdad*, he replied deadpan: "He just picked me up and flew me." Fleischer's comment: "Good for Sabu." I agree; I've no time for those who explain how screen miracles are achieved, and I shouldn't have asked. Mark walked round Mark, and I don't mind not knowing how it was done.

Cardiff has the rights to Jeffery Farnol's *Jade of Destiny*, and wants me to write it for Olly in some kind of co-production deal. I make non-committal noises. It could be fun to write, and might make a good swashbuckler, but I wonder if the market will bear

---

* For those who may wonder what this means, in Bing Crosby musicals the scripts simply noted "Bing sings" – two words representing several minutes of screen time.

another Tudor adventure so soon after *Prince and Pauper*. Also, production isn't my style. I'm a hired typewriter.

Back to the I.o.M., and a call from one Harold Hecht: am I interested in writing a sequel to *The Crimson Pirate* for Burt Lancaster, and will I go to a screening of the original movie (which I haven't seen) in London with Lancaster, who is coming to England shortly? I'm taken with the idea of working with Lancaster, who has the reputation of being an unusually intelligent actor, but I'm not sure about the job. Without knowing what *The Crimson Pirate* was like, I doubt if there's much chancing of doing an M3 (or a P and P) with a sequel. But who knows?*

To Pinewood with Fleischer to see the rough-cut. It seems that Olly took to turning up legless during the last two weeks in Budapest; once he had roared at Fleischer, explaining how he was going to do a fight scene, stabbing the air, flinging himself on the ground, and simply failing to register when Dick said: "But, Olly, we've shot that fight, remember?" Olly didn't, no doubt because he had been entirely gassed when he did it, plunging about and trying to kill everybody. Barry had had to scrap his carefully choreographed fight and ad-lib the whole thing, which looked suitably shambolic on screen.

Plainly booze is going to be the ruin of a fine but undisciplined actor. What makes it so painful is that Dick had golden opinions of Olly the actor before he saw Olly the drunk.

At lunch in the Pinewood restaurant (Table One, whee-whew! that's what directorial giants get) I learn to my horror that most of Rex Harrison has been removed from the film. The logic is that Rex's part was artificially built up (which I did on instruction because he is who he is) and that this unbalances the film as a

---

* The meeting with Lancaster, and discussion of *Crimson Pirate II*, eventually took place in Hollywood, and is described in a subsequent chapter.

whole; the built-up part is judged to be "obtrusive". My feeling is that Rex can never be obtrusive – and, dammit, I wrote the part specially for him, he liked it and does it beautifully, and for my money it's the best dialogue in the film. So I say, the hell with whether it's obtrusive or not – if you're lucky enough to have Harrison doing his thing as only he can, *use* him, and who cares if the picture runs ten minutes over?

Pierre arrives with his sister, a pretty, quiet girl. Alex and Ilya are at the Dorchester, cooking up big deals, but will arrive by executive transport, air-conditioned chauffeur, etc., in time for the showing at 3 p.m. We go to the viewing theatre – no Salkinds at three. Pierre phones in all directions, the chauffeur is still outside the Dorchester, but Alex and Ilya have vanished. Dick contains what must be white-hot fury under a bright-eyed calm. We continue to wait . . . and wait. Dick says if they don't arrive by three thirty, forget it, because he won't try to crowd the showing into the time available before the theatre is booked for another film.

We wait some more, Pierre's sister brings coffee, we drink it in silence, I deliver a brief lecture on the manners of film producers, and Dick nods with gritted teeth – much more delay and he'll burst.

At the last minute Alex and Ilya arrive, in trench coats, Alex apologising profusely and Ilya shaking his head. Coffee finished, Dick cocks an eye and asks: "Are we all . . . reddee?", and we take our seats, myself at the end of the back row, well away from massed Salkinds with Dick in their midst. He must be a masochist; sitting beside Michel le Grand with a heavy cold is bad enough, but how he's going to cope with Alex's stertorous breathing and muttered translations of English into French via Russian, I hate to think.

Dick, using what I imagine is an age-old Hollywood formula, makes a nice little set speech from his seat, telling us the form: we'll see the movie, and think a while, and then exchange views, right? Enthusiastic grunts from Alex, frowning malignantly from the depths of his trench coat (this is his "concentration" expression) and the film rolls.

Well, my first reaction is one of disappointment.* The overall direction is vintage Fleischer, and Jack Cardiff's photography is immaculate as always, but some of the acting isn't that good, and I'm not all that struck with some of my screenplay, either – but in self-defence there are lines I'd have played differently. But the main fault, dwarfing any others, is in the casting: Mark just isn't right for the parts. Now and then he sounds like a school-play rehearsal – and yet sometimes that crack-voiced boyish intensity hits exactly the right note. It's not his fault; it's simply not his role – for one thing, he's far too tall, six feet if he's an inch.

Harrison's reduction aside, I'm annoyed that the editor has dropped the long shot of Henry dying, which I liked because it was historically accurate and rather moving, with the whispered "Monks, monks, monks!" and the haunting music of "The Hunt is Up" coming in softly, and substituted a jarring close shot in which Charlton's head drops alarmingly, and he does a great slump.†

Borgnine is excellent . . . I think – is he too much, with that mad glint? – Olly as good as always, Heston v. good, and the most believable Henry I've ever seen, Raleigh's tyrant to the life; he manages something which I wouldn't have thought Heston could have done, namely, make my eyes moist. Lalla Ward gives Young Bess the message, on all cylinders. George Scott looks even better the second time.

Surprisingly, the scene at the stocks between Olly and Raquel plays well, possibly helped by Korngold's music, which Dick has used for the nonce. I rewrote the scene, on request, but the principals liked the original better. Mark's finest hour is his "They shall

* Leslie Halliwell's verdict: "Moderately well-made swashbuckler with an old-fashioned air, not really helped by stars in cameo roles or by the poor playing of the title roles." I'd say its strength is the stars in cameo roles, but otherwise I can't disagree.
† The original shot was restored in the finished film.

have right" speech, which he does superbly, with Olly reacting perfectly – that whole sequence, beside a dreary river in half-light, is Jack Cardiff photography at its wondrous best.

Westminster Abbey has got out of control – long pauses, Mark looking serene, Raquel doing her damnedest with that bloody Great Seal – I hate the sequence, always did, gave them what they asked for against my better judgment, and it doesn't work.

They haven't shot the last fight, by the way, which is as well; I had doubts at the time, and we're better without it. So Dick won his battle with the producers, the Abbey set wasn't rebuilt, tons of cotton and beetroot found a happy home, and Eddie Fowlie and his workers were spared a maddening job.

Lovely finish to the film, with Rex speaking the end pieces and Lalla Ward sweeping off to take care of England, and looking as though she's just the girl to do it, too.

Worst mistake – taking most of Harrison out. He could give the thing just the lift it needs. My overall judgment: it could go either way, good or bad, probably on the bad side. I'm a harsh critic, and it may be better than I think. But I doubt if we'll have a hit. Respectable at the box office, perhaps, but no better. And yet, who knows? I had serious doubts about the M3, and how wrong I was.

Dead silence when the lights go up. Salkind murmurings, comments like "Yes … very good … Yes …" (At least no one gives the ultimate thumbs down of "Great locations".*) I move behind Dick and say "Well done", and he says thanks. He's disappointed at their reaction, but he probably expected to be. Talk of restoring Harrison, which will mean cuts. I make the case for keeping Scott and Young Bess intact, and Dick agrees.

*

* This is the stock comment if you want to say something nice about someone's film when there's really nothing nice to say.

Some time later, in Paris, I hear that Harrison is to be restored, thank God. Ilya tells me the feeling is that Rex put bags of pathos and oomph into the thing, and that his removal would cut out all the good emotion. He then horrifies me by wanting to remove Lalla Ward's final magnificent exit, his reasoning being who the hell knows about Queen Elizabeth I anyway, and look at the state of the pound, for Christ's sake. They want to fake in some appalling nonsense of two hands shaking, indicating friendship and love or something equally bizarre and meaningless. I suspect Ilya of froggy prejudice against English history. I tell him he's mad – that America at least knows about Good Queen Bess, even if the garlic-eaters don't, and the final shot will not be lost on them. But he insists.

Fleischer says that over his dead body will they cut the Bess finale, and even Ilya agrees that it should stay for the British version. Fair enough, I don't really mind what they show in Venezuela, although I think it's a damned shame if it isn't kept for the US version too.

The Bess finale was retained, and a curious medallion-like decoration was also inserted, showing two hands shaking, which did no harm if it did no good. The film took a critical pasting in Britain, one reviewer apparently taking offence at the Ruffler's attitude to religion. I've heard of weird, but that's ridiculous. However, it was better received in the United States, where it was called Crossed Swords, *God alone knows why. Mark Twain's title wasn't deemed right for American audiences? But the change of title didn't keep the audiences away, and the film achieved a rare distinction. Radio City Music Hall was to close, and for the final week* Crossed Swords *was chosen as being a good family film. Result: it ran for six weeks, and Radio City Music Hall stayed open.*

The screenwriting credit on the picture was unique in my experience. The authors of the first script, none of which was used, were credited with "original screenplay", and I with "final screenplay".

The Westminster Farce

To call members of Parliament the dregs of society is the kind of hasty judgment one makes at every new revelation of folly or corruption at Westminster, but the sober truth is that no group except criminals and illegal immigrants ranks lower in public esteem. Journalists, lawyers, and even chat-show hosts attract less odium. The reasons are plain: parliament has become increasingly untrustworthy and incompetent, and there is a natural instinct that anyone with the brazen cheek and monumental conceit to say: "Vote for me, for I am fit to govern you, decide your destiny, set your taxes, and make your laws" is patently unfit for election, and in an ideal world would be pelted in the street. People know this, and hold MPs in contempt, but thanks to the inevitable evil of the party system have no option but to vote for them or effectively disenfranchise themselves by abstention.

That is not to say that there are not worthy men and women in the Commons, but it would be rash to think they are a majority. The remainder you would, at best, hesitate to rely on for their ability, courage, and probity, and, at worst, be unwilling to trust with doing more than sweep your steps or, in an emergency, remove your refuse.

Conspicuous among the honourable exceptions, imbued by the old ideals of service to country and constituents, and (don't laugh, there are such folk) putting party second and self a distant third, are those admirable Left-wingers with an independent streak born sometimes of wealth, but also of their personal reputation which puts them beyond deselection. Some may be more noteworthy for their integrity than for their intellect – indeed, some may be described as eccentric to say the least. You know who they are; be thankful for them, and for those others who know that to be a good MP it is first necessary to be a lady or a gentleman.*

But they are well outnumbered by the lobby fodder of all parties whose first loyalty is to themselves, their positions, and their purses, which means in effect loyalty to the party until the time seems right to defect or stab the leader in the back. There is little to choose between the sides, but one remembers with particular distaste the rat-like behaviour of Conservative members when Mrs Thatcher was brought down. For those who still retain any illusions about Parliament as a whole, study of the diaries of the late Alan Clark will prove instructive and disgusting.

But it is not to be wondered at, when one considers the muddy path that aspiring politicians must follow to reach Westminster. To win selection as candidates they must be able convincingly to dissemble, to toady, to cozen, and, when necessary, to lie outright; given these essential defects of character, and a sufficient supply of platitudinous wind to deceive the voters, all they need is luck and grovelling loyalty to the leader, obedience to the Whips, and an ability to suppress conscience, common sense, and decency as the need arises.

It was not always so. As recently as fifty years ago, Members of Parliament at least presented a more dignified and worthy appearance. They were, to a fair extent, respected and not entirely dis-

---

* Admittedly, Commons tradition militates against this. Bad manners is deeply ingrained, as we see from the constant heckling, childish braying, waving of papers, and general kindergarten behaviour for which the Chamber is noted. If anything, M.P.s seem to be quite proud of this, and defend it as part of the parliamentary system. Indeed it is nothing new, but what was an unwelcome novelty was the playground "nyah-nyah-nyah" technique lately employed by party leaders who mistook stridence for oratory and insult for wit.

trusted; they were thought of as sound, largely decent, dependable people, a cut above the ordinary. Tories might be a bit pompous, Labour passionate, and Liberals rather quaint, but no one doubted, really, that they were men (and very occasionally women) of bottom and common sense. They were the subject of jokes, lampoons, and caricatures, and their worthlessness was taken for granted by comedians, but it was a fairly kindly humour; if Parliament was regarded with cynicism, it was of a tolerant kind. It might be derided, but not despised, and it was expected, by and large, to do right.

How far this tolerant-cynical view was justified it is hard to say. MPs were not under the intense spotlight they endure today; their faults were not seen in close-up, and they had the sense to limit their public utterances to political meetings, and not run off at the mouth as politicians nowadays seem to feel obliged to do, God knows why. Possibly we were less critical of them than we should have been; there were rogues among them, but not that many so far as the public could see, and their conduct was generally thought to be above the national average. They were certainly not at the bottom of the league table of the despised.

All that has changed. It is no longer taken for granted that a politician will bear a level dish. There used to be occasional scandals; now one follows hard on another, with shady deals and loans and honours for the boys and brown envelopes and cash for questions and favours in return for party contributions and blatant buying of influence and feverish attempts to hide personal interests.

It is a sorry tale, made worse by the contempt which the Commons plainly feel for the electorate, as we see when a married MP, detected in infidelity, protests indignantly that it is none of his constituents' business what he does in his private life – and in this arrogance he does not lack support among his parliamentary colleagues. What turns the stomach is not the adultery, which is usually good for a laugh, but the lofty assumption that the voters have no right to know that he is not a man to be trusted; he has broken the most solemn promise a man ever makes, but when it is asked "If his wife couldn't trust him, who can?" there comes the inevitable whine about privacy, and the childish attempt at justification: "Everybody does it," which is a lie. Everybody doesn't. Without being unduly sanctimonious, one may remark that time was when unsavoury personal character, like poor performance, was a matter for resignation, but no longer. We have government from the gutter, and neither the detected transgressor nor the incompetent minister feels it incumbent on himself to do the honourable thing. They seldom jump; they have to be shoved. No wonder Parliament has fallen into disrepute.

The tragedy is that not Parliament alone, but the very matter of government, has been besmirched. God knows democracy, that much-trumpeted and venerated myth, has faults enough; the notion of government of the people, by the people, and for the people, was silly enough when Lincoln said it, but later generations of politicians have turned it into an obscene farce. It is worth defining democracy, not in its literal* sense or in the swollen meaningless terms beloved of demagogues, but as it exists in fact: the opportunity, every four or five years, to choose among a few party hacks of doubtful character and ability in whose selection the voter has had no say. That is democracy, Western style.

None of Lincoln's conditions for government exists in fact. There is government of the people only in the sense that they are governed, but not in the sense that government comes of the people, and only a crook or a madman would say we have government *by* the people, when the truth is that it is in the hands of a dishonest, self-serving clique under unbreakable party control. As for government *for* the people, don't make me laugh: the people's will is

---

* The much vaunted "democracy" of ancient Greece was not a democracy in any sense. About 5 per cent only of the population were entitled to vote, and women were excluded altogether. More than 60 per cent of the population were slaves.

flouted at every turn, on Europe, capital punishment, and the promotion of sexual perversion by government, to take only three issues. The politicians' attitude is, bluntly, that the public are sheep who don't know what's good for them, and need to be led by a pack of second-rate lawyers, trade union activists, career opportunists, student agitators, and crazed feminists. That is democracy, British style.

A striking illustration of this was given by one MP, a former minister, speaking on television, when he made clear his contempt for "grass roots opinion", dismissing it as an unsound basis for decision-making; it was, he declared, a negation of political leadership.

The arrogance of this, coming from a failed politician whose judgment one would not have trusted to buy a jar of marmalade, was almost stupefying. He actually saw himself as a leader, fit to take decisions, in defiance of the public will if necessary. I had the same kind of pompous claptrap trotted out to me on a radio chat-show by another MP when I taxed him with refusing to meet the public wish on capital punishment; it was for him and his fellows, he assured me earnestly, to supply a lead, not to follow popular opinion.

Now, this kind of haughty pretension may have been well enough in the days of Burke and the Pitts, when there was genuine force to the argument that the country was best governed by an educated elite, trained and fit to lead and make the many-headed's decisions for them. Many MPs then looked on public service as something to which they were devoted by tradition; they could also, with some justice, consider themselves the intellectual as well as the social superiors of their constituents and the unenfranchised masses. Those days are long dead. No one in his right mind would suggest that today's MPs are superior in intellect, morality, education, or judgment, to the people they represent; many of them are plainly inferior on all four counts. Some cannot even talk grammatically, and by their speech shall ye know them – assuming you can interpret the half-educated proletarian noises they make.

I have mentioned Burke, and those who defend the practice of MPs following their own judgment against the voters' wishes can quote, if they are familiar with his works or have even heard of him, his warning to the people of Bristol that their MP owed them his judgment, "and betrays . . . you if he sacrifices it to your opinion." Fair enough for the eighteenth century, no doubt, but it was also this same Burke who said: "In all forms of government the people is the true legislator", and, most tellingly: "I am not one of those who think that the people are never wrong . . . but I do say that in all disputes between them and their rulers, the presumption is . . . in favour of the people."

It appears that the great Parliamentarian was no more consistent than any other politician, but he would repay study by those who, in their complacent self-admiration, have so little regard for the wishes of those whose judgment they were only too delighted to accept when it sent them to Westminster.

An excellent way of demonstrating the unfitness of MPs is to compare them to ourselves. I think I know my capacity and limitations, and I doubt if I have ever been competent to run a department of state, but I led an infantry section in war when I was nineteen, commanded a platoon when I was twenty-one, and in middle age edited a great daily newspaper. Now all these jobs required some degree of what is called leadership – a gift which people like Blair seem to think is automatically conferred by election. I hold no very high opinion of myself as a leader, but can it be contended that the sorry collection of placemen and party hacks and p.c. women and semi-literate nonentities who have crawled and toadied and lied their way to Westminster are fit to lead me and millions like me – educated professionals and workers and artisans and craftsmen who have made their way in the world by real skill and perseverance, not by blathering and caballing?

If I weren't so outraged at the idea, I'd be helpless with laughter. Blair, a junior barrister who has never done a real job in the real world, to lead me? I wouldn't follow him round the corner. Or any of his Cabinet of freaks and oddballs. Or the sorry parcel of yuppies and businessmen opposite.

It may be asked, what's the alternative, and the answer is that there isn't one. The British political system has been defended as the least bad polity yet invented, and there is something in it – *but only so long as the people who operate it play the game.* I don't apologise for using an old, perhaps outworn, expression; what I am saying is that our "democracy" is acceptable only if our elected rulers are honest, tell the truth, behave with decency, and strive to remember that they are there to serve the people as the people wish to be served.

That is not what we have, or have had for thirty years, or look like having for a long time to come. Politics has become the preserve of the second-rate, a career primarily seen as a means of advancing personal ambition and lining the pocket; service is the last thing an aspiring parliamentarian has in mind. I must say again that I speak of the majority, not of the handful who have not forgotten what honour means.

Occasionally, and more often since we became involved in the European folly, it is suggested that we need a constitution. This is puerile. There is not, and never has been, a written constitution worth powder to blow it to hell, including the collection of platitudes and wishful thinking by which Americans set such misguided store. Why it should be supposed that a document drawn up by a group of eighteenth-century English squires and merchants for a largely agricultural country should be thought suitable for the governance of a modern, highly industrialised, multi-national state, has never been clear to me, but then I have always been mistrustful of vague, high-sounding, and sometimes downright daffy pontifications, and uncomfortably aware that a constitution means what you want it to mean. We have seen the US Constitution twisted and distorted and turned inside out by slick lawyers to a degree which Jefferson and Co. wouldn't believe; to take one small example, they wouldn't have equated pornography with freedom of speech.

We must remember also that any constitution endures only until someone comes along who is powerful enough to tear it up, as the history of Germany, and others, bears witness.

That, of course, is the ever-present danger, and it applies regardless of whether a country has a constitution or not. Any democracy which plays its people false is liable to find itself displaced by tyranny, and don't think it couldn't happen in dear, sane, sensible old Britain. All it takes is enough betrayal by dishonest government, and enough public disillusion, and suddenly Wodehouse's wonderful fun about "Spode swanking about in his footer bags" is funny no longer.

We can only hope for the best, reminding ourselves that our creaky old "democracy" can work, given integrity and courage in those charged with operating it; even the ghastly party system needn't be an insuperable obstacle to good government. It's a bloody awful manifestation of the worst in human and political nature, but it's inevitable, as is the lure of politics to the corrupt and venal personality. The days when Cincinnatus could be called from the plough are long gone – and if he could be called he would be derided as a comic figure at Westminster.

In closing, I must cite a prime example of hypocrisy in the so-called mother of Parliaments: the clamour from the Liberal Democrat benches for proportional representation. They demand it as the only fair, equitable, sensible, honourable, etc., etc., system. In fact, fairness, equity, sense, and most of all honour, have nothing to do with it; the Liberals want it because it's the only possible way by which their clapped-out party can ever hope to get a share of power. Strange that their cry was never heard in the days (now some time ago, fortunately) when the Liberal Party meant something; was it not fair and equitable then? The truth is that today's Liberal Democrats are like a football team fed up and resentful at languishing permanently at the bottom of the league, crying: "The rules must be changed, so that we can win." It is a pathetic, typically dishonest plea.

Quite apart from the moral one, there are many reasons why proportional representation, in any form, would be an extremely bad thing. One is that in Britain we traditionally vote for people, not parties, and the notion of party lists of candidates, chosen by the party hierarchy, is totally odious to any serious democrat. Not only is it wrong in principle; in fact it would mean that you could never get rid of those parliamentary disasters who so often rise to the top in their parties; p.r. would guarantee them permanent seats.

On that last ground alone p.r. is abominable, but we may add the equally convincing objection, namely that it doesn't work, as consideration of the havoc it has wreaked in various continental countries shows all too clearly. Fortunately, thus far New Labour has resisted the Liberal Democrat demand; the danger is that if ever they suffer a reduced majority they may bring it in to ensure the survival of Left-wing government – and its probable continuance until the day when Scotland becomes fully independent, and England, spared the presence of the Clydeside rabble at Westminster, will get the conservative (I emphasise the small "c") English government it wants.

Orcs and Goblins

W ITH THE FIRST FILM OF *The Lord of the Rings* trilogy having rekindled the controversies about allegories and symbolism which broke out after the books' publication more than forty years ago, and new disputes about where Tolkien got his inspiration (the Warwickshire countryside? the Ribble Valley? the Western Front?) it is highly satisfactory to be able to settle absolutely one minor question in the great panorama of Tolkienery. Namely, are the goblins of *The Hobbit* the same creatures as the orcs of the *Ring* stories, or are they of different species?

This debate divided the canteen of *The Glasgow Herald* in the 1960s, so I wrote to Tolkien for a ruling and received a courteous and detailed reply, written in the famous spidery hand so familiar to students of his works. Yes, orcs and goblins were identical, and he added the fascinating information that they had been inspired by his childhood reading of *The Princess and the Goblin* and *The Princess and Curdie*, eerie spellbinders which had helped to freshen my own infant nightmares. Their author was a Scottish minister named George MacDonald (I was about to say "no relation" until I discovered that he was descended from a survivor of the Massacre of Glencoe, and therefore kin to my paternal grandmother).

That is my tiny contribution to Tolkien scholarship. His orcs and goblins are George MacDonald's, but as to other inspirations, who knows? It is a common mistake to think that one can spot with certainty the wellsprings of an author's imagination, as I know only too well, having had a critic state flatly that I was plainly much influenced by Conrad – of whom I had not read a single word at that time. I will not enrage Tolkien admirers by noting that Conan the Barbarian preceded the *Ring* books by many years in the field of sword-and-sorcery, since I would bet heavily that Tolkien never even heard of Conan, but I have wondered if he ever encountered that remarkable fantasy of E. R. Eddison's, *The Worm Ouroboros*, which has been casting its spell for more than seventy years. Probably not, but I'm fairly certain that Tolkien enthusiasts would find Eddison to their taste.

Gene Hackman Should Have Blown up Vesuvius

SOMETIME AFTER the Musketeer movies had been released, Pierre Spengler asked if I was interested in doing Superman, which Ilya Salkind was determined to bring to the screen. I had my doubts but said 'yes' on principle; however, later Pierre phoned me to say that they thought an American writer would be more appropriate, and I couldn't argue with that; in fact, I was rather relieved.

After that nothing happened until the scripts of *Superman I* and *II* were written by David and Leslie Newman, and Robert Benton. Pierre told me they had some slight problems with the script; would I go to Rome to meet Guy Hamilton, who was to direct? So I went, staying at the Cavalieri Hilton, outside Rome (notable for excellent ball-point pens which wrote very finely). Guy and his wife (formerly the actress Kerima, in *Outcast of the Islands*) were staying at a palazzo (Lanzerotti?) in the middle of Rome, one of those magnificent marble interiors which looks like a slum from the outside. We had dinner, and I quickly realised that this was a director I could get on with splendidly; a tall, genial, educated Anglo-Scot who had learned his trade sweeping the studio floor for René Clair.* He was slightly older than I; Kerima, who was about my age (early fifties) he referred to as "my child-bride".

---

* The *Macmillan Film Encyclopedia* describes Guy as "among England's most technically proficient craftsmen", which is an understatement. After his apprenticeship with Rene Clair

The production at that time was planned for Cinecittà, and there I was given the two scripts – really one long script, split in the middle à la Musketeers. Guy said: "I want twenty-five minutes out of the first one, eighteen out of the other, and any improvements will be gratefully received."

In fact they were splendid scripts – fast, inventive, and thoroughly well-written, and I hated the idea of cutting them at all. But I did, in consultation with Guy – which means that I explained where I would abbreviate and connect up, got his agreement, and made my notes for the actual work, which I would do at home. There was no question of improving them; I just had to cut and rework so that no one could see the joins.

I had previously been sent Mario Puzo's script, which is still in my attic somewhere. It was enormous, with very long speeches, and I didn't refer to it again: my impression is that if its storyline bore any resemblance to the Newmans–Benton job, the actual treatment and dialogue didn't, but I never read it closely. Puzo got the principal credit on the first two movies, but for my money the moral credit belongs to the N–B version. At this stage I doubt if I contributed much new material at all – maybe a rephrasing of dialogue to accommodate a cut, maybe a different ending-opening of scenes for the same reason, but nothing original. Anyway, I did the work, getting the scripts down to size, and that, I thought, would be that.

At this stage, incidentally, there were four super-villains in the movies, to be played, it was hoped, by Christopher Lee (as Zod), Ursula Andress, Charles Bronson (as the goon) and Mickey Rooney as a sort of evil jester, Jakel. The Rooney character had to go, alas, and in the end the villains were played by Terence Stamp, Sarah Douglas, and Jack O'Halloran.

---

he graduated to assistant director with Carol Reed and John Huston, and worked on such prestigious films as *The Third Man* and *The African Queen* before going on to direct a string of major pictures, including four James Bonds – one of which, *Goldfinger,* I regard as the best in the series.

Time passed, in which I wrote books and worked on various other films – *Royal Flash* (with Dick Lester), *Prince and Pauper* (Fleischer), *Force Ten from Navarone* (Hamilton, of which more anon), and at least as many others which never got made, such being the way of this crazy industry. Five films written and actually screened in five years was unusually good going, but in my novice ignorance I didn't appreciate this.

And then, *Superman* re-surfaced and I was invited to Paris, but exactly why I can't remember – presumably to consult with Guy on the edited scripts, although I don't recall our doing so. What I do remember vividly is a series of long meetings with Alex and Ilya Salkind and Pierre in the Hotel Lancaster, where the great question was: who would play Superman? Christopher Reeve wasn't heard of at this point, and one of the names that came up was Muhammad Ali, the boxer. I'm not sure who suggested him – Alex, I think, but not I, anyway. He got a brief canvass, God alone knows why, because even in that black-is-beautiful era, the idea of a black Superman was, on the face of it, crazy. Fans of the comics would have been outraged, and there was no evidence that Ali, fine showman though he was, could act his way out of a paper bag.*

If this kind of discussion sounds lunatic, it isn't; indeed, it's par for the course. The front runner for the part at that time was, believe it or not, a New York dentist who was said to be physically perfect, but I never saw him. Paul Newman was mentioned, and I think Redford also, but it was agreed that the hunt would be a long one. They eventually landed right on their feet with Reeve, who could not have been bettered.

I don't know how many times I was in Paris for conferences with the Salkinds, but it was at one of them that Brando came into

---

* But we may have underestimated his talent; many professional boxers have acted, and acted well, since James J. Corbett and his fellow-champion John L. Sullivan trod the boards a century ago. Rocky Graziano, Max Baer, and Maxie Rosenbloom were all good comic actors, and more recently Jersey Joe Walcott, Tony Galento, and Henry Cooper have acquitted themselves well in supporting parts.

the picture, at a reported $3 million, which was thought excessive at the time, although when I think of the $10 million contracted for but never paid to Steve McQueen for *Taipan* a couple of years later, it seems quite modest. Since then, of course, fees for the top names have become astronomical, if you believe the figures, which frankly I don't, knowing the press agents' talent for hyperbole. But if some of them *are* true, I doubt if they turn out to be justified at the box office.

Anyway, Brando was coming aboard, and his part, that of Superman's father, was going to have to be expanded, said Alex, looking at me meaningly. How could we make the most of his remarkable talent? As it stood, Superman senior, Jor-El, wasn't much of a part; he was out of the movie for long stretches, and what he had to do was nothing out of the ordinary, looking solemn in a toga, mostly. No one wanted to alter the structure of the pictures just to accommodate Brando, so it was a question of improving the scenes Jor-El had already, and beefing up his dialogue accordingly.

Could Brando, Alex wondered, play Jor-El in different guises? I said Brando was good at accents . . . and the next thing I remember Alex saying (this is God's truth) was: "You know, maybe we could see him coming in from golf." Golf? On the planet Krypton? How the talk went after that I don't recall, but I came away from that meeting with a vision of Brando in a kilt with a set of clubs slung over his shoulder. Quite seriously, I know that various possible changes of costume for Jor-El were mentioned – Roman tunic, Louis Quattorze, armour, just about every dam' thing except paint and feathers. But that is how such conferences sometimes go, to the lunatic fringe and back.

In any event, I expanded Jor-El's part – and when I saw the movie his role was, indeed, larger than it had been, but did not include a philosophic moment in which I had him quoting from Wordsworth's "Daffodils", I can't think why. I can't lay claim to any of his other dialogue because what I wrote has simply faded from my mind – it wasn't memorable, that's for sure, but neither were the words which came out of Brando on screen, so it may have been my stuff, for all I know. Or the tea-lady's.

A curious and rather worrying thing resulted from one of our talks. Alex wondered how the trial of the super-villains would be shown on screen. Possibly with a sub-conscious memory of *A Matter of Life and Death*, I said it would have to take place in a huge stadium in outer space – bags of milky way and wide blue yonder, with this tribunal blending into the vastness of the firmament, blah-blah. Alex asked what it would look like, and I had a vision of a pale blue bowl in the great up-yonder, its upper rim fading vaguely into nothing, and the judges seated in soft dimple-niches in its sides, with the Super-villains down in the bottom of the bowl in a solid glass cube, or cubes. There were to be millions of eyes, too.

Alex got very excited, and asked me to say it again.

"An enormous bowl," I said.

"A bowel!" cried Alex, enthusiastic, and sounding very Russian. "Great idea! A great big bowel in the sky!"

I elaborated, and thought no more about it, but Alex must have passed it on, and somewhere along the way his "bowel" was picked up by some unfortunate as "ball". Whether they actually began to build an enormous ball at Pinewood, I can't say, but I was told that it at least got to the drawing-board stage. In the end the Super-villains finished up trapped in a one-dimensional piece of glass, which was very effective, and the judges (Harry Andrews, Trevor Howard, et al.) appeared in a disembodied way, but I don't recall whether they were seated in a bowl or not.

Somewhere along the line Guy Hamilton dropped out, and various directors were discussed – Lester, Fleischer, Donner, and several others. This, of course, was not my business, but when you find yourself at one of these discussions you just sit back and listen, making what observations seem appropriate. I supported the idea of Lester and Fleischer both, they being buddies with whom I'd worked happily – I was thinking all the time of the script, of which I had come to think of myself as the guardian, although I hadn't written it. I wanted to see the Newmans–Benton screenplay faithfully translated to the screen, because it was first-rate as it stood, and I knew that either Richard could be relied on to do that.

My doubt was whether Lester would take the job. I'd gathered that he'd not been altogether happy with the way his deal on the Musketeers had worked out. I'd had my own much smaller disappointment, but I'm not sure that legally speaking I was entitled to anything beyond my fee except in special circumstances – if the films were shown on the planet Jupiter, probably. As everyone knows, getting a cut of the profits (to which you may be entitled if your agent is sharp enough) is next to impossible if the producers are determined to freeze you out; heart-rending stories are told of creative accounting denying worthy actors, writers, and directors their just deserts. My own policy has always been: get it up front, and the only regular residuals I've ever collected have been from *Red Sonja*, a Schwarzenegger sword-and-sorcery epic, which continues to provide small dollar cheques now and then, thank you, Dino De Laurentiis.

It soon became evident that whoever was going to direct, the Salkinds wanted Dick on the picture in some capacity, and I can only assume that they made him an offer he couldn't refuse, and he finished up on the picture with some kind of production title, I think.

Richard Donner is the credited director on *Superman I*, and Lester on *Superman II*, and it was Lester who phoned me after the completion of *I*, inviting me to meet him at Pinewood to discuss what remained to be done for *Superman II*. As in the Musketeers, where the two films were shot as one, so on *Superman* much of *II* had already been shot when *I* was completed.

"I've used the ending of *Superman II*, on *Superman I*," he told me.

"You mean Superman flying through the earth's core, etc?" I said. "What the hell did you do that for?"

He said it had seemed like a good way to finish *I*, and I asked how did he now propose to end *II*.

"I was hoping," said he blithely, "that you could tell me."

This is why I love the film business, incidentally. *Ex Hollywood* (or Pinewood) *semper aliquid novi*. I was rather excited at the prospect – not that I supposed I could tell him anything. We would talk about it, and I would make suggestions, and he would make other suggestions, and by God's grace something would emerge, and I would go away and write it. In this case, it didn't quite work out that way, because there were other factors that we knew not of (at least I didn't).

I asked what had happened to the volcano scene which had been at the end of *I* in the script. He said they hadn't done it; changes had been made to the script. I cursed a bit, because that volcano scene had been the Newmans and Benton on top form – Gene Hackman at the bottom of the Vesuvius crater with some Heath Robinson machine which would fake an eruption (in furtherance of some dastardly Lex Luthor ploy to blackmail the Italian Government, if I remember rightly). Anyway, the point was that in the middle of all this, Vesuvius would erupt in fact, and Luthor would be embarrassed. Well, that was out – and so, if I remember rightly, was a sequence in which Superman penetrated a vault which was guarded by 1) a zone a jillion degrees below zero, 2) a zone a jillion degrees *above* zero, and 3) a belt of super-radioactivity, through all of which the Man of Steel would pass unscathed. There was another sequence in which Superman lost his power, and went out and bought a Superman suit at a pawnshop, trying to kid Luthor that he still had his power intact, but it was changed, to remove the comic element.

Which reminds me, I *did* contribute a scene, adapted from the N–B script, in which Luthor stole Kryptonite from a museum; I had him, the ultra-technological villain, smashing a glass case with a brick, brown paper, and treacle, but it vanished along the way.

Incidentally, while *I* and *II* were exceptionally successful films, on every level, I maintain they would have been better still if the N–B script had been left entirely alone. That's a personal opinion, and an objective one, since my contribution was minimal, and wasn't affected by the changes.

Anyway, I set off for Pinewood, and encountered a hazard that we have to face on the Isle of Man occasionally: fog had descended, the aircraft that would have taken me to Heathrow couldn't get in, and all that was available was the flight to Blackpool, which I shared with an eccentric peer who had to get to the House of Lords for some vital vote or other. We got a taxi at Blackpool and drove at speed to Runcorn, where my companion, who I think had been a big wheel in the LMS or something in the old days, used his influence to get a southbound train halted, and we climbed aboard. There wasn't a taxi to be had at Euston, and his lordship was in despair, but fortunately I was being met by a studio car, and got him to Westminster in the nick of time. So not only did he manage to vote; he excited the admiration and envy of his fellow peers by drawing up at the Lords entrance in a limousine emblazoned in psychedelic colours with the legend: SUPERMAN! and the Man of Steel hurtling across the windscreen.

It was a bit of an anti-climax to get to Pinewood, where Dick and I sat in the viewing theatre watching a good two hours of material which had either already been shot for *Superman II* or left over from *Superman I*. I have no coherent memory of it, but I know there seemed to be endless shots of Gene Hackman and Valerie Perrine floating around in a hot-air balloon, and Reeve jumping off boxes, and the whole escape sequence which I remember only because it featured Angus MacInnes, with whom I'd worked on *Force Ten from Navarone*. My one thought as we left the theatre was: how the hell do we make sense out of *that* lot?

We conferred with the Salkinds and Pierre, and my first questions were: can you get Brando and Hackman back for the remainder of the shooting? They couldn't, of course, which caused me some concern, since I couldn't see how they were going to complete *II* without Hackman; Brando could be got round by using, in place of one Jor-El, a group of starry Kryptonian elders (Andrews, Howard, Susannah York, et al.). Dick was fairly quiet at our little conference, which took place in the lobby outside the theatre; when I asked him privately what he thought he sighed and spoke with feeling about discouraging shots of E. G. Marshall kneeling in the ruins of the Oval Office – I don't know what he didn't like about them; they were used in the film. Mind you, all that we had seen was fairly discouraging; I had a list of all the takes, and it struck me that an awful lot of it was going to prove superfluous.

Alex obviously assumed that we would now start sorting it all out; Dick was non-committal, and said he would phone me next day. What else was said, I don't remember, but I have a memory of Dick standing, saying very little, looking extremely formal in a very nice tweed suit (which wasn't like his usual casual style at all), and for some reason I thought, this is as far as we go.

Which proved to be true, in a way. Dick rang me next day and said he wasn't going on with the project. So that was that, and I prepared to turn my attention to whatever other work I was doing at the time. I wasn't all that interested in the project myself by this time, and when Pierre called me and asked if I would go to Paris to confer with Guy Hamilton, who was to come back on to the picture, I wasn't enthusiastic, and if it had been anyone but Guy I think I might have bowed out.

But, let's face it, I would be getting paid, and I can stand a couple of nights in the George V or Prince de Galles any time. I met Guy and his wife in London and we flew over. Come to think of it, I don't recall why we were working in Paris; possibly because we had to confer with Alex. Anyway, for two days we worked on the thing employing 1) my list of the material already shot; 2) the unshot material from the script of *II*; 3) our own ideas. These last we kept to a minimum, because the less new material, the better; the job was to link what was shot with what was unshot into a coherent story with as little fuss as possible. New stuff obviously had to go in for the Kryptonian elders, but Hackman's part was a real problem, since at first sight it didn't seem to be complete, and would take careful rearrangement.

I covered sheets of foolscap with notes in red, green, blue, and various other colours, denoting filmed material, unshot material, possible plot links, new material, etc., etc.; we cut and spliced and arranged and rearranged and somehow arrived at a synopsis which satisfied us both. Neither of us got a credit on the finished film, but we didn't expect it – there is no such credit as "script cobbler" or "script fixer" or "plot arranger", and the writing credit went to Puzo and the Newmans – why Benton was left off, I've no idea. By this time I just wanted to get home, and insisted on catching an early plane; I packed in haste, with Pierre helping, and as I was about to close my case he suddenly produced a book and asked me to read it on the flight. It was called *The Ice People*, of which more anon.

That was the end of my connection with *Superman*. Dick came back on to the picture, and although I was summoned in haste to Pinewood during the shooting, it was simply to do a very minor tinker on one part of the plot which could easily have been accomplished without me. I watched one daytime scene being shot – an announcer talking to camera, and a couple of cars being wrecked – and one night scene involving the enormous New York street which had been built on the back-lot – life-size at one end, and dwindling down in size at the other to give a sense of perspective. It was a smashing set; I heard it was eventually demolished by a high wind, much to the annoyance of a later production which had hoped to use it. Pierre and I stood in the dark eating endless hot dogs and watching them rehearse and then shoot the bit in which a woman with a pram doesn't get hit by a falling girder.

There was a royal premiere attended by the Queen, followed by a dinner, but I confess that my chief interest was in recognising little bits and thinking "I did that" or "I was responsible for that," or "Well, I sort of influenced that", which is the only personal satisfaction you can get from a movie in which your participation has been limited to tinkering little things, script-snipping and arranging and so on. Critical opinion of it has changed; at the time, the flying sequences were regarded as terrific, there was much praise for the music and the opening credits, and the end titles provoked mirth for being of such length that they even included the breakfast cereal used by Clark Kent's earthly parents. The early "earth" scenes were interminable, and I came out asking myself why the hell they hadn't just been content to shoot the original N–B scripts, instead of padding it out with unnecessary junk. But it was obviously going to gross a jillion, which it did.

Superman II was the better movie, probably because Dick had the direction all to himself. But I like to think back to that Paris hotel room, with Hamilton and me up to our ankles in coloured paper, and tell myself that our labours were not in vain.

The Europe Fiasco

SUPPOSE THAT IN 1945, with the Nazi war machine smashed and Britain rejoicing after the greatest victory in her history, we had been told: "Of course, fifty years hence your leaders will have surrendered your sovereignty to the people you've just defeated and those you've liberated. In effect they will be your masters, your lawmakers – oh, and incidentally, it will be a crime to sell in pounds and ounces . . ." The prophet would have been ridiculed, perhaps even reviled as a traitor, and probably put in a padded cell.

Well, it has happened. Since 1972, when the country was dragooned into the Common Market by Edward Heath,* successive governments, with a cynical disregard for public opinion, have squandered countless millions of treasure for the benefit of the

---

* The holding of a referendum more than a year *after* entry was a cynical fraud, and not only because it was preceded by a massive campaign to ensure a "yes" vote. The claim that this was a fair procedure was rather like pretending that there is no difference between giving a man on shore a free choice of getting into a boat or remaining on land, and forcing him aboard, rowing him out to sea, and then asking him if he wants to get out or not.

It is interesting to speculate what would have happened if, in 1972, Her Majesty the Queen had taken the unprecedented step of refusing to sign the original Bill into law. The howls of its supporters would have been deafening at this breach of Parliament's sacred rights, and a constitutional crisis would have arisen – a crisis which would certainly have seen Heath's government broken, because however unconstitutional the royal refusal, it would have commanded overwhelming support in the country, and we would have seen the welcome spectacle of Parliament, which in the 1640s had to defend the people against the throne, being in the 1970s defeated by the Throne's intervention to protect the people against Parliament's abuse of power. A nice point which would not have been lost on King Charles I and Cromwell – and would, incidentally, have guaranteed the future of the monarchy for generations to come.

moocher nations of the EU, and in return our farming and fishing industries have been brought to the brink of ruin, our constitution undermined, and our laws, passed by properly elected Britons, brushed aside whenever they are at odds with the directives of unelected foreign bureaucrats whose corruption is a byword, in whose appointment we had no say, but whose will is sovereign while ours goes for nothing. Having been sold out not just tamely, but positively eagerly, we have seen despatched to the governing bodies of Europe our sorriest political failures, cast-offs, and has-beens, who of course are pro-European to a man, since Europe has provided them (and in some cases, their families) from time to time with a gravy-soaked alternative to the unemployment they deserve.

We, and the other European nations, have to pay for a "Parliament" which has rather flatteringly been described as "an unspeakable assembly . . . of self-important nonentities", and which not only performs no useful function but is a positively harmful and colossally expensive dead weight existing for nothing but the benefit of its members.

Worse still, our leaders have been criminally stupid in embracing, and enshrining in our law, the wicked and misguided twaddle of European "human rights", submitting to the ruling of that unqualified kangaroo assembly, the European Court, and using all this farrago of Continental nonsense as an excuse for destroying the fabric of our nation. "We have to do it because Brussels says we must." How often have we heard this pathetic whine from a gutless government.

Is it not remarkable that Britain, with a record on human rights superior to any other nation's, Britain which has done more to spread honest law and democracy than all the European states together, Britain whose ideas and ideals have been adopted by every respectable people on earth, should be lectured on "human rights" by the Continent which gave us the Holocaust, the Inquisition, the

French Revolution and subsequent horrors of Napoleonic aggression, the police state, fascism, communism, and other benefits too numerous to mention – to say nothing of being so wicked, corrupt, and feeble that within living memory it had to be rescued by Britain, America, and Russia.

Brazen impudence is too mild a phrase for the effrontery of the European Court in issuing its diktats to us, and all the epithets of cowardice are insufficient to describe the British governments of both parties who have been so craven and witless as to accept them.

I am ranting, no doubt about it. But then, I am enraged at what has been done to my country by the contemptible dross elected to Westminster in evil hours, worst of all the Heath government which gave Britain its death blow, and New Labour who have trampled on the corpse. But not half so angry, I dare swear, as our forefathers would be if they could see the betrayal, by worthless politicians, of the country they worked so hard to build, and the surrender of the precious freedoms won by better men at Gravelines and Trafalgar and Waterloo and Flanders and Alamein and in the skies above Kent.

"Oh, emotive drum-beating!" I can hear the snoopopaths cry. "Jingoism of the most Victorian kind, a bellow from a bygone age!" That is how they see their country's past, and are too stupid and complacent to look to its future. But even they would do well to ask themselves what Churchill and the first Elizabeth and Chatham and William Wallace and the Unknown Soldier (yes, and Washington and Jefferson and Lincoln) would have thought of the pass to which Britain has been brought in the past half-century.

It will be said that these worthies belonged to other times, and their notions are out of date. Not so. The freedoms they believed in are eternal, and we will lose them forever if we allow ourselves to be conned or bullied into, first, joining the ludicrous euro, and inevitably thereafter, railroaded into a European superstate, a union of European soviets controlled by people whose ways are not our ways, whose values are not our values, and whose polities have shown themselves inferior to ours at any time in the past millennium.

Consider how willingly they accept dictatorship, whether of Louis XIV or Napoleon or Hitler or Mussolini or Franco, and compare their pathetic record with ours, who tolerated even such an enlightened despot as Cromwell for a bare decade. Europe is simply not fit to have any say in British affairs, and if one recalls Kipling's line about "lesser breeds" it is not as a racist slur but as a simple truth, and because one questions their competence, their reliability, and above all, their honesty.

Corruption is plainly endemic, not only in great matters at the very top in the European Parliament, but in such trivia as the World Cup 2006 scandal; the bribe, the backhander, the favour, the nepotism, the freebie at public expense – these are the air that the EU breathes, and there are signs in our own political establishment that the infection is spreading, although we still, fortunately, have some way to go before our scandals reach European proportions.

How unfit the Continental politicos are for government is patent from such indecent proposals as that emanating from Strasbourg which would have "undemocratic" parties blacklisted – this stemming from the propaganda campaign against the inclusion of Haider's Right-wing party in the Austrian coalition. "Undemocratic" meaning any party or politician of whom the Left wing disapprove. Had it been a Communist party, the party of Stalin and the Gulag and an even greater bloodbath than the Holocaust, not a word would have been said;* Left is right, and Right is wrong, you understand, and the fact that Haider's party, whatever one may think of them and him, had been democratically elected, went for nothing. The irony is that nothing could be more Fascist than the attempt

---

* Nor was a word said when the Communist pasts of German ministers were revealed.

to ban a political party; so much for the EU view of democracy. To quote Brecht on Hitler: "The bitch that bore him is in heat again", in Brussels and Strasbourg – and these are the people who dare call their opponents Fascists.

The totalitarian dangers of Europeanisation are to be seen at every turn. It is European gospel that EU Commissioners must put Europe ahead of their national loyalties; it is European doctrine that we have the "strongest obligation" to the Communist countries of Eastern Europe, who must be brought into the union without delay. Personally, I am conscious of no obligation to Bulgaria or Romania, to name but two, and the last thing I want to see is these sponger nations consuming our national wealth and, in time no doubt, imposing on us the "democratic ideals" they learned under communism.

The great mystery is why the Eurofanatics want to see us under the sway of Brussels. It has already cost us a fortune and done us untold damage: why should they wish to cost us more and damage us still further? The motive of those on the European gravy-train is plain enough, but what's in it for those commercial interest spokesmen who clamour for the euro and closer integration? Short-term profit? Perhaps; there are those quite base and stupid enough to think the loss of national sovereignty a small price to pay for lining their pockets. They would probably be on the Right, but what attracts the Left? Being part of a glorious union of Socialist Republics? Surely not, at this time of day.

There are some, to be sure, who have entirely different notions about independence and national honour and integrity from the rest of us. The child of, say, Balkan immigrants may well have a different concept of what it means to be British (supposing he has any at all beyond possession of a passport) than the man or woman whose ancestors have been here for a thousand years. (And that will be denounced by liberals as an abominably racist thing to say. Which doesn't stop it being true.)

One way or another, the question whether Britain remains a free nation or becomes the vassal of a totalitarian Europe will be settled soon, and those who oppose our further integration would do well to remember, and proclaim as widely and as loudly as possible, the unashamed dishonesty that has characterised the pro-European movement from the beginning. Not since Lenin and Hitler cast their obscene spells has there been a political campaign so blatantly deceitful. In 1972 we were assured it was merely a Common Market, and that no political union was envisaged: it is now shamelessly admitted that this was untrue, that political union was the aim from the start. Whether one can trace this back to Vichy France's collaboration with Nazi Germany and the plan drawn up by the defeated Nazi generals in 1946 for an armed and united Europe dominated and led by Germany, is a matter for conjecture; what is certain is that the last thirty years has seen the mischief moving into high gear: lie has been piled on lie, deceit on deceit, and folly on folly, and there can be no one, surely, so naive as to suppose that the underlying motives of the Euromaniacs are pure and altruistic.

It has actually been pretended that European union has kept the peace for half a century. This is one of the silliest lies; the peace has been kept by nuclear deterrence – and the fact that Germany has been in no position to flex its military muscles.

One need cite only a few examples of the Europhiles' lack of scruple: the refusal to accept the original Danish "no" vote, with the referendum being rerun so that the Eurocrooks could get the right answer; the sorry lie that failure to join the euro could jeopardise eight million jobs; and the disgraceful conduct of the Conservative government in bullying and blackmailing their backbench sheep at the time of Maastricht.

But the most dishonourable ploy of all has been the red herring thrown in the public's face by the European lobby implying that the sovereignty issue is irrelevant, and all that matters is satisfying the five economic criteria for Britain's entry into the euro. In fact, this is the least of what matters, except to the money-grubbers;

economic conditions change like the tide, but the right to freedom does not. What matters above all is sovereignty, the right to make our own laws (thrown away with the incorporation of the mad and disgusting European Convention on Human Rights into our domestic law, which has already caused disruption in our courts), the right to remain independent of the unworthy, undemocratic, unprincipled, authoritarian, bureaucratic rabble of Brussels. That, first, last, and every time, is what matters, and "economic criteria" pale into irrelevance.

We do not need the euro, the Monopoly money which begins to bear a close resemblance to the French Revolutionary *assignat* and the Weimar currency. Those who do want it parrot the cry that common currency will not lead to political union, but that is a falsehood wasted, for everyone knows that political union, the declared aim, would be inevitable. The British people have shown that they want neither, and a growing number (including a former prime minister) would like to see us out of Europe altogether. It is probably the knowledge of this that has driven the scaremongering of the Europhiles to the point of desperation.

My fear, and it is a growing one, is that pusillanimous, foolish, and dishonest politicians will complete the process begun by Heath in 1972, and that Britain will become a helpless cog in the European machine, a mere province of the Holy Brussels Empire without real power or influence in the face of our traditional enemies. Babble about being "at the heart of Europe" is wishful thinking.

My hope, and it is a fervent but slender one, is in two stages. First, I hope to see the British public resist the propaganda onslaught of the pro-Europeans, in which the broadcast media, led by the BBC, have shown themselves willing tools of the government, and vote a resounding "no" in the referendum, if and when it comes. I believe they will, in spite of Blair's patronising arrogance in suggesting that Britons can be "educated" into compliance once he has explained things to them.

Given a "no" vote it is unlikely that Blair, even under the bullying of his French and German friends, would have the nerve to reject it, much as he might like to. If it were anything better than wafer-thin he would be perfectly capable of leaping on the pro-British bandwagon, no doubt trying to pretend that he had only been with the Europeans to spy on them.

My second stage, whether a referendum were "no" or not, is less probable. I want to see the whole rotten edifice of the EU collapse in ruin, and if Britain can emerge from the wreck with her nationhood intact, then whatever temporary damage she has suffered by her ill-starred involvement will have been a small price to pay for independence.

I suppose it is just a pipe-dream, but if we must, in the mysterious future, belong to any bloc, for God's sake let it be the North American one. However the ethnic mix of the United States may have changed, they are our people still, in language and culture and ideals. Nothing but good could come of a reunion of the English-speaking peoples – not only Britain and America but the old Empire and Commonwealth countries, our kinsfolk, who stood by us when Europe crumpled, and who, we may hope, would be magnanimous enough to forgive and forget our betrayal of them in 1972.

This may seem at odds with my earlier strictures on US policy in Afghanistan, but it's not. The present crisis is a passing thing, and the special relationship with America, while it has undoubtedly received a tremendous shot in the arm from Blair's "shoulder to shoulder" stance, would not have suffered lasting damage if we had given America every support short of fighting. After all, our contribution is a drop in the bucket, and Blair might have employed his time as an honest broker rather than as a co-belligerent.

As to closer association with the US in years to come, I am aware of the affected-intellectual school who recoil with revulsion from "American culture" (while being all too ready to accept its benefits). I have heard the weary argument about "the 51st state"; well, assuming that our association with the US flourished to that extent, we would be not one state but ten at least – and with the growth of non-white population in America, we would probably be welcome. (Oh dear, I've told another politically incorrect truth; when will I learn to fudge and falsify?)

Alas, it is probably too late, not only to hope for a North Atlantic Union, but to prevent Britain being sucked into Europe. The poor stewardship of the Conservatives, no less than the apostasy of the Labour Party, has left the pass wide open for sale. While Labour stood firm, and there were enough Tory patriots to stand too, we could hope, but that hope is fading now. How tragic, how degrading, that the marvellous thing that was Britain, the wonder of the world, should after all the travail and suffering and heroism and sacrifice and sheer bloody genius of centuries, end with the sorriest of whimpers, sold down the river by mere politicians, unworthy and third rate. And then it will be bye-bye Magna Carta, fare ye well Declaration of Arbroath, so long Bill of Rights and Constitution. You were great while you lasted.

If you have read the foregoing, it will come as no surprise if I repeat a phrase which I used in my introduction: that I have no wish to see our British laws and life influenced by the children of those wonderful people who gave us Belsen and Dachau. A reasonable outlook, I'd have thought, which would have commanded universal support at any time before 1970, and which I'm sure is still the view of a majority of my countrymen.

But not of the columnist A. N. Wilson, who in an article headed "We mustn't believe all Germans are Nazis" was critical of what he called my school of thought, and by implication likened my opinions to those of Captain Mainwaring of *Dad's Army*.

Now I admire Mr Wilson's writing, agree with many of his opinions, and am not one of those who delight in crossing swords with other writers. But his piece made me realise that what I have just written about Europe is incomplete, since it doesn't deal fully with one of my particular reasons for loathing the EU and all its works. For that reason I take him up – or rather, use his piece as a peg to discuss my apparent affinity with the hero of "Dad's Army", or at least with his outlook.

Well, Captain Mainwaring may be nothing more than a pompous buffoon to the snug, safe modern generation, but even from the comedy series he emerged as an extremely brave and patriotic, if hilarious, figure, and remembering the old men and youths parading in school playgrounds and drill halls in 1940, I'd say there were worse role models, and my immediate reaction was to give Mr Wilson the obvious and appropriate retort: "You stupid boy!" I refrained, preferring to point out that I never said, and don't believe, that all Germans are Nazis. I'm just pretty sure that they're all Germans, and that is the point.

You see, while I don't wish to tar a whole nation with the same brush, and have the liveliest admiration for Wagner, Marlene Dietrich, Beethoven, von Lettow-Vorbeck (whom my father helped to chase all over East Africa, without success), Marshal Blucher, Franz Beckenbauer, Conrad Veidt, Kurt Weill, Gert Froebe, Ute Lemper, the great Sig Ruman of *Ninotchka* fame, and others too numerous to mention, including Goethe and Schiller (whom I'm sure I would admire if I ever read them) – despite all these worthy folk, I still cannot overlook the German national record which, I suggest, has few if any equals for brutality, atrocity, and aggression. Consider the Thirty Years War, Frederick the Great, Bismarck, the Kaiser, Hitler, and all that they add up to; it's an impressive roll-call of barbarism, and hardly mitigated by all those fine composers, authors, philosophers, poets, artistes, and the countless millions of decent Germans who, alas, have apparently been powerless to prevent their country becoming, from time to time, the abomination of the world.

A. N. Wilson deplored the fact that, for the Mainwaring generation, the German character seemed to be defined by the period 1933–45; we should, he said, know better, which is an interesting reproach from someone born in 1950. Twelve years in a shared German history is not, as he pointed out, a long time, but it happens to be the period of which we Mainwarings have bitter experience, and it seems to us not entirely inconsistent with the rest of German history. And while one doesn't want to harp on about Hitler and the Holocaust and the Gestapo too much, it has to be remembered that they did happen, and were unique; no other nation, no other people, has ever done the like.

I don't want to be unreasonable about this. It may be, as A. N. Wilson plainly believed, that the German nature, character, or whatever you care to call it, has changed in fifty years, and that the instability (for want of a better word) which led the German people to give overwhelming support to Hitler, follow him in his attempt to crush all Europe underfoot, abet with vigour his ghastly policy of genocide, reprisal, and total war, and attempt to remove him only when the war was plainly lost, has been eradicated entirely. But we shouldn't take it for granted, as I think Mr Wilson wished us to do. He wrote of the "total extinction" of National Socialism; has he visited the Saltzkammergut lately, and seen the swastikas? Has he not read of alarm, in Germany itself, at the resurgence of neo-Nazism? Does he really believe that there is no nostalgia for the triumphant days of the Third Reich among that proud and valorous race, or that they have forgiven and forgotten that in two great wars the English-speaking people beat the hell out of them, humiliated them, conquered them?

Apparently he does. He has assured us that German invasion or domination are not a threat, and while one may agree with him that invasion isn't (for the moment, anyway; they haven't got the muscle yet, for one thing), domination may be another matter. Who needs to invade, when they can win the long struggle two generations after the war by dominating, politically and economically, a Europe into which Britain has been tamely absorbed? It is happening, and the German Foreign Minister is intent on securing more votes in the European Council of Ministers than Britain (or France or Italy for that matter) on account of Germany's size. After which, no doubt, he will have no further territorial (sorry, political) claims to make.

But then, I'm just a bloody dinosaur, living in the past, unable to understand that humanity (and expediency) demand that we forget that past, and pretend the Nazi era was just a glitch in German history, and couldn't possibly, by any stretch of the imagination, ever happen again, because we're all friends and good Europeans nowadays, and the last thing any modern German wants is to get his own back, and let's have another rousing chorus of Beethoven's "Ode to Joy".

Yes, I'm a Mainwaring, a blimp, a chauvinist or whatever, quite out of step with the joyous fraternal Europe of today. I know I'm very wrong and reactionary and pessimistic – but the trouble is that I remember (as Mr Wilson cannot), the thunder, hour after ghastly hour, of the blitz that almost abolished Clydebank, and the horror of hearing the news of Lidice and Oradour, and the sickening spectacle of those ghastly emaciated wretches stumbling out of Belsen, and knowing what it was like to live in a country besieged, and hear in imagination the tramp of jack-boots on our streets, and know we were in the most mortal peril we had ever faced, and that if we failed or even faltered or ran out of luck we would be a Nazi – no, a German slave-state. That is what the Germans wanted and did their damnedest to do to us – not just Hitler, the Germans. Is it wrong to keep it in mind?

What prompted Mr Wilson's article was the German Ambassador's anxiety about what he saw as a British obsession with 1939–45. Well, considering that Germany caused the greatest mass slaughter in human history in those years, and wreaked carnage on us, and committed the most abominable crimes, it would be no wonder if we were obsessed. But the word is ridiculously strong, and the Ambassador's complaint seems to me to reflect a wondrously Teutonic insensitivity, rather as though the son of a convicted rapist and killer should wonder what the victim's family have got to beef about. But as I've already made clear, it is not only the last war that colours our view, but a perfectly rational feeling that Germany, whatever her statesmen and our Europhiles may say, has shown by her history that she is not a country to be trusted. And if I am prejudiced (which I am not, but *post*-judiced), it may be because I can still hear the words:

"Our countries are friends now; we can never fight each other again."

They were spoken in my presence by a member of the Hitler Youth when he visited our school on a goodwill exchange in 1935. The tragic irony is that he may have spoken them with complete sincerity.

"Oh, grow up!" was Mr Wilson's reaction to my Mainwaringish reservations about Germany. My difficulty is that, unlike him, I did grow up, but in my time, not his, and I want my grandchildren to grow up in theirs. I believe they have a better chance of doing that if Germany is carefully watched, kept within bounds, and above all not allowed the least influence in our affairs. To put it mildly, they haven't earned the privilege. A dominant Germany is not, and never has been, a safe thing for the peace of the world, and we would do well to remember that – and reflect on the thought that came to me on the night the Berlin Wall came down, and all the politicians and pundits and media cheer-leaders threw up their sweaty nightcaps: I know one man who'd have exulted tonight, and his name was Adolf Hitler.

It's too late for me and my generation to grow up; our government cannot hope to "educate" us into what Mr Wilson called "a different perspective on things". We know too much, and are hardly to be instructed by second-rate politicians who have still (we can only hope) to reach maturity.

Nor, I have to say, by A. N. Wilson. He does not see Germany as a potential menace, but thinks the most obvious threat to our civilisation is "creeping Americanism." Well, I don't care for McDonalds or the US Constitution or the Jerry Springer show or cheeseburgers (whatever they are) myself, and I do try to make allowances for the youthful folly of columnists, but there are limits to my tolerance.

It's no use, I've got to say it: "You stupid boy!"

Act of Settlement

CONTRARY TO FASHIONABLE, ill-considered opinion, the Act of Settlement, which in effect bars Roman Catholics from the throne, must be retained.

On the face of it the Act is discriminatory, unfair, archaic, bigoted, wicked, and all the other epithets its opponents can throw at it, and the case for removal seems obvious. There is, however, one excellent and over-riding reason for keeping the Act: the British monarch must never be subservient, spiritually or otherwise, to a foreigner, usually an Italian though at present a Pole.

It is that simple. I know little of Roman Catholic doctrine, and am not in sympathy with what I understand of Catholic beliefs and practices, but since I'm not in sympathy with anyone else's religious beliefs either, I hope I may be acquitted of partisanship. But I confess I find it difficult to accept the plea for toleration from a Church whose intolerance is a byword.

If a Catholic wishes to reign in Britain, he or she must somehow discover (possibly with Jesuitical assistance) a means whereby he or she continues in his or her faith, but at the same time ceases to recognise the Pope's superiority. (I think we've been here before, in Henry VIII's time, but that's by the way.) If such spiritual agility is impossible for a devout Catholic aspirant to the throne, then forget it.

"Not a Bad Bismarck, Was I?"

I WORKED ON FIVE FILMS with Oliver Reed, but I didn't get to know him well. We weren't just of different generations, but of different worlds, and had little in common beyond our work. Yet with the possible exceptions of George C. Scott and Edward Fox, he was the most rewarding actor I ever wrote for, and one of the best. He is remembered chiefly as what is called, usually with admiration, a hell-raiser – though why anyone should admire a loud-mouthed, violent, drunken nuisance (which is all a hell-raiser is) I can't imagine. Oliver may have been all of that; I have seen him make an immortal ass of himself on television, and had well-documented accounts of his excesses from mutual acquaintances, but of his legendary aggression I had no personal experience. Eccentric behaviour, yes, but violence, no. And he could be, and often was, a perfect gentleman.

I can't recall my first sight of him on film, but I know he struck me as one of the ugliest men I'd ever seen, and when he was cast as Athos, with top billing in that astoundingly starry Musketeer cast, I was disappointed, especially as Heston had been mentioned for the part, before his inspired casting as Richelieu. My disappointment turned to alarm when I heard that during shooting in Spain Oliver had been arrested after a hotel brawl and dragged to the slammer by five policemen, roaring: "Leave me alone! I'm Athos of *The Three Musketeers*! I don't want any problems!" He escaped prosecution, but it was a worrying beginning.

However, doubt and disappointment didn't last five seconds after I had heard his first lines when the showing of the rough-cut took place at Twickenham. He had to say, with facetious sarcasm, that the gash on his arm was not a wound, but small-pox, and when the sycophantic surgeon agreed, to retort: "Don't pretend you would know one from the other, or that it would make any difference to your treatment if you did."

Not the easiest line for an actor to manage, as I'd known when I wrote it; Oliver rasped it out at speed with splendid throwaway contempt, and I felt that surge of delight that comes when you hear your words spoken far better than you thought they could be. (Good actors can send a writer out of the cinema convinced that he's a genius.)

I knew then that Lester had found the perfect Athos, and when I met Reed for the first time I thanked him for the way he'd handled those opening lines. Roy Kinnear, typically, couldn't resist adding: "He means the rest of your lines weren't so hot," but Oliver just smiled and said: "Thanks for the opportunity."

I did my best to give him the opportunity again in later films because it was such a pleasure to hear and watch him at work. He could always be relied on to give lines full value (and often more than they were worth), and he was blessed with that rare quality that is beyond mere acting: style. He had it by the bucket; Flynn and Fairbanks never swept a cloak or threw out a challenge with greater panache. On the Parkinson show he got his interviewer to deliver a "Musketeer line", and very well Parkinson did it; he had the best exemplar in the business.

When you know whom you're writing for, you obviously try to play to his strength. Olly had remarkable breath control, and frequently I deliberately gave him quite long passages rising to a crescendo, because he did them so well. He didn't always care for this; on one occasion, faced with a tirade, he complained to Dick Fleischer about "George adjective Fraser's adjective dialogue" being "too adjective much."

"Then don't say it," said cunning Fleischer, knowing that such a remark is about the most deflating thing an actor can hear, especially an actor without formal training. Oliver snarled – and once in front of the camera, said the speech perfectly.

He had the most menacing whisper in the business, and, unlike many whispers, it was always audible; he would vary it with sudden, unexpected roars, and took a special delight in pejoratives and insults which he could spit out – I recall him on location in Spain, bellowing with laughter as he rehearsed, with immense gusto, a line which he had to fling at Bob Todd (he of Benny Hill fame): "Take your damned summons and soak it in wine and choke on it, you time-serving pimp!" He brought the same energy to his action sequences, and I often felt a pang for the extras and stuntmen who got in his way when he was really motoring. He met his match on *Royal Flash*, in which he had to trade punches with Henry Cooper, who was playing John Gully, a champion of the Napoleonic era,[*] to Oliver's Bismarck. I wasn't present, but I understand that Oliver got ambitious until Cooper gave him what is technically known as "a sweetener", to calm him down.

That movie was the only film made from one of my Flashman books. Dick Lester directed my script, with Malcolm McDowell in the lead, Britt Ekland as the heroine, and Alan Bates as Oliver's assistant villain – the first time they had appeared together, I believe, since their notorious nude fight in Ken Russell's *Women in Love*. The supporting case included Alastair Sim in his penultimate film, and a number of minor players who have since become very big names, among them David Jason and, in a lovely two-minute cameo as a London policeman, Bob Hoskins.

It wasn't a box-office success, but Oliver was one of the best things in it, and was, as I discovered later, unusually proud of his performance – when we met again in Budapest he hailed me with

[*] There had been a minor crisis when Equity had objected to Henry Cooper playing an acting role, since he wasn't a member, but it was smoothed over and he gave an excellent performance.

a cry of "Not a bad Bismarck, was I?" and I still have a card bearing his sketch of a rapier and plumed hat labelled "Ath" and a top hat and moustache captioned "Bis", signed "Olly Reed". He sent it to me in Hollywood when he was working on *Sting II* and I on *Octopussy*, and it's a remarkably neat piece of work, considering that he did it, according to the messenger who brought it to me, in an advanced state of inebriation.

As I have already recounted, Hungary, where much of *Prince and Pauper* was shot, saw Oliver at his spectacular worst, brawling, boozing, being ejected from hotels and threatened with deportation, and wading the Danube by night. I have to say that it also saw him at his best, patient and cheerful during long and difficult days on set, a model diner in the hotel restaurant, at his most charming when I introduced him to Kathy, and showing no more than mild suspicion as he sat in the corner of the bar watching Fleischer and me conferring – the sight of writer and director together seems to unsettle actors, who probably think no good can come of it.

He was also on his best behaviour at the big party in Budapest, moderately elevated as the evening wore on, but not unpleasantly so, merely inviting passers-by to feel his biceps, airing what sounded like fluent French to a female hotel guest, reminding me again what a splendidly square-headed Bismarck he had been, that he was thirty-eight and fighting fit, and suddenly waxing confidential with dark hints that *they* (the press, the public, the gremlins?) seemed to think that he was over the hill and would be lucky to get the part of bloody Santa Claus next Christmas outside bloody Harrods.

"Just you wait – let 'em go to bloody Harrods next Christmas, get hold of bleeding Santa and whip off his beard, and what'll they find?" Explosive shout of laughter. "Bloody Steve McQueen!"

I gathered then that there was no love lost between him and McQueen, and this was confirmed by McQueen when I worked with him some months later on *Taipan*. There was a part which I thought Oliver would be right for, but Steve frowned and wrinkled his nose. "Ferdinand the Bull," he said. "You know why they call him that? Because he's always being put on his ass." Pause. "Matter of fact, I almost put him on his ass once myself."

The idea of McQueen, who was fairly slight in build and of no more than middle height, putting that hulking mass of muscle* on any part of its anatomy, was not worthy of comment, so I didn't. I have since been told that the reason for their mutual dislike was that Oliver had thrown up over Steve during a meeting in London, which might account for it, but I suspect that even if Oliver's internal economy had been under control they would still have been poles apart, the quiet, plain-spoken, pretty egotistical American, and the ebullient, beautifully accented Englishman. Thinking of them together, I have no difficulty understanding the events of 1776.

I had left Budapest before Oliver's final fall from grace, when he arrived on the set in a highly alcoholic condition, falling down and rolling on the floor. Fleischer was adamant that he would never work with him again, but knowing Dick I rather think he would have relented if the occasion had ever arisen.

Olly was not the only actor on *Prince and Pauper* with a drink problem. George C. Scott's appetite for the sauce was well known, and when he was cast as the Ruffler I received a hurried instruction to rewrite one of his scenes – this, I discovered later, was to ensure that he and Oliver would not be called on to perform together; some risks are just too great to run.

Ten years passed before I saw Oliver again – in the flesh, anyway. I watched him falling off couches and performing an ape-like dance on TV chat shows, and felt anger at the creeps who plainly had invited him to appear in the hope that he would make an idiot of himself. And then *The Return of the Musketeers* brought us together again, and on the Spanish locations he was back in his old uproari-

* Oliver certainly had an impressive physique, but I was told that when he managed to get hold of the shirt worn by Errol Flynn in the 1937 version of *The Prince and the Pauper*, he found to his astonishment that it was too big for him.

ously good-natured form, bellowing with laughter as he was yanked up to dizzy heights and down again on a mobile platform, enacting a brawl in which he hurled stuntmen about with rare abandon, and giving his lines all the force and energy of old. Off the set he was quieter and more placid than I had known him; perhaps a happy marriage and middle age were having their effect.

We had dinner one night at Pierre Spengler's house, with Billy Connolly and Pamela Stephenson (and their new baby in a cot hard by), and afterwards Oliver and I talked away in a corner – about Max Beerbohm's *Zuleika Dobson*, of which apparently he owned the rights (and supposed gloomily that I would be too expensive to write him a screenplay; I assured him that for friends I gave a discount), and Alf Gover's cricket school, which he had attended, and what might have been if Jack Cardiff had succeeded in getting Farnol's *Jade of Destiny* off the ground, and what was it like living on the Isle of Man – he was then on Guernsey, and feeling restless – and much else that I've forgotten; he was on his best behaviour again, entirely on the wagon, he assured me.

He declined a cigarette, saying he didn't smoke, and when I reminded him that he'd smoked between takes while seated in the stocks at Sopron, he said: "Sure it wasn't a joint?" That I couldn't tell him, but somehow our talk veered from the fatal potential of tobacco to the subject of death, on which we had a spirited argument, he taking exception to my fatalistic attitude. "Rage, rage against the fading of the light" was Olly's style – but then, it would be, wouldn't it?

Our conversation came back to me when I heard the news of his sudden death in Malta; it reached me in hospital, where I was recovering from a heart attack of my own. At such times one naturally conjures up memories: I saw him again, sweeping his Musketeer cloak round his shoulders and telling Frank Finlay to "kill the fellow and come after us"; sitting, sad and heavy, with Michael York, intoning in that beautiful voice "There was a man once . . ."; pronouncing sentence of death on Faye Dunaway with a sudden catch in his throat; bellowing a welcome with that gleaming grin through his beard when we met again in Spain – and our final meeting, at the *Return of the Musketeers* premiere, when he told me he was making *Treasure Island* with Charlton Heston: "I'm playing Billy Bones, playing him as a Jock, what d'you think?" I said I was sure Stevenson would have had no objection.

And for some reason his last words to me after the premiere have stuck in my memory: "Right, George, you know where the sausage rolls are?" before the photographers hauled him away to pose, bearded and beaming and slightly dishevelled.

I was lucky to get the chance to write parts for him; very lucky indeed. He was a remarkable screen presence, and among those for whom I've been privileged to write, he ranks with any, Heston, Harrison, Scott, Lee, Brando, and the rest.

Last thought: if he had been born twenty years earlier, what a war he might have had, for he was the very marrow of those mad, outrageous, insubordinate subalterns one encountered now and then in the forties, wild men frequently in trouble, admired almost to worship by their platoons who thought them hell of a fellows, bull-at-a-gate reckless in the hour of battle, tolerated by an Army that knew when it was well off and when to turn a blind eye, and all too often ending up as names carved in marble. I think Oliver might have been such a one; in his own words, he was true blue.

The Day of the Pygmies

THERE MAY HAVE BEEN worse governments in our history than New Labour, but offhand I can't think of one. Ethelred the Unready was less of a ditherer, Henry VI was useless but never actually had much chance to govern, Tumbledown Dick Cromwell at least made way for the Restoration, and James II had the sense to know when he wasn't wanted. Which leaves us with Lord North, Clement Attlee, and Heath's railroaders of the early seventies who not only brought about the European fiasco, but clashed disastrously with the miners, reduced us to a three-day week, and gave me the humbling experience of flying out from a power-cut London where people were reduced to pinching candle-ends in darkened restaurants, and arriving in a Moscow ablaze with light. It takes a real talent for disaster to go one worse than Communist Russia.

But bad as these were, they didn't have the all-embracing, widespread incompetence, fuelled by conceit and ignorance, of New Labour, who rocketed to power on the strength of an Andy Pandy grin, a Tory administration which had long outstayed its welcome, and a gullible electorate who weren't all old enough to know how awful Labour government invariably is. To be fair, New Labour has managed the economy well, thanks to Gordon Brown, a novelty among Labour Chancellors in that he knew what he was doing, and in mitigation it has to be said that the Blair Government has not been notably lucky.

Even so, one searches our annals in vain for a record of bungling, dogma-driven amateurism to match that of the unhappy crew who in a mere five years achieved the atrocious mess of Kosovo, the mishandling of Scottish and Welsh devolution, the shameful episode of Pinochet, the hypocrisy displayed over Clause 28, the fox-hunting farce, the sleaze which (unlike the Tories' back-bench scandals) was at the heart of government, the failure (shared by their predecessors) to stand up to Brussels, the mendacity of describing a surrender to terrorism as a "peace process", the misguided and unnecessary intervention in Afghanistan, the weak reliance on unelected advisers, and the general impression given of middle-aged boys hopelessly out of their depth in a man's job ... it's quite a catalogue. But all pales into comparative insignificance beside the irreparable wrecking of the Constitution.

No doubt there was a case, if something better could be devised, for reforming the Lords, but there was no excuse for New Labour's undisciplined rush to abolish the only legislative body in the world that could truly be called independent – unbound by party discipline, free to ignore the whips, fearful of no leader's displeasure, or of deselection. None of which, of course, endeared it to a premier impatient of the restraints of Parliament, who has shown disturbing dictatorial tendencies.* He undid at a stroke a Constitution it had taken a thousand years to build, through civil war, revolution, and national peril, breaking it like a petulant child with a toy he doesn't like.

A sensible reformer would have gone about it warily, taking into account, among other things, that the House of Lords embodied

* And incredible delusions of grandeur, if one can believe the extraordinary report that he said in a complimentary message to our troops: "No leader is better served by his armed forces than the British Prime Minister." It is disturbing when a premier doesn't realise that they are not *his* armed forces but the Queen's and that while governments may make war and commit troops, those troops in the last analysis are the Queen's men, owing loyalty to her, not to the government or its head. This relationship of the Services to the Crown is much misunderstood, but vitally important. Which is why the monarchy, not a presidential system, is essential to our security – but that's another question.

probably a greater variety of expertise, knowledge, experience, and talent than any other political assembly on earth. Name a calling, a profession, a qualification academic or practical, and you would likely find it in the old Lords, simply because it was composed not of politicians fit only for politics, but of people who lived and worked in the real world. Privileged indeed, aristocratic relics in some cases, but infinitely preferable to a House packed with cronies and placemen, or an elected assembly of party hacks who couldn't get into the Commons or the European Parliament. For the time being at least the Lords should have been left alone; it might have been frustrating for a Labour government to have an upper house right of centre, but better that than the destruction of an admitted anachronism which was, paradoxically, a true bulwark of democracy. It was a long time since the Lords had been the Tory Party asleep; its restraints on the Commons more often than not had the approval of the country, however much they might infuriate the Left.

But if the reforming (or rather, the deforming) of the Lords was New Labour's most wicked act of mischief in its first term, it at least did not make me ashamed to be British – something I wouldn't have thought possible. New Labour managed it, dishonouring my country and its people by behaving like savages and trying to pretend that they were doing something noble.

I'm talking about Kosovo, a war crime by any standards, for which, in a civilised world, the Labour leaders would have been arraigned and convicted, a brutal slaughter for which the pathetic excuse was that it was necessary because "we could not walk away from a humanitarian catastrophe" – the ethnic cleansing by Milosovic. So they created another humanitarian catastrophe every bit as ghastly, blowing up children with cluster bombs, hammering civilian convoys, blitzing Belgrade (and the Chinese Embassy), acting illegally in defiance of the UN while telling the world that their beastly campaign was just and necessary – and successful, when in fact it failed miserably, with our bombers hitting just 2 per cent of their targets.

And these are the people who demanded the trial of Milosovic* while posing as saviours. To paraphrase *Henry V*, I was not angry till that moment.

It can be argued that a cabinet whose training for office consisted mostly of union politics and student agitation, could have no real conception of the horror they were inflicting. But that won't wash. True, they had no experience of war, and lacked the imagination to put themselves in their victims' shoes (supposing they gave them a thought), but inexperience and ignorance are no excuse in today's well-informed, graphically reported world. They knew very well what they were doing, and did it regardless.

No old soldier likes to use the word cowardice, but that was one of the most distasteful aspects of the Kosovo bombing. We know that had there been the least possibility of Serb retaliation the heroes of the White House and Westminster would never have dared military action – the genuine and justified fear they showed of engaging the Serbs on the ground told us all we needed to know about the repulsive poltroon of Pennsylvania Avenue, for whom the campaign was a heaven-sent distraction from the scandals of his presidency, and the worth of our own government spokesmen's mock-Churchillian posturing. (There's a thought to brighten your nightmares: suppose New Labour had been in office in 1940 . . .)

For some reason which escapes me, there seems to be a feeling now that we have a moral duty to interfere in foreign disputes, and tell other countries how they should govern themselves, especially

---

* Personally, I'd shoot the bastard out of hand, but I come from a generation often regarded as homicidal by the liberal Left, and sometimes even reviled as Fascist. Which reminds me, it was fascinating to hear the then Foreign Secretary, Robin Cook, denounce Milosovic, in fervent tones, as a Fascist; he actually said it twice, presumably in case people found it incredible, which it was. Milosovic is not and was not a Fascist; he is and was a Communist, and while the two are closer together than political rhetoric will ever admit, there is a difference. So why did Cook talk nonsense? Because to him, as to all socialists, "Communist" is not an insult in the same league as Fascist; indeed it is not an insult at all.

if so-called democracy is thought to be in danger. This has led us into costly misadventures in Yugoslavia and Afghanistan – where we had absolutely no right to be, sticking our nose into other people's quarrels – and in Sierra Leone. But not, curiously, in Zimbabwe, where our people were actually being attacked and dispossessed by a most unsavoury tyrant. But then, one perhaps shouldn't expect New Labour to worry about ethnic Britons in Zimbabwe, whom they probably regard as the despised remnant of a colonial era, and therefore unworthy of concern.

As to our "moral duty" elsewhere, isn't it ironic that today's liberals, who throw up their hands in horror at our interferences overseas in previous centuries, seem to approve of them in a modern context – no matter how unjustified, and no matter that they produce atrocities like the cluster bombs of Kosovo?

If anything, the Pinochet affair was even more dishonourable than Kosovo, being a mixture of treachery and sheer bad manners. His arrest and detention were said to be justified by his crimes against humanity and the demand for extradition from a Spanish lawyer, but both in fact were irrelevant, and would not even have been considered if he had been a Mao or a Castro or even a Stalin with full Left-wing credentials, instead of a monster of the hated Right.

The real issue was British honour, and New Labour's failure to observe a code respected by the lowliest savage. Admit someone to your home, let him eat your metaphorical salt, and you are bound to treat him as a guest and see him safe. It doesn't matter if he's Hitler (or Stalin); if you found his crimes gut-churning (to use the felicitous expression of Mr Mandelson), you should have refused to admit him. To let him come in good faith and then seize him is simply despicable.

In the event, as nasty a betrayal as we have seen since Quisling's day turned out to be a monumental piece of bungling. For after months in which odium was heaped on the government, curious kangaroo procedures took place, Pinochet's health and Chile's political situation both deteriorated, vast amounts of time and money and credit were wasted – after all that, they had to let him go, having achieved nothing.

No, I'm wrong, they had achieved something. They had ensured that a saying once proverbial and honoured in Latin America would vanish thenceforth, or be used only in sarcastic contempt: "Word of an Englishman".

I've confined myself to New Labour's three worst offences because the others – the sleaze, the spin, the devolution fiasco, the foot-and-mouth debacle, the disgrace of having to send NHS patients abroad for treatment, the truckling to Brussels, the hypocrisy of waging war on Muslim terrorists while surrendering to Irish ones and even welcoming tham at No. 10 and Westminster – aren't worth the waste of further words. The Pinochet affair was disgusting, the Kosovo atrocity enraging, and the assault on the Constitution appalling, but looking over this chapter my chief feeling is one of depressed regret. What a sorry tale to have to tell about a British government.

And the most galling sorrow, to me and millions like me (not only my fellow-dinosaurs but more young folk than New Labour suspects) who love our country and its past and all that it has done for the world with a fervour and pride this government can never feel or understand, who hope and fear for its future, is that we can only stand helpless while unworthy nonentities spoil what generations of good and great men and women built and defended and died for. It's hard to see the things you gave your life to broken, as Kipling said, and know that not all the tools in the world, worn-out or new, can build them up again.

What a bitter irony that Britain, which fought so many giants and sent them packing, should be brought low by pygmies.

Well, we must bristle our courage up, hope for better days for our children and grandchildren, and never lose sight of the glorious certainty that New Labour, too, shall pass away.

A Writer, a Soldier,
a Comedian, a Football Hero,
a Beverly Hillbilly

PARENTAL-FILIAL jealousy is a phenomenon worth studying. It's natural, I guess, for a son to resent, or at least feel over-shadowed by, a famous parent: I remember Maurice Macmillan, son of Prime Minister Harold, addressing a luncheon in Glasgow chaired by young Hugh Fraser, son of the celebrated old bandit who bought Harrods, and saying that he sympathised with young Hugh because he too knew, none better, what it meant to be the son of a giant. It is particularly hard when the son finds himself in the same field of endeavour as Papa, and is less successful.

But more interesting is the case of the jealous father – or perhaps I should say the father who sees his son as a competitor. Douglas Fairbanks, Senior, is said to have discouraged film producers from employing Douglas Junior because "there's only one Fairbanks". It sounds like desperation, and was rather pathetic, for the truth was that Fairbanks Senior, while highly regarded in his day, was a pos-turing little ham unfit to polish the sabre of his son, the one and only Rupert of Hentzau. And there have been others who have seemed uncomfortable at the thought that junior might outstrip them.

I believe this was the case with Amis père et fils. My first encoun-ter with them was when Martin, then literary editor of the *New*

Statesman, asked me to do book reviews for him. I did, and we had a most happy relationship by correspondence. What was odd was that my work, not noticeably left of centre, was appearing in a famously socialist journal.

"Which is probably why my son is no longer literary editor of the *New Statesman*", was Kingsley's comment when we met for the first time at a *Sunday Express* literary thrash, and I mentioned that I had worked for Martin. The younger Amis was at that time beginning to make a name as a novelist, and I remember Kingsley remarking "I wish him well," and adding, as he reached for another drink: "Not too well."

An odd attitude, if you ask me. I wonder if, being a Scot, I have that Caledonian lust of ambition for my children, and want them to do well, and better than I have done. When my son was appointed Sheriff in Scotland, my only regret was that his grandfather – and my grandmother, to whom I always felt that I was a disappointment – were not there to see it. I fairly burst with pride, as I did when my other son somehow masterminded those enormous dinosaurs into the Natural History Museum. Ah well, it will be said, they weren't in your line, they weren't competing.

True, but hold the phone; my daughter is on her way to becoming one of the leading women novelists, with nine books behind her, a growing readership, and a professional talent which I didn't have at her age. She owes me absolutely nothing except perhaps that because of my work she grew up with the idea that writing was the natural thing to do; her career has been a one-woman show, and if I have a hope in old age it is that she will knock the old man's socks off and become a name in modern literature.

I'm not trying to make comparisons between my parental outlook and those of Fairbanks and Amis; I can't help the way I feel, and that's all there is to it. Indeed the subject has always been one for comedy in our family: let one of the children do well at school or in any intellectual pursuit, and somebody would invariably quote

A. J. Cronin's Mr Brodie: "It's a great thing for a man to see his brains come out in his own child." The jest is compounded by the fact, as the little blighters well know, that I haven't even a vestige of an official educational qualification to my name.

So I simply don't understand Kingsley's attitude – or the astonishing fact that he didn't try to conceal it. To judge from his letters, he seems to have been above-average unpleasant, and even on brief acquaintance I saw examples of his rudeness and cantankerousness, but I wouldn't be human if I didn't have a soft spot for a man who was so enthusiastic about my work. At our last meeting, a lunch for *Flashman and the Angel of the Lord*, he surprised me by asking suddenly: "Which is the best of the Flashman books, then?"

I said I had no idea, and had no favourites; all I was sure of was that I always disliked the most recent one. I added that my former agent, George Greenfield, thought *Flashman at the Charge* satisfied the canons better than any of the others. Kingsley shook his head firmly. "It's got to be *Flashman and the Redskins*," said he, and proceeded to tell me why, in some detail – and if I seem unduly self-admiring in recounting this, my excuse is that it isn't every day that you hear that kind of thing from arguably the leading writer of his time.

He was probably a man of unexpected enthusiasms. He told me that he had recently developed a mild passion for Scottish folk-songs, "The Flowers of the Forest" in particular, and we discovered an interesting (to me, anyway) piece of common ground: neither of us had the foggiest idea what R. L. Stevenson's *The Suicide Club* was about, and we weren't too sure about *Jekyll and Hyde*, either.

All writers are proud and delighted to have kind things said about their work, but few things have moved me more than learning that in the last days of Kingsley's life, Flashman was his favourite companion. That shook me, and led me to wonder what I would like to read when preparing to meet the Great Perhaps, and came to the conclusion that I'd be happiest with something funny, like

Leacock or Wodehouse, or perhaps a good robust piece of sensational fiction. *Synthetic Men of Mars*, for instance, or any James Hadley Chase.* No, even better, any back numbers from the 1930s of the *Wizard, Hotspur, Rover*, etc. . . . Who needs Proust when you can go over the edge and into the undiscovered country with the Wolf of Kabul and Clicky-ba?

I worried a moment ago about self-admiration, but how one is to write autobiographical material without a modicum of smirking swank, I'm damned if I know. So, just to get the vanity bit out of the way, I shall record that I have been proud to number among Flashman fans not only Kingsley but such celebrities as Charlton Heston, Johnnie Cash, Burt Lancaster, Wodehouse (how lucky can you get?), and a plump, smiling, white-haired old gentleman to whom I was introduced in Trader Vic's by the late Bob Parrish, film director, many years ago. Bob presented me, the old chap cried: "Flashman!" and I realised I was shaking hands with Charlie Chaplin. I'm sorry mentioning it, but wouldn't you?

Which brings me to memorable (to me) encounters with great men, the first being Field-Marshal (then General) Slim, of whom I have written elsewhere; we didn't meet, exactly, but I was one of a rifle company whom he addressed in Central Burma, and he was unforgettable. I never saw a more honest, human, and indestructible

---

* Sensational, but far from trivial. In his Martian romances Edgar Rice Burroughs foresaw transplant surgery with uncanny accuracy, as well as radar, electronic tagging, and the autopilot, and in one of his Tarzan books introduced cloning long before it was known to science. His imagination of space travel was much closer to today's truth than either Verne's or Wells's, and his vision of "hot-house cities", enormous glassed-in communities, will no doubt be realised as our atmosphere deteriorates.

As to Hadley Chase, I find it remarkable that in all the learned discussion of "the most influential books" of the century, or the millennium, no mention is ever made of *No Orchids for Miss Blandish*, which probably did more to shape popular attitudes in its time (and consequently in our own) than anything from the fashionable literary icons. That most perceptive of prophets, George Orwell, singled it out in one of his best essays; he detested *No Orchids* ("a header into the cesspool"), admired its author's skill, and was plainly disturbed by it, and by other of Chase's works, which he had evidently studied closely.

For the uninitiated I should explain that the Wolf of Kabul was a British agent on the pre-1939 Northwest Frontier, and that "Clicky-ba" was a bloodstained cricket bat used as a club by his faithful attendant, Chung. They were not politically correct.

man. My mate Grandarse, a walking mass of Cumbrian brawn, used to say: "Neebody's tough. Ah could put doon Joe Louis, easy – aye, and he could put me doon, an' a'. See what Ah mean? Naw, neebody's tough." He added, after seeing Slim: "Mind, Ah'll mek an exception in that booger's case."

From "the greatest battlefield general since Wellington" to perhaps the best-loved funny man of the last century may seem an odd leap, but it was only a few years after seeing Slim that I was fortunate enough to meet Oliver Hardy. He and Stan Laurel were at the end of their joint career, touring British theatres, and in due course arrived at Her Majesty's, Carlisle, where they were to be the penultimate act in the second half of the bill. As usual with Carlisle audiences, there was a pessimistic critic in the gents, observing glumly to whoever would listen: "They say Laurel an' 'Ardy spoil this show. Aye, that's what they're saying." To my delight, when the two great men took the stage and put on an act whose simple brilliance and comic timing were close to genius, the prophet of gloom was to be seen having hysterics of mirth.

I was a young reporter, but it wasn't journalistic zeal that sent me backstage during the last act; I just wanted to meet Hardy. I knocked on his door, the well-known voice called: "Come in!", and there he was, bowler on head, blue suit crumpled, sitting on a chair, looking rather weary in that resigned, patient way that all the world knew and smiled to see.

I told him that I just wanted to say thanks for all the fun and laughter of years, and would have withdrawn quickly, but he bade me to a chair, shook hands, and thanked me with old-world courtesy for coming in to see him. I must have asked him some question or other, for he began to talk, of his Scottish ancestry, and of two of his film colleagues whom I especially admired, Dennis King, that splendid baritone of *Fra Diavolo* fame, and pop-eyed Jimmy Finlayson, the master of suppressed fury. I didn't want to linger, for he looked truly tired, but as I was making for the door he called

"God bless!", and I turned to find that he was giving me the Hardy farewell, beaming and twiddling his tie with those plump fingers. Memories don't come any better, and whenever I recall that stout, kindly figure sitting in that seedy dressing-room, I hear the words of the cinema narrator: "Laurel and Hardy, two very funny gentlemen. Two very funny, gentle men."

No one would call Bill Shankly gentle; I have heard some of his Liverpool players call him the very reverse, and his manner was certainly brisk and frequently abrasive. But he was a merry man, too, loud and lively, with a good understanding and, on occasion, something suspiciously like a kind heart.

I knew him when I was a sports reporter on the *Carlisle Journal* and he was the novice manager of Carlisle United, the club with whom he had made his playing debut in English football, after an apprenticeship in his native Scotland with the splendidly named Glenbuck Cherrypickers. It is an acquaintance which has given Kathy and me enormous status on holiday cruises, with waiters who seem to come mostly from Liverpool; nothing has been too good for those fortunates who have actually *known* and *spoken to* one who in his day was the uncrowned king of Merseyside.

Kathy's first meeting with him – she too was a reporter – was at some function which he was to open, and provided her first acquaintance with what I can only call the West of Scotland industrial accent. Bill beamed affably and asked: "Hoo ye gonnon?" and it took her a moment to translate this as: "How are you going on?", a common Glasgow greeting. In fact, although his accent was strange to unaccustomed ears, he was an unusually clear speaker, with a decisive, rapid-fire delivery; Shankly meant what he said, after a moment's thought usually accompanied by a drawn-out exclamation of the letter "a", something like "Eh-h-h-h-" followed by a rapid patter of speech.

He spoke as he was, and as he had played: a bundle of energy who never let up. The first sight I ever had of him was in a newsreel of the England–Scotland match at Wembley in 1938; it had been a dull game, and in the last minute, with a Scottish victory foregone, the players were moving lackadaisically – except for one, chasing the ball up to the final whistle: Shankly. I played against him once, in a knock-up game at Brunton Park, and was ill-advised enough to shoulder-charge him. It was like hitting a brick wall, and I doubt if he even noticed.

I have heard that he was a tyrant at Liverpool, and indeed he imposed a discipline at Carlisle which would probably seem excessive today. Football was his life, his abiding passion, and he expected (and got) a dedication to it from his players. I remember him seeing off a coach carrying the Carlisle team to an away match in the charge of his assistant; as it pulled away, Shankly had an afterthought, and ran after it, beating on the side and shouting "Fred, Fred, don't stop at yon restaurant in Hellifield or the gannets'll eat themselves stupid!" His training methods might seem primitive to modern eyes, but they were uncompromising.

He could be very human. At a reserve game a young trialist was playing deplorably, and apparently deaf to the instructions roared at him from the touchline; late in the game he put the finishing touch to his lamentable display by scoring an own goal, and when the final whistle blew I expected a Shankly explosion. But when Bill took his accustomed place at the tunnel mouth, patting each Carlisle player with a muttered encouragement as they trooped past (a typical Shanklyism), and the offender came off last, hangdog and plainly apprehensive, he too received a pat and "On ye go, son." I must have shown my surprise, for Bill shrugged and muttered, "Ach, whit the hell, the boy wis daein' his best."

He retained an affection for Carlisle long after he had become a household name, and when the club won promotion to the First Division (now the Premiership), and topped the table after three games, he described it as "the greatest day in the history of fitba'!"

How nice a man he could be I discovered when Kathy and I,

having emigrated to Canada and worked as reporters through a freezing Saskatchewan winter, returned to Britain after a year. On our departure Bill had bidden me good-bye with a crushing hand-shake and an emphatic Shankly benison: "Eh-h-h-h, ye're daein' the right thing, Geordie! There's far more opportunities in Canada than there is here! On ye go, son, and a' the best!"

Now, on our return, and the inevitable reaction from various well-wishers of oh-so-you-didn't-make-good-and-here-you-are-back-with-your-tail-between-your-legs, it was an unexpected plea-sure to meet Shankly on English Street and be told: "Ye're back? Ye've done the right thing, Geordie – there's far more opportunities here than there is ower yonder! Good for you, son!"

A hard man? Hardly.

Lastly, a genial old gentleman now living in retirement in Cali-fornia and delighting our household each year with his Christmas cards, which he paints himself. Seventy years ago he was a popular supporting player in Hollywood musicals, a tall, gangling, loose-jointed, country-bumpkin-style comedian with a slow humorous drawl, puzzled expression, and brilliantly relaxed dancing style. After a memorable failure to appear in *The Wizard of Oz* he became a respected character actor, and gained international celebrity as the archetypal hillbilly in one of the most popular TV series of the sixties. If that were not enough, he is also an authority on Mary Queen of Scots, and is probably one of the few people who know *exactly* where the Battle of Evesham was fought. He is Buddy Ebsen.

He was at the peak of his career as the yokel turned millionaire, Jed Clampett, and detective Barnaby Jones, when he phoned to introduce himself, announce his arrival in Cumberland, and ask me to be his guide on a brief tour of the Border country. He had read my history of the sixteenth-century reivers, *The Steel Bonnets*, which dealt in part with Mary Stuart, Bothwell, and their adventures in the wild frontier country; as an enthusiast on the subject, he wanted to see the land and people at first hand.

We met in the dining-room of a Carlisle hotel where he was trying to finish breakfast while detaching himself politely from admiring American tourists, with many a "Gee!" and "Gosh!" and "Waal, ye don't say!" to the delight of both guests and attentive waitresses; all fans of the *Beverly Hillbillies* knew the grizzled head and rumpled features, and were enjoying the happy discovery that he was as nice and funny off screen as he was on.

He was also a most satisfactory tourist, exclaiming eagerly at the scenery as I drove him north through the Debatable Land to Liddesdale, the cockpit of the Borderland, and the grim fortress of Hermitage, where Bothwell had been bushwhacked and wounded by the Elliots, and Mary had risked life and limb on a hectic ride to be with him. Buddy knew all about this, and stalked round the ruined castle photographing and murmuring: "Boy, that's an impressive hunk o' stone!"

He was indefatigable, too, insisting on tracking down Johnnie Armstrong's gravestone at Carlanrig, assuring me that it wasn't nearly as tough to find as the site of the Battle of Evesham, which he'd done recently, hacking his way through bracken and bramble to the marker stone, and consequently arriving late for a Shakespeare production at Stratford ("but my wife's talking to me again now"). We visited Hollows Tower, one of the best Border peles, dating from 1492, and he stood in awe-stricken silence at the thought that it had been there when Columbus discovered the New World. Accosted by tourists (as he was at every stop we made), he flourished his copy of *The Steel Bonnets*, advertising it in the most shameless fashion ("Publicity, that's the name o' the game").

Naturally, he wanted to talk about Border history, and I wanted to talk about his movies, of which he had little to say, but recalled a production of *HMS Pinafore* when he was at sea in the US Navy; he was to play Sir Joseph Porter, KCB, and was already in Admiral's costume when action stations sounded, so he'd served through the engagement in the full fig of a Victorian Royal Navy officer. I still think it's a shame the Japanese didn't take him prisoner; their reaction to Buddy Ebsen in cocked hat and tail coat would have been something to see.

We had tea in Hawick, and watching the people pass by outside the cafe, he asked me about the racial origins of the Borderers; I told him they were part Viking and he nodded contentedly. "So that's why I feel at home here. My people are Danish."

We didn't meet again for several years, when we had lunch in Century City. Jim Hill, Burt Lancaster's partner, joined us, and afterwards told me about Buddy's famous non-appearance in *The Wizard of Oz*. I knew the authorised version, that he had been cast as the Tin Man, but had suffered an allergic reaction to the silver paint make-up, and was replaced by Jack Haley.

Not so, said Jim. What had really happened was that Buddy had *refused* to be painted silver, even defying the great Louis B. Mayer himself. The result was that for eight years Buddy did no film work; after the war he and his sister, with whom he had appeared in vaudeville, resumed their stage partnership, touring the country. Once, in a New England winter, their car got bogged down in a snowdrift, and Buddy laboured in a blizzard to dig them out, heaving heroically and finally breaking off in a state of near-exhaustion to stagger round and address his sister through the car window: "Boy, I sure told Louis B. Mayer, didn't I?"

That's Jim Hill's version, and it fits. If it's not true, it should be.

The Truth that Dare not Speak its Name

THAT POLITICAL CORRECTNESS should have become acceptable in Britain is a glaring symptom of the country's decline. For America . . . well, a country that could tolerate Clinton in the White House and Edward Kennedy in public view will buy anything, as P. T. Barnum observed, and the transatlantic tendency to embrace the latest craze is one of their more endearing traits, but for Britain to swallow – or at least to accept at the prompting of its media and supposed intelligentsia – the most pernicious doctrine to threaten the world since communism and fascism, with both of which it has much in common . . . that truly beggars belief. But it's here, in all its deceitful wickedness, and it's a brave soul who will dare to lift two fingers in its direction.

Political correctness, whatever form it takes, almost always involves a denial of truth, or at best a refusal to recognise it; it may be the lie downright, or a dishonest, even cowardly, reluctance to face reality. In both these senses it would have been anathema in Britain fifty years ago – or more probably submerged in gales of scornful laughter. For political correctness would be a total hoot if it were not undermining the concept of truth as we have always understood it – until now, when truth is acceptable only if it suits the prejudices and false doctrines of the powerful and unscrupulous p.c. lobby.

Its chief weapons are censorship and taboo, often employed far beyond the limits of lunacy, as in the case of the council which called for Christmas decorations to be "restrained" in case they gave offence to "non-Christians". (And mosques? And synagogues? Would the same council be concerned in case they gave offence to non-Muslims and non-Jews? One suspects not.)

The list of such evil imbecilities is, of course, endless, but before describing my own encounters, as a writer, with political correctness, I cannot resist a few random examples as a reminder of how low we have sunk. Even thirty years ago they would have been greeted with incredulous derision, but now they are enshrined in the p.c. code.

The word "black" must be used with care, or even removed from the vocabulary. Expressions like black market, blackspot (as in reference to accidents), black economy, and blackguard must be avoided in case they upset some racist bigot whose antennae are attuned to take offence where none, obviously, is intended. In one instance, a person of African descent actually objected to being called "a black man" and "black friend". The nursery rhyme "Ba-ba black sheep" is banned in at least one infant school to my knowledge, and there exists a council-run canteen where (wait for it) black coffee must be referred to as "coffee without milk".

Elsewhere, references to war and victory were censored from a plaque commemorating the little ships of Dunkirk, in case foreigners (guess who) were offended. Concern for the tender feelings of the same people inspired the removal of a Spitfire from a beer advertisement.*

"Guidelines" from the Lord Chancellor's office to judges have discouraged the use of the word "British", and leniency has been

---

* But only temporarily. There were nineteen complaints (none from Germans) and London Underground had the advertisements removed from trains, but the Advertising Standards Authority rejected the complaints saying the posters were unlikely to cause offence. The German Embassy said it was a misconception that Germans had no sense of humour.

urged in dealing with Rastafarians convicted of smoking pot, apparently on the ground that it is part of their culture. (I resist the temptation to speculate facetiously on what guidelines the Lord Chancellor's office might suggest if some enterprising worshippers of the Indian goddess Kali decided to revive the ancient cult of *thugee*, whose culture included ritual murder.)

In view of the above it is perhaps not surprising to hear that the Foreign Office, whose record of blunder, stupidity, and sheer perversity is unmatched in the history of British institutions, should have considered changing "British Embassy" to "United Kingdom Embassy" for fear of wounding the devolved parliamentary bodies of Scotland, Wales and Northern Ireland.

The Archbishops of Canterbury and York are instructed in "race awareness". It would be interesting to know just who is considered fit to teach their Graces anything on a subject which is surely at the very heart of Christian thought.

Policemen are cautioned against asking outrageous questions like "Are you married?" and "Do you have a girlfriend?" in case they wound the feelings of homosexuals. The use of nicknames is discouraged so that people of different races may be spared such wounding appellations as Mick, Jock, and Taffy, and feminist sensibilities are catered for by changing "manning the phone" to "staffing the phone" to avoid "sexism", which also substitutes the nonsensical "chair" for "chairman", and prohibits such disgusting words as policeman, fireman, foreman, and, presumably, mankind. And "Ploughperson's lunch" has appeared on a pub menu.

The length to which the p.c. lobby will go not only in discovering, but inventing causes of offence has been demonstrated by the college which reportedly frowned on "taking the mickey" and "nitty-gritty" on the entirely false grounds that one is anti-Irish and the other refers to sexual intercourse with black women. In fact, "taking the mickey" has nothing at all to do with Ireland or the Irish, but derives from a vulgar piece of rhyming slang anent one "Mickey

Bliss", while "nitty-gritty", though possibly from black American vernacular, carries no sexual connotation whatever, being simply an expressive piece of slang, slightly onomatopoeic, meaning the heart of the matter, the essential.

The same seat of learning, incidentally, disapproved of "lady", "gentleman", "crazy", "mad", and even "history" (which presumably is sexist in excluding the alternative "hertory").

Nor should we forget the diktat that those working with infants must not use the word "naughty" because of its negative quality. So a magnificent, expressive, universally respected word with a currency of five centuries in English, is banned at the whim of some trendy idiot; this is as splendid an example of p.c. as one could wish – perverse, stupid, and thoroughly dishonest. At this rate, no word in the language is safe.

A mad world, my masters? Yes, but along with the misguided, frightened, and brain-dead, it has some very nasty, unscrupulous people in it, intent on destroying traditional values and established truth – but for what reason is not clear. Perhaps simply sheer perversity, or an obsessive dislike of Western (and especially British and American) civilisation, or possibly the p.c. brigade are carried away by that destructive impulse so often detectable in supposedly progressive and enlightened thought. It should be noted that p.c. is rarely found on the Right; it is almost entirely a psychopathy of the Left, and if it seems too dramatic to suggest that they are out to overthrow democratic society, one should bear in mind those liberal apologists for communism who used to pooh-pooh "reds under the bed" with such amused disdain, and managed to overlook the fact that the doctrine they so admired was dedicated to just such an overthrow, by any means, violent, criminal, or deceitful.

But the "why?" of p.c. is less important than the thing itself, with all those subversive and malevolent fatuities which it has tried to impose, with considerable success, on a society frightened to stand up for sanity and honesty and simple decency in case it incurs the hostility of the new children of Goebbels. Even the British press, while denouncing them, is not immune to their influence, or to the incessant, insidious propaganda with its weight of censorships, proscriptions, and downright follies dreamed up to pander to the prejudices of special interest groups such as feminists, racists, animal rights activists, and every vocal crank and mischief-maker clamouring to assume the role of victim.

Many of them, of course, are good for a laugh – or were, in the days when W. S. Gilbert, casting about for the most nonsensical taboo he could imagine, conceived of the death penalty for "all who flirted, leered or winked".

Gilbert, thou shouldst be living at this hour, when a glance or a compliment or the most inoffensive of gestures can be described as "sexual harassment", often with demands for compensation.* Whatever became of the girls (oh dear, female persons) of fifty years ago, who responded to unwelcome attentions with a wisecrack, a sarcasm, or, in extreme cases, a left hook? And no hard feelings or whines for protection; they could take care of themselves, and if anyone had recommended that they complain in p.c. terms, they would have fallen about, the brazen little hussies.

Come to think of it, Gilbert would have had a field day with Cool Britannia, ethical foreign policies, Lord Robertson and Mr Hoon sticking close to their desks as they ruled the Queen's navee, people recommending themselves for peerages, asylum-seekers costing more to keep than Etonians, and the word going forth to museums and galleries that they must meet quotas of visitors from ethnic minorities and the poorer classes – a decree which raised the spectre of Asians, Africans, and ragged bums being rounded up and forced to stare at glass cases of Roman coins, while museum police barred the doors against Anglo-Saxons and the wealthy. (How would they deal, we wondered, with a Pakistani who arrived in a Rolls Royce?)

---

* Which, incredibly, can result in pay-outs of hundreds of thousands of pounds (rather more than a war widow's pension or the pittance paid to disabled war veterans).

This lunacy, designed to achieve a racial and social balance to satisfy the Secretary of State for Culture (a title which told us we had been delivered into the hands of the Philistines) was introduced in 2000, to the horror of museum and gallery directors: some were told that 40 per cent of their visitors should be from "non-wealthy" backgrounds, and the Tate Gallery was warned that its annual £25 million grant was conditional on its ability to prove that 5 per cent of its visitors were from ethnic minorities.

Sanity prevailed the following year and the decree was dropped after the museums had pointed out the difficulty of determining what an ethnic minority was (Scots? Welsh? parties of French schoolchildren?) and the further problem posed by some of those officially categorised as poor (pensioners, students, et al.) who in defiance of bureaucratic definition were actually quite well off, and even rich, damn their impudence. The Secretary for Culture, Mr Smith, described the abandonment of the scheme as a "move away from lots of detail".

So that was all right, and what this p.c. experiment cost in money, time, and stress, it is best not to ask. But we may wonder what kind of moron thought of it, blind to its obvious impossibility, and thank heaven that the Culture Department, which is also responsible for sport, didn't think to apply the percentage demanded of the Tate Gallery to the England football team, since this would have limited it to .55 of a black player. (And if a racial yardstick can be applied, why not a feminist or ageist one – why are there no women or pensioners in the England team?)

It's all very well my being facetious. The politically correct ding-a-lings are perfectly capable of demanding these things, and a few more I haven't thought of.

My personal encounters with p.c. are of comparatively recent date. Thirty years ago, when I resurrected Thomas Hughes' bully, Flashman, p.c. hadn't been heard of – not by me, at any rate – and no exception was taken (apart from one mildly concerned American publisher) to my adopted hero's character, behaviour, attitude to women and subject races (indeed, any races, including his own) and general awfulness; in fact, it soon became evident that these were his main attractions. He was politically incorrect with a vengeance, and nowhere more flagrantly than in his descriptions of native peoples, of whom he used language which, while perfectly acceptable in the Victorian era, has been outlawed (quite literally) in our own time.

Through the seventies and eighties I led him on his disgraceful way, toadying, lying, cheating, running away, treating women as chattels, reviling and abusing inferiors of all colours, with only one redeeming virtue, the unsparing honesty with which he admitted to his faults, and even gloried in them. And no one minded, or if they did, they didn't tell me. In all the many thousands of readers' letters I received, not one objected.

In the nineties, a change began to take place. Reviewers, interviewers and commentators started describing Flashman (and me) as politically incorrect, which we are, though by no means in the same way. This is fine by me; it's my bread and butter, and if Flashman wasn't an elitist, racist, sexist swine, I'd be selling bootlaces at street corners. But what I notice with amusement is that many reviewers and interviews now feel themselves obliged to draw attention to Flashy's (and my) political incorrectness in order to make a point of distancing themselves from it. This isn't to say that they dislike the books; they have been much more than generous, but where once the non-p.c. thing could pass unremarked, they now feel that they must warn readers that some may find Flashman offensive, and that his views are certainly not those of the reviewer or interviewer, God forbid.

I find the disclaimers interesting and just a little alarming. They are a novelty of a new age, almost a knee-jerk reaction, often rather a nervous one, as though the writer were saying: "Look, whatever I may say about Fraser's books, please understand that I feel a proper loathing for Flashman's character and behaviour. I'm not a racist or a sexist, and hold the right views, and I'm in line with modern enlightened thought, honestly . . ." They don't admit to being politically correct, and indeed I'm quite sure they're not, and despise p.c. for the dishonesty it is; some may even sympathise secretly with Flashman's dreadful outlook – but they will say nothing to which the p.c. lobby could take exception. That is what alarms me: the fear evident in so many sincere and honest folk of being thought out of step.

But that, thank God, is as far as the British literary world goes in the direction of p.c. – an acknowledgement that it exists, no more. In America, it seems, the cancer has gone much deeper, as I discovered when I wrote a book called *Black Ajax* in 1997. It was based on the life of Tom Molineaux, a former slave in the US, who came to England in 1810 to try to wrest the heavyweight championship from Tom Cribb, was cheated out of the prize, and died after a rapid decline into drink and debauchery. A sad tale, but one which I thought, in my innocence, that the American public would respond to with enthusiasm, since its central figure was a simple black man exploited, patronised, cheated, and ruined by villainous whites. In view of the racial climate in America, it seemed a natural.

But it wasn't. It was readily accepted by British reviewers, who took no exception to the subject matter, and sold reasonably well, but in America it couldn't even find a publisher at first; one described it as offensive, and seemed to think I was trying to make racist jokes, and only after much work by my agent was it taken on by a small publisher, who did well enough with it. That doyen of boxing writers, Budd Schulberg, wrote not unkindly of it in the *New Yorker*, and I received a favourable post from American readers. So how to explain the blank refusal of leading US publishers to have anything to do with it?

The answer, of course, was p.c. I had written the book in the first person, or rather persons, using witnesses such as Cribb himself, William Hazlitt, various English pugilists, and other voices, real and fictitious. They told Molineaux's story, and since they were pre-Regency Englishmen for the most part, their language and attitudes, being of their time, were politically incorrect, to say the least. They used words like "nigger", and treated Molineaux with contempt, mostly, and while this was an absolutely true and fair reflection of the time and place and state of mind, American publishers could not see beyond the awful words and racist behaviour; no use to tell them that this was how it was, and that any historical novel which pretended otherwise would be false and useless.

But even if they understood that, and that a writer either presents historic truth or fails in his duty, they were still in the grip of p.c., and victims of what I believe is nowadays called "denial". They knew the book was true, but they didn't want to believe it, because of this ridiculous obsessive guilt that they seem to have about their country's past, with its slavery and cruelty and exploitation and oppression of black people; they would rather forget that, or pretend it was different, and so they chose the easy road, and just ignored it.

I am not complaining. I wouldn't want my book published by that kind of publisher, and it did perfectly well without them. What alarmed and depressed me was to discover what a grip p.c. had taken in the US; that truth was no defence if that truth was deemed offensive to modern fashionable taste and reminded it of a history it would rather forget. It's profoundly worrying when people refuse to look history in the face because they're frightened of what they'll see there, and feel uncomfortable. It is akin to the kind of prejudice that bans *Huckleberry Finn* and *Oliver Twist* from library shelves because the politically correct are offended by what they call racial stereotypes, true though they may be.

I have run across the same sort of thing in Hollywood, where the Roman Catholic Church, and fear of picketing by ethnic minorities, both wield a powerful influence. I fell slightly foul of the churchmen when, in a TV movie about Casanova for Richard Chamberlain, I depicted the debauchery and corruption of certain clerics – which was historically true, and I had chapter and verse, but that didn't matter. It had to go, so the bishops and others in my *Casanova* behaved themselves, more or less, but the film, while it did well on US television in its bowdlerised form, has never to my knowledge been shown in Britain.

The Lone Ranger, on the other hand, never even reached production, and while the weird vagaries of the movie industry, contractual foul-ups, etc., were to blame for that, political correctness stormed onto the scene, red in tooth and claw, at an early stage in the writing. I had given John Landis a script in which I had used a piece of Western history which had never been shown on screen, and which was as spectacular as it was shocking – and true. The whisky traders of the plains used to build little stockades, from which they passed out their ghastly rot-gut liquor through a small hatch to the Indians, who paid by shoving furs back through the hatch. The result was that in short order, frenzied, drunken Indians who had run out of furs were besieging the stockade while the traders sat snug inside, and did not emerge until the Indians had either gone away or passed out, leaving the little fort surrounded by intoxicated aborigines.

Landis was all for it – and then informed me that word had come down from on high that the scene wouldn't do. It would offend "Native Americans".* Their ancestors might have got pie-eyed on moonshine, but they didn't want to know it, and it must not be shown on the screen. Damn history, in fact; let's pretend it didn't happen, because we don't like the look of it. I still say it would have made a splendid sequence, and I think little of people

---

* The application of this clumsy expression solely to those who used to be called Red Indians is quite wrong: anyone born in the United States is obviously a native American. In fact the phrase appears to have been coined in the nineteenth century by Theodore Roosevelt, referring to Americans of British and Dutch descent.

who will deny their history because it doesn't present the picture they would like. Hang it, my Highland forebears were a fairly primitive, treacherous, bloodthirsty bunch, and as David Balfour said, would have been none the worse of washing. Fine, let them be so depicted, if any film-maker feels like it; better that than insulting, inaccurate and dishonest drivel like *Braveheart*.

But that's another story, equally politically correct in its way, in that it pandered to false prejudices and myths. P.c. comes in many guises, some of them so effective that the p.c. can be difficult to detect – the silly euphemisms, apparently harmless, but forever dripping to wear away common sense; the naïveté of the phrase "a caring force for the future" on poppy trays, which suggests that the army is some kind of peace corps, when in fact its true function is killing; the continual attempt to soften and sanitise the harsh realities of life in the name of liberalism, in an effort to suppress truths unwelcome to the p.c. mind; the social engineering which plays down Christianity, demanding equal status for alien religions; the selective distortions of history, so beloved by New Labour, denigrating Britain's past with such propaganda as hopelessly unbalanced accounts of the slave trade, laying all the blame on the white races but carefully censoring the truth that not a slave could have come out of Africa without the active assistance of black slavers, and that the trade was only finally suppressed by the Royal Navy virtually single-handed; the waging of war against examinations as "elitist" exercises which will undermine the confidence of those who fail – what an intelligent way to prepare children for real life in which competition and failure are inevitable, since both are what life, if not liberal lunacy, is about.

P.c. also demands that "stress", which used to be coped with by less sensitive generations, should now be compensated by huge cash payments, lavished on griping incompetents who can't do their jobs, and on policemen and firemen "traumatised" by the normal hazards of work which their predecessors took for granted; that "grieving" should become part of the national culture, as it did on such a nauseating scale when large areas were carpeted in rotting vegetation in trumped-up "mourning" for the Princess of Wales; and that anyone suffering even ordinary hardship should be regarded as a "victim" – and, of course, be paid for it.

Closely related to the grieving craze (for it is no less) is that of forgiveness. P.c. does not permit anyone to harbour resentment or hatred for an injury, however malicious and atrocious, or to seek retribution. This is also part of the Christian ethic (doing good to those that despitefully use you, turning the other cheek, and so on), and I suppose it's a bit late in the day to point out that it's an often contradictory philosophy* imposed only by centuries of religious browbeating on Northern peoples whose natures are more in tune with the Old Testament and who believe that the best reply to an injury is retaliation in kind, preferably with interest. That is politically *in*correct (with a vengeance, literally). It is also natural and human and logical, and anathema to the new p.c. morality which requires expressions of forgiveness from victims or relatives when some peculiarly vile crime has been committed. It's as though there were a deliberate attempt to institutionalise forgiveness, to create a climate in which a good old-fashioned hatred of evil is never expressed. Forgiveness has become a wonderful excuse for inertia in the face of wickedness; indeed, it makes tolerance of wickedness a virtue – and that is the road to hell.

It is some years since I heard, with disbelief, an Irish father whose daughter had been killed in the unspeakable atrocity of the

---

* Not the least of the inconsistencies in Christian teaching lies in the contrast between the Good Shepherd who blessed the meek and preached brotherly love, and the furious roughneck who beat up the moneychangers in the temple. Whether his violence was justified is by the way; the significance is that Jesus, far from being the rather delicate figure of religious art, must have been an unusually tough, powerfully built, and aggressive bruiser: I have seen the kind of muscle employed by Middle Eastern moneychangers, and if the Saviour could tackle that lot single-handed and come out on his feet, he had nothing to learn about unarmed combat. This evidence of his strength and vigour, with other indications in the Gospels, leads me to believe that he probably survived the Crucifixion and that the Resurrection was simply a reappearance.

Enniskillen Cenotaph bombing, say that he forgave her killers. He is dead now, poor soul, and I have no wish to offend, but I have to say that I don't think he was fit to be a father. A man who can forgive his child's murderers may be a Christian, but he is something less than human, and he sets a dreadful example by, in effect, absolving them. I hate to think that my own father would have been so lost to his parental duty as to forgive anyone who had murdered me – but then I know it would never have crossed his mind. Vengeance, legal or otherwise, would have been his one thought, and if you think that un-Christian, just be thankful that it was a creed to which previous generations held. Because if they hadn't, you wouldn't be here.

"Grieving" and "forgiving" are both heads of the same Hydra of political correctness, and there are many, many more, although few quite as fatuous, dishonest, and maliciously provocative as the great cult of apology. This is part of the guilt industry so carefully nurtured by the liberal Left, which sees no evil save in the past of the white race (as already noted in the slavery question), and is strident in demanding that it should grovel for "crimes" committed in the past.

Thus we have Mr Blair apologising for the Irish famine (as though he personally was responsible for it, and there was the least cause for Britain to feel guilt about it), while the Pope regrets the Roman Catholic Church's failure to denounce the Nazis, and a member of the British royal family says sorry for the destruction of Dresden. Then there is the bawling of the "Native Americans" for atonement (and compensation, naturally) by white America, the disgraceful demand from Indian sources that the Queen should apologise for "atrocities" allegedly committed by the Raj, and the even more contemptible cry from Afrikaners (a people whose record of beastliness is matched only by Germany, Belgium, and various banana republics) that she should apologise for the Boer War.

Words fail me, but it is necessary in the face of all this impertinent and dishonourable whining that one should approach the matter calmly, as I do.

To begin with, it should be obvious that only the person who has done a wrong can apologise for it. For anyone else to take it on himself is not only wrong but impudent, since it may well be that the original perpetrator would not himself feel obliged to apologise if he were still here. But it is also wicked, for it is racism of the most repulsive kind, since to apologise for an act committed by one's ancestors, or kinsmen, or co-religionists, is to accept the concept of racial guilt – and that is the kind of thinking which results in American-Italian children pursuing small Jews with cries of "You killed Christ!"

It is doubtful if this occurred to Mr Blair, intent on parading his p.c. virtue, and no doubt, in his pursuit of the chimera of a "peace process", it seemed wise to placate Irish nationalism. His Holiness probably bowed to similar political pressure, although in his case he may have felt himself the embodiment of Catholicism, and so responsible for its crimes and misdemeanours. They were both misguided, to say the least; apologies, if they were ever due, would be the concern of Pius XI and Pius XII, not of John Paul; and of Sir Robert Peel and Lord John Russell, not Mr Blair, who is obviously unaware that, far from feeling guilt over the Great Hunger, Britain can feel pride at the huge efforts which its people made to alleviate it.

Similarly, apology for Dresden is an insult to Bomber Command; if apology were due (which it patently is not) it would have to come from them, no one else. And the suggestion that the Queen should apologise for acts committed in previous centuries is as foolish as it is insolent. Nor is the Archbishop of Canterbury in a position to apologise for "wars, racism, and other sins committed in the name of Christianity" during the last millennium. Nor is the Pope, who seems to have an obsession with apology, to make one to Africa for the slave trade.

To put it bluntly, it is none of their business, and they do wrong to take it upon themselves to speak for the dead. George Carey slaughtered no prisoners at the Siege of Acre, and John Paul did not work his ticket on the Middle Passage. And it is doubtful if the Crusaders or the slave-runners felt any reason to apologise. So condemn them by all means, if it makes you feel better, but don't have the effrontery to apologise for them.

All this is crashingly obvious – unless you believe in racial guilt and inherited guilt, and it is hard to think of a more wicked, dangerous doctrine. It makes for enmity, hatred, and mistrust – between black and white, Catholic and Protestant, Jew and Muslim, German and practically everybody. The list is endless, and while such mutual antipathies are inevitable, that is no reason for going through the bogus and thoroughly hypocritical farce of apology. It serves only to keep the hatreds alive.

Which is why, while I cannot help feeling a dislike for the Japanese en masse, I cannot for a moment subscribe to the suggestion that modern Japan should apologise for atrocities committed by their fathers and grandparents. Those were the guilty ones, not their descendants.

The sickest joke about the apology racket is its complete one-sidedness. Some modern Indians demand apology from Britain for the Amritsar massacre – but does it occur to them that, if such apologies are due, they must cut both ways? Is modern India prepared to apologise for the appalling atrocities of Cawnpore, Meerut, and Jhansi? Do the "Native Americans", beating their breasts about Sand Creek and Wounded Knee, feel like owning up to the massacre of helpless white prisoners at Fort William Henry and Fort Venango, or atoning for the abominations practised by the Apaches on the Rio Grande settlements, or the shattered wagon trains and butchered immigrants? Are the Irish republicans, keening over Drogheda and Cromwell, ready to apologise for the burned-out Protestants and the foul crimes of the IRA? Do we hear sincere apology, for their part in the slave trade, from the descendants of those Africans who made such a good thing out of it?

Don't be naive. Political correctness demands that blame should lie on one side only, usually the British and American, and that no non-whites can ever be taxed with past crimes, the rationale being that if they committed them, they were justified, and it was all the whites' fault anyway. Incidentally, I doubt if many "Native Americans" have even heard of Fort William Henry, and you can be sure that no p.c. historian is going to enlighten them.

So much for the apology industry, one of the most truly rotten manifestations of p.c. And yet great and good people are stupid enough, and pressured enough, to subscribe to it; they feel they ought to, and not having considered the dreadful implications of the concept of racial guilt, they accept meekly the vilification from ethnic minority agitators and liberal bigots. The black humour of it all is that they believe they are living in the most enlightened age this country has ever seen, when the truth is that we have to look back to the days of supremacy of the Roman Catholic Church and the excesses of the Puritans to find spiritual tyrannies to compare with political correctness. Common to all is the abominable doctrine: "Thou shalt not speak, nor even think for thyself, but only as thou art told."

(Oh, shame on me. I have used the phrase "black humour", and must apologise for the deep offence this must have given to all non-whites. It was entirely unintentional – which of course is no excuse. Sick humour, then. I'll just have to risk offending everyone in hospital.)

119

To Scotland, with Love

"THERE'S LITTLE GOOD in an English Whig; in a Scotch Whig there's none," says John Law of Laurieston in Sabatini's *The Gamester*. For Whig read politician, and consider, in support of this, that the most Scottish government ever to sit at Westminster is manifestly the worst. Whether the new Scottish Parliament will prove to be a burdensome and expensive disaster it is still too early to say, but the eagerness with which its members have voted for a colossally expensive and entirely unnecessary new parliament building which will be an architectural atrocity as well as a monument to its occupiers' self-importance, does not bode well.

I was, and remain, a firm anti-Scottish Nationalist, but whereas my enmity thirty-five years ago was unqualified, and expressed through the columns of *The Glasgow Herald* at every opportunity, it has been modified of late. I can no longer blame any inhabitant of Scotland for wanting to get rid of Westminster rule, although whether King Stork will be any better than King Log (assuming full independence does come) is doubtful. He'll be a dam' sight more expensive, with the loss of the Westminster subsidy and inevitable increased taxation – and this, I confess, was what I found most baffling about the vote (minority one though it was) to set up the Edinburgh Parliament in the first place. If my countrymen had a virtue, I always thought, it was thrift, and yet they voted for something which would inevitably lighten their pockets – and to no good purpose that I can see.

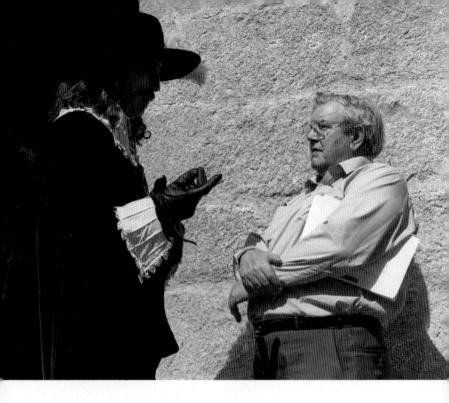

On location in Spain for *The Return of the Musketeers*. Above, Christopher Lee (Rochefort) with GMF. Left, Pierre Spengler, GMF, and Michael York (Dartagnan). Overleaf, Bill Paterson (King Charles I) drives off under the critical eye of caddie Billy Connolly.

The leading players in *The Prince and the Pauper*. Front, seated: Charlton Heston (Henry VIII) and George C. Scott ("The Ruffler"). Behind, standing: David Hemming

(Hugh Hendon), Raquel Welch (Edith), Rex Harrison (Norfolk), Mark Lester
(Tom Canty), Ernest Borgnine (John Canty), and Oliver Reed (Miles Hendon).

A trio of brilliant directors.
Left, Richard Lester; right, Richard Fleischer; below left, Guy Hamilton, and below right, Richard Lester at his most persuasive during lunch on *The Return of the Musketeers*. Pierre Spengler is on the left.

Two faces of Steve McQueen. Above, the familiar look as Hilts in *The Great Escape*, and right, bearded and bespectacled as Stockmann in Ibsen's *An Enemy of the People*.

Of course, the cry will be that self-government, whether by the present half-parliament or a fully independent one, is to be preferred to government from London, and there's something in it, if not much. Certain matters can probably be better settled by Scots in Scotland than by Westminster. But the real reason for Scottish satisfaction in devolution is that it feeds the national *amour propre*, and may be seen as raising two fingers to England – or, as the more virulent Sassenach-baiters like to say, "the English".

Well, it will certainly be an expensive gesture, and to me it seems to be a symptom not of Scottish pride, but rather of a lack of it. There is something wrong, I feel, with a country whose nationalism seems to be based, to some extent if not entirely, on dislike of another country. I never hear that God-awful dirge, "Flower of Scotland", which must be the most pathetic whine ever set to music, without reflecting on the inferiority complex which it reflects. You don't, if you have any national pride, have as your anthem a prolonged greet against an enemy whom you last defeated on a large scale seven centuries ago. "Sent them homeward to think again," indeed; well, they did think again, and beat the hell out of us on more than one subsequent occasion, and we only held on by dint of a ferocious refusal to be subdued which I'm not sure still exists in Scotland today. If Scotland proves to be pro-European, I can be sure it doesn't.

The damnable thing about this poor-mouthed resentment of England, which so often finds an unworthy echo in the shawl-over-the-head complaint that Scotland has been oppressed and held down, is that it's so much rubbish. Until recently, no self-respecting Scot felt anything but superiority towards his southern neighbour. After all, Flodden and Falkirk and Solway Moss notwithstanding, we had stood toe to toe with the most formidable foe on earth and seen them off as no other nation ever had (and if this seems at odds with my sneer at "Flower of Scotland", it isn't, because it's said with pride and not with whimpering self-pity). We weren't just good, we were the best, the little, poverty-stricken corner of Europe that gave the world a lion's share of great inventions and discoveries, rivalled only by Greece among the small nations of genius, whose scholars and adventurers and fighting men and explorers and scientists were household words, and nowhere more respected, be it noted, than in England; was it not Barrie who, in addition to observing that there was nothing more impressive than a Scotsman on the make, also remarked that there was nothing a Scot could not achieve, especially if he went among the English – and he should have known. He was echoing that closet Scot Nat, Lord Macaulay, who had pointed out that the sergeants and the foremen were invariably Scots – and yet today there are Scots who will rail against the England which was so necessary to them, and which they came, if not to dominate, at least to influence out of all proportion to Scotland's size and numbers.

So, that's that. Here's tae us, wha's like us? (Dam' few, and they're a' deid.) Having got that off my chest, not only to show my pride in my race and country, but also because (like "Celtic 1, Partick Thistle 4") it's something that cannot be said too often, I have to add that my feeling towards England and the English is almost, though not quite, equally strong. Perhaps if you're born in England, as I was, if you grow up there, and marry an Englishwoman of the English, and soldier with Englishmen, and have children who are half-English, half-Scottish, then England becomes part of you, and you of England. No doubt it's a sentimental thing, based on misty ideas of Robin Hood and the bowmen of Agincourt, of Runymede and the Armada, of Gray's *Elegy* and Shakespeare's prose, of Squire Western and G. K. Chesterton and Falstaff and the Pilgrims and the Londoners unbroken by the Blitz and my fellow-Cumbrians walking into the Japanese shellfire – hopelessly romantic, you will agree, but very real too.

Unlike the Scottish internationalist who said he was impartial, he didn't care who beat England, I am for England against anyone

– except Scotland. I know that I am an unusual Scot in this respect. I didn't use to be; I can remember Scottish supporters carrying Stanley Matthews shoulder-high, but that was many years ago, and the world was different then.

The sudden increase in anti-English feeling, ranging from mild resentment to naked hatred, has saddened and sometimes shamed me. It is stronger now than it has been in my lifetime or, I suspect, since the Darien fiasco.* Why, is not difficult to understand: the partnership with England, the greatest and most beneficent of its kind in human history, lost its reason for existence with the passing of empire. The high road to England which Dr Johnson rightly described as the noblest prospect a Scot ever sees, no longer led on to the ends of the earth; the huge opportunities of imperialism, from which Scotland profited so greatly in wealth and achievement, had gone; that partnership essential to Scotland's development was essential no more. So dissolution was inevitable, and to inward-looking people the old animosities come all the more easily when accompanied by a general decline in power and status. It's the end of an old song, indeed; the best song the world ever heard, I think – but then, I remember it in all its glory.

It will be seen that my feeling is a nostalgic one, for a time when Scotland was the junior but never the lesser partner in a Britain that mattered in the world. Well, that time's gone, and it may be that Scotland will be well-advised to go it alone hereafter; I just don't know, and I confess my opposition to devolution, and to possible future independence, is not based on sound foundations of polity or economy or social philosophy; like most Scottish feelings it is based on prejudice and passion.

* Equally alarming are the signs that England, that most tolerant and easygoing of nations, is beginning to get fed up with Scotland. This is not surprising. They are ruled by a Scottish cabinet, and a most inferior one. They have no say in Scottish affairs, but Scottish M.P.s sitting at Westminster (where they are grossly over-represented) can vote on purely English matters. And England continues to foot a disproportionate amount of the bill. One wonders when English patience will finally wear through.

For example, my principal objection to a Scottish Parliament goes back to the opening sentence of this piece: I know my fellow-countryman, and the ghastly change that can come over him when he is elevated to political office, his delight in his own voice, his tendency to swell visibly like a cock on a midden, his evident conviction that he is worthy and wise beyond his fellows – you know him well, from Burns and Scott and (if you're old enough) Willie McCulloch's record of the "worthy baillie". The thought of him being given a Parliament of his own, to strut and bore and feel important in, was enough to make me regret that I no longer had a newspaper's leader column at my command.

As to those who have full independence in their sights, I suspect that they cherish private dreams not only of rolling in limousines and refreshing themselves at the troughs of office, but even of aspiring to the role (dare we say it?) of Scottish Ambassador to Washington or Paris or even the Court of St James. In this they resemble the leaders of almost every independence movement since time began – full of fine slogans and lofty ideals for the voters, but not without occasional thought to their own advantage. Garibaldis have always been thin on the ground.

My second objection was that Scotland needed another layer of government like a dose of influenza. It does nothing but clutter the corridors of power with more red tape, serving no purpose but the aggrandisement of politicians, the waste of money on the salaries of unnecessary civil servants, and the impoverishment of the unfortunate Scots who are going to have to foot an ever-lengthening bill.

That the leaders of an independent Scotland will be only too happy to trade away that independence in return for admission to the fleshpots of Brussels for themselves and their families, goes without saying; they have the example of Westminster to copy.

So while hoping against hope for the best for the dear old country, and wishing her people a greatness to match their ancestors', I fear the worst – and that's a right Scotch characteristic, too. I do hope it comes right for her, because she deserves it, and I, like the rest of mankind, owe her so much. She gave me my blood and bone and being, and that loyalty, so strong in the Highlander, that comes from clanship and pride in those forefathers who were the centre of the charge in the last brave cry of "Claymore!" at Culloden, and a few years later were Wolfe's pathfinders up the Heights of Abraham. "Aye, indeed," as my MacDonald grandmother used to say, "it's no small thing to be a *Friseal*, a black Fraser, one of the smiling folk – and don't you forget it." I shan't, honest, and neither will Simon and Nick and young Andrew.

And yet, despite the pull of blood and history, and having finished my schooldays in Scotland, and served in a famous Highland regiment, and worked on its greatest newspaper while my children grew, and turned back at last to those western shores of my Viking MacNeill ancestors (for what is the Isle of Man but the most southerly of the Hebrides?) – despite all that, Scotland has never been home. A place to dream of returning to, perhaps, as the "Wandering Star" song has it, but above all a place to remember, although I know that the Scotland in my mind, the Scotland of summer holidays in childhood, is a never-never land that no longer exists.

But it did, and I have never felt closer to it than I did then, running with bare feet squelching inside sodden gym-shoes, splashing through shallow burns the colour of whisky, slipping on stones fringed with brown slimy weed, and scrambling up the earthy scree beyond. It was dangerous work, for that scree was the side of the Khyber Pass, and the whole countryside was hotching with Afridis; how they hadn't picked me off as I crossed the burn was a miracle. There were always at least two of them waiting in ambush when I scrambled over the heathery lip of the scree, but I disposed of them in a hectic tussle on the springy turf, wiped my sheath-knife in the grass, chased their baaing sheep deep into the bracken, and then raced full tilt down the hillside to the fort (my parents' caravan) to refresh myself with Creamola Foam and biscuits. When you've been without food or water for three days, you need your Creamola Foam.

Caravans were quite rare in those days. The car which pulled ours was an old Argyle, with carbide lamps, a hood, and a petrol-can strapped to the running-board; many of the roads we travelled were unmetalled and maintained by solitary men with red-rimmed eyes, shovelling chips into the pot-holes from their wheelbarrows. It was a Scotland of AA scouts and tweedy men in plus-fours, of occasional hikers and quiet farm-folk who sold us milk and eggs and spoke in strange, mincing accents, of still lochs like glass in the sunlight, and bakers' vans chugging through empty glens to our camp sites. All you needed was a level patch to pull up on at the roadside, close to a burn, sufficient flat stones to build a fireplace, a grassy stretch for cricket and rounders, and screes to climb. Pine woods were essential, too, for kindling – if you could get it before the Iroquois got you, for the cool dark depths were haunted by their war-parties, and you needed to steal softly from tree to tree, making no sound on the carpet of pine needles.

It will be gathered that I had a vivid imagination, fed by the "tuppenny bloods" which I devoured in the back of the car as we drove north from England each August, when I should have been drinking in the beauties of the scenery. "You'll hurt your eyes," my parents would say. "Look, there's Ben Hooligan, and Tilliegollacher Castle, and just over that hill is where your great-grandfather broke his leg." Often they would bicker gently about whether it was, in fact, Tilliegollacher or some other unpronounceable place – it might have been Glengoolicky or Aberinver or the wee house where Donald was sick after eating the cheese or the Camerons massacred somebody; I would leave them to it and get on with the Wolf of Kabul or Red Circle School, or fratch with my big sister on the back seat.

For sadly I was something of a Philistine about Caledonia. I have no idea of where those magical camp-sites were, except for one that was always our first and last stop, in Dumfriesshire, where the misty rain would come sweeping over Glen Elven at dusk, and another at Halfway House on the Dalwhinnie road. Another was in Sutherland, at a place pronounced Scootchy Hall (how it was spelled, heaven knows, but there was a Wee Free kirk with a corrugated iron roof that we went to, where a precentor who must have been a hundred and ten years old would line out the psalms in an ecstatic, quavering falsetto, and I disgraced the family by giggling and had to be put out).

I think I almost had a resistance to my national heritage, born no doubt of having to wear the kilt on Sundays in England – something which should not happen to any right-thinking seven year old. I was conscious of being half a stranger when we went to Scotland, and yet I knew I was a Highlander of the Highlands, and felt resentful of the natives who regarded me as an outsider. I had a knack of putting my infant foot in it: there were incidents like the precentor, and the occasion when I fled in terror at the sight and sound of an old crone in a shawl whining Gaelic songs by the roadside; I thought she was a witch (and still do), but I was rebuked by my grandmother for not showing a proper appreciation of "your country's songs".

She was at pains to instruct me in my traditions; I remember when we visited my great-grandfather's grave (to my shame, I don't know whether it was at Balquhidder or Blair Atholl), and it was pointed out to me that he rested alongside the great Rob Roy MacGregor – and I suspect that one has graves in half the kirkyards in the southern Highlands – I asked, in my childish innocence: "Rob Roy was a robber, wasn't he?" Granny's basilisk eye turned on me. "He was no more a robber," she said sternly, "than those who hunted him."

I learned something about the Highlands in that moment, and even more when we visited Killiecrankie, and stood by Dundee's stone, with my father murmuring Aytoun's verse and Granny, brooding grimly as she watched the mist swirling over the Garry, told me how the broadsword charge had shattered the government army in five minutes, and that was right, but the clansmen had been fighting for the Papist king, and that was wrong.

"What's the difference between us and the Catholics, Granny?" I asked, and my father coughed and sauntered off, whistling vaguely, while Granny took a deep breath. "The difference," she said, and I wish John Knox (and Sir Thomas More) had been there to hear it, "is that we're going to be saved, and they're going to be damned."

She was, as you may gather, a very old and very formidable lady of strong opinions. I went in awe of her, and would listen wide-eyed on those golden August evenings to her stories of Campbell iniquity and MacGregor cunning, of Cameron subtlety, Stewart treachery, and MacDougall general wickedness. And I remember her moved, in a very strange way, when we visited the Field of Shirts, where in 1544 my Fraser ancestors deliberately put themselves in the way of a superior force of MacDonalds whose land they had been raiding, and fought all through a sweltering summer's day until the MacDonalds were exhausted and there were only three Frasers left.

"Only three," said Granny, with tears in her eyes. "And you are all their people." As I've said, she was a MacDonald.

But for the most part those summers were running about the hills, and falling in deep brown pools, and building dams, and helping my father fry the breakfast on damp mornings, wriggling through bracken, learning to take "heather steps", fishing from boats on Loch Leven and Loch Awe, catching trout in the Breckachy burn by Halfway House, listening to my father reading *Kidnapped* and *Blackcock's Feather*, shuddering at the huge red heather spiders spinning their webs among rotten branches, and jumping from boulder to boulder or rolling down grassy slopes, and collecting the milk from a farm at Portsonachan and watching the great crabs scuttling through the cool green depths of a Highland harbour, and seeing the glorious sunset behind Duncan Ban's monument.

It's getting close to seventy years since, and I've hardly been back, except to the fringes, with my wife and my own children, picnicking by Loch Chon and skiting flat stones across the water and beating off the midges. We went to Glencoe once, my grandmother's valley, to enjoy the gloom of that awesome place, and when we stopped by the roadside the children scattered into the wild like gulls. A busload of American tourists pulled up just as our younger son, aged four, emerged from the bracken in his tiny kilt and shirt, bare-legged and tousled, looking like a very small Highland bull. There were squeals of delight from the American females at the sight of a genuine little Scotch laddie – they probably imagined he lived in a cave somewhere up the hill – and cameras clicked while he surveyed them stonily before turning silently and plunging back into the undergrowth, no doubt going off to find a scree to climb.

I should have warned him about the Afridis, perhaps – but on second thoughts I probably didn't need to.

"Phlam with Cheese" for the Stars

I DON'T KNOW where Djablak is, and at this stage of the game I don't much care. I don't even know how to spell it, although I've hunted every conceivable combination of Dj-, Jh-, Dy-, Zh-, and even Dzh- through all my maps and gazetteers. Its pronunciation lies between Zh- and Dj-, and it's somewhere in Yugoslavia, several hours drive up the road from Titograd, but whether it is in Montenegro or Serbia or Kosovo I cannot say. No doubt clued-up people like Edward Fox and Harrison Ford could place it immediately, but they were there longer than I was, and probably it is burned more deeply in their memories.

It's no more than a village of a few houses and the most eccentric hotel in the world, all in a beautiful mountain setting, lofty peaks, springy turf, rocky outcrops, and air so pure you can almost drink it. But it contains something which is worth going a long way to see, and is one of the most moving sights I've ever been privileged to look at. Zhablak cemetery is much too large for such a little mountain village, row upon row upon row of tombstones, each with the photograph of the buried person glazed into the stone by that astonishing process which I've seen only in Eastern Europe. So far as I remember, they are all men, young and middle-aged for the most part, but some are old and white-haired and some are boys no more than children.

They have one thing in common: the year of death in every case is 1943. For Zhablak is the place where the Yugoslav partisans, driven back into their mountains by the German advance, made their last stand, and stopped the invaders in their tracks. They did it at terrible cost, and every year Marshal Tito used to come to honour the heroes who sleep in the hillside cemetery.

In 1977 there was a sort of fictional re-enactment of the Yugoslav Thermopylae, filmed under the title of *Force Ten from Navarone*. It was a sequel to *The Guns of Navarone*, and starred Robert Shaw, Harrison Ford, Barbara Bach, Edward Fox, Franco Nero, the late and much lamented Alan Badel, and Carl Weathers (Apollo Creed of the Rocky films). Guy Hamilton directed, assisted by the irrepressible Bert Batt (singled out by John Huston as one of *the* assistant directors). They had a script but weren't satisfied with it, and I was called in, probably because Guy and I had already worked together on *Superman* and found ourselves to be highly compatible.

It was a very sudden summons that took me to Yugoslavia, and in the short interval between a signing session at Hatchards and the flight to Zagreb I was briefed at his Jermyn Street office by Carl Foreman, who had done the original screen story from Alistair MacLean's novel. I say briefed: we spent most of the time discussing a project which he thought I might like to write, about Phileas Fogg's American son going round the world in eighty hours or eighty minutes or whatever. But he did find time to tell me that in addition to making adjustments to the beginning, middle, and end of the story, which was about British and American parachutists helping the partisans to blow up a bridge, I would have to write a new part for Edward Fox, a last-minute replacement for another actor who, during a phone call to the producer, had become so incensed with his employer that he had wrenched the phone off the wall. This had concluded their conversation and the actor's connection with the picture. Edward, the ultimate laid-back Englishman, was as different as could be from the phone-wrencher, a volatile Scot, so adjusting the part would be an interesting exercise.

Oh, and one other thing: there would have to be two versions of the final script, one for shooting and the other for the Yugoslav authorities. (This was a not uncommon procedure at the time, when regimes, especially totalitarian ones, tended to be terribly sensitive about how they were portrayed in the movies.) I asked Carl, no doubt sarcastically, if that was all; he said, please, would I give the Phileas Fogg idea serious thought, lent me his typewriter, and wished me luck.

Guy Hamilton was waiting in Zagreb, where we started work at the hotel. Every director has his own methods, and I knew one of Guy's from our time on *Superman*: where practicable, and a scene seemed to call for it, he liked to work out positions, movements, lines of sight, perspectives, and so on, in as much detail as possible, before the scene was even written. For example, A and B are hiding in a railway wagon, watching their comrade C, disguised as a German, talking to an enemy sentry D, who mustn't see A and B, so C has to block his line of sight, but since C is actually a traitor, he must use looks and body language to convey this to D, without giving himself away to A and B, etc., etc. . . . you get the idea (I hope).

So Guy and I spent much time walking around a hotel room, manoeuvring for position, looking at each other over our shoulders, peering round furniture. working out who could see (or not see) what from where, and even getting carried away to such an extent that we finished up improvising dialogue, acting it up with cries of "Das is not correct, schweinhund!" and "Barnsby, I think the bastard's selling us out!" or words to that effect. Anyone, say a waiter or cleaner, who had happened in on us would have thought us certifiable – but it worked marvellously, for I could then write the scene knowing exactly how it would play physically, to the last look or turn of the head.

At the other extreme were such scenes as the closing moment

in the picture, when the bridge had been destroyed, the Germans foiled, and we were looking for an ending. I suggested that since our heroes were cut off behind German lines, their mutual congratulations could be interrupted by their leader pointing out that they were going to have a hell of a long walk home; without hesitation, Guy said "Sold", and no further discussion was needed. (Robert Shaw loved it, did it as only he could, and it worked.)

Given his film background, it wasn't surprising that Guy treated absolute clarity as a priority – if only more modern directors did likewise. He went to what some film-makers might have thought an odd length, showing the rough-cut of a picture to the cleaning ladies of Pinewood, or whatever studio he was at, looking not for a critique, but to satisfy himself that an ordinary audience would understand everything they saw and heard.

We drove up to Zhablak on a bleak winter evening, through endless gloomy forests fringing deep ravines and surrounded by towering cliffs. There seemed to be no other vehicles on the road, and the only sign of life was the occasional gleam of a light deep in the woods; it was real Dracula country, the road wound on and on and ever upwards, civilisation seemed to be dwindling away behind us, and we beguiled the time imagining how the gigantic size, flowing beard, and menacing appearance of Richard Kiel (Jaws of the Bond films) who was in the cast, could be used to advantage by having him lumber out of the woods by night, dressed à la Karloff, for the benefit of any American tourists who might chance by. Our facetious speculations didn't seem quite so amusing when we arrived, after hours of weary driving, on the Zhablak plateau in the dead of night, with its double line of villagers' houses and the Hotel Zhablak, presently to be rechristened the Hotel Japlacquered, standing in sinister isolation at the end of the street.

For a mountain-top in Montenegro, or wherever, I guess it wasn't bad, and certainly worth more stars than some I have struck, like the old Hotel Tashkent with its bathrooms from whose bourne no traveller returned. But it wasn't the Savoy or the Ritz either, being constructed, so far as I could see, entirely of wood, with tiny bare rooms, no heating, medieval mattresses, and as for porters, don't make me laugh. I can still hear Bert Batt's plaintive Cockney cry as we dragged our luggage up the darkened stairs: "Why are we 'ere, George? Why are we 'ere?" As C. P. Snow would say, I had no comfort to give him.

But the glory of the Hotel Zhablak was its dining room, a curious long chamber divided halfway by an open fireplace, with communicating arches either side – not that anyone in his right mind would have wanted to communicate, for while we occupied the VIP end, the popular side was patronised by the locals, a typically Balkan clientele, which is to say they were an armed, passionate, and occasionally violent crew whom Blackbeard Teach would have thought twice about enlisting. On two occasions fighting broke out beyond the fireplace, and while no shots were fired it may have been a near thing – the catering manager of our company, touring the countryside in search of delicacies to supplement the Hotel Zhablak's eccentric menu (of which more in a moment) returned to report that at one of the farms he had visited, his host had kept a loaded revolver on the table and kept glancing hopefully out of the window, waiting for a neighbour who had displeased him to pass by.

I wish our government, and indeed all those who hold views on the tragic events in Yugoslavia, could spend some time in the Zhablak area, absorbing the atmosphere and studying the natives. It might cure them of their deplorable habit of regarding Yugoslavia as a country where there are "goodies" and "baddies", and it behoves the West to take sides. Speaking from brief experience which seems to be borne out by recent history, I'd say that if they're not all savages, they are certainly capable of savagery, regardless of race, religion, and political outlook. So when I hear of "ethnic cleansing" I am in no doubt that given time and opportunity the ethnically cleansed will clean up their oppressors in turn, and so on ad infinitum, and if we had any sense we'd let them get on with it and mind our own business.

For the first day or so we subsisted chiefly on prosciutto ham and chips, but as more of the cast and crew arrived the maître d'hôtel, who introduced himself, in fractured English, as Samuel Becket, decided that a more extensive menu was called for. He was a genial, expansive character, and I was told that he had done time for homicide; I would not malign the man, and repeat only what was common report; if rumour lied, I can only apologise.

He accosted Edward Fox and me on the hotel steps, fixing Edward with a glittering eye. "You", he said accusingly, "are great film star."

"No," said Edward, "I am an actor."

"Ah, no," cried Samuel Becket, "you are the famous Fox. And you," he rounded on me, "are writer. Must have fine bill of fare for film stars. You help me, so good food may be preparrit." ("Preparrit" was a favourite word of his, sometimes pronounced "preparrate". I do not mock his English. My Serbian or Bosnian or Croatian should be half so good.)

The upshot was that I found myself in his office, trying to translate, with his assistance, the hotel's menu into English; he had already had a shot at it on his own, and after some study I realised that "Hemmadeks" was "ham and eggs", while "ships patato" was easy, since we had them with prosciutto ham each night. But as we worked our way through the à la carte Sammy's English began to flag, and I had recourse to a system which I don't expect anyone to believe, but it's true, and I'm sure Fox and Hamilton would bear me out.

I would point to an item in Yugoslav, and Sammy would make an appropriate noise. When he went moo, I knew we were discussing beef, grunts and baa's indicated ham, bacon, and mutton, and his spirited clucking I took to mean chicken until, by employing a mime which I have no intention of describing, he convinced me that he meant eggs.

It was a crude system, but it worked nicely until we came to the last item, in Anglo-Yugoslav: "phlam with cheese". I pointed to it and, so help me, he barked. Further investigation confirmed the appalling truth: the Hotel Zhablak served dog meat with cheese. I did not append an English translation when I typed the menu out, but warned the company to avoid the phlam at all costs. Their reactions were interesting: Harrison Ford registered horrified disbelief, Carl Weathers roared with laughter and Edward Fox raised one eyebrow. Robert Shaw arrived late, and when he had scowled his way through the menu, tossed it aside, and demanded: "Is that all there is, then?", I was tempted to recommend the phlam, but desisted. After all, he was the star, and shooting would have been held up if he'd been taken ill.

I spent the first few days huddled over Carl Foreman's typewriter in my room, trying to keep out the cold with one of Hamilton's jerseys. It's always difficult, looking back on a script which you've revised, to recall how much and what you altered, but I know I changed the ending, fiddled the beginning slightly, invented a new treachery (and a new death) for Franco Nero, and thoroughly enjoyed myself with the relationship between the British sergeant (Fox) and his American counterpart (Weathers). Fox's casting was a wonderful piece of luck; his urbane, languid style was a splendid contrast to Weathers' massive black presence, and they played off each other perfectly.

A problem arose with the scene in which Richard Kiel, playing a partisan, had to greet Weathers with the line: "Hallo, nigger!" and make a great show of trying to wipe his colour away. The producers were worried about "nigger", but Weathers wasn't – he had been coaching me in black slang, some of which you wouldn't believe – and as I hadn't written the scene, I was neutral, as was Hamilton. We tried various other terms, including "darkie" and "sambo", and finally settled on "blackie", which I'd have thought just as offensive to anyone who was going to take offence.

I'm surprised that Weathers hasn't gone farther. He is a fine actor with expressive eyes, good looking, and with the physique of the pro footballer he once was, but he has contented himself with mostly supporting parts. He had a good idea for a film about a black American who by chance finds himself back with an African tribe, and encounters complex cultural and social problems; we talked it over at some length, but I haven't heard that he pursued it.

I finished the scripts, and what the difference was between the "official" version for the Yugoslavs, and the "real" one I have long forgotten. Shaw's daughter, Debbie, beavered away duplicating them, they were distributed to the cast at supper, Hamilton, the recreant, took evasive action, and I was left to deal with the actors. There wasn't too much trouble; Harrison Ford, I remember, took me through his part with a professional care which I found impressive; Alan Badel, God bless him, shook his head at me in admiration, exclaiming: "Marvellous! What a difference!" I must have changed at least two words from the original part which he'd already seen, but that was Alan all over, and explains why I liked him as much as any actor I've ever worked with.

We had a read through – Shaw, Ford, Fox, Weathers, and Nero, the five principals, while Hamilton stood in for Barbara Bach and others, and I did the occasional German sentry being strangled. It went nicely, with little discussion, the highlight being the abandon with which Shaw threw back his head and bellowed a line at Fox: "Miller, you stupid git!" Why do actors love shouting? Possibly it breaks the monotony. And at the finish he delighted me by remarking: "Well, you've got the best part, Eddie – as usual."

The only major problem was: who was going to kill the traitor, Franco Nero? I know I rewrote the scene, but I don't remember whether I changed the identity of the killer or not. Anyway, in the final script the execution was to be carried out by the American colonel, Barnsby, played by Ford, and Shaw objected, not altogether unreasonably.

"I ought to kill him," he said, when we had adjourned for dinner. "I'm the man he betrayed in the first place, and the audience will expect me to kill him."

I suggested that was a good reason for having Barnsby do it, to take the audience by surprise, Hamilton agreed, and Shaw, having growled and glared in the direction of Ford, who was sitting innocently at the next table, finally said: "Oh, well, all right ... but you've got to give me *a line!*" This was accompanied by a fist on the table – a dramatic gesture timed to perfection. Guy and I suggested a few lines, none of which was well received, I had to fight down my fatal impulse to propose something really facetious, and finally Shaw said in a grating voice:

"So Barnsby shoots him, and the audience don't know who's fired the shot until I say: 'Thank you, Colonel!'"

Neat, you have to admit, and so it was done. He was, I realised, an intensely competitive actor – goodness knows why, since he could hold his own with the best in the business, and act most of them off the screen. I think back to him as Henry VIII, and Lord Randolph Churchill, or eyeing Paul Newman across the card table in *The Sting*, dominating the scene simply by his presence.

Perhaps he was just a natural competitor. There was to be a scene involving cliff-climbing (which didn't get into the movie), and Shaw champed at the bit beforehand, muttering: "I'm going to bloody well kill Franco Nero at this." In the event, which I didn't witness, the fastest man up the cliff, ahead even of the stuntmen, was Harrison Ford. Which surprised me, for Harrison had struck me as quite the gentlest of the cast, soft-spoken and quietly courteous, and not the one you'd expect to be first as an action man.

He had just become internationally famous with *Star Wars*, and his part in *Force Ten* was modest by comparison, but he took great pains over it. He and I shared an acquaintance in Dick Fleischer; Harrison, who during a hiatus in his film career had become a carpenter, had been engaged on building a projection room at Dick's Hollywood home on South Rockingham when he suddenly had the chance to appear in George Lucas's *American Graffiti*, and the projection room was abandoned half-finished, which had not endeared Harrison to Dick's wife, Mickey. I gather that Harrison had emerged somewhat shaken, but eventually it all came right, for I learned later from Mickey that he had completed the projection room, which is an extremely handsome one.

Edward Fox and Alan Badel and I gravitated together, when Edward was not in his room studying to be Edward VIII in the TV series which won so much acclaim. He was one of those actors whose personality off-screen is in keeping with his professional image: quiet, humorous, unfailingly polite. Badel, on the other hand, was the opposite of his acting persona: on screen he was usually the coldest of cold fish, icy-eyed and with a voice to match, the kind of heavy who could make Rathbone or Henry Daniell seem positively jolly – and that last word is a good description of him as he really was, exuberant, talkative, given to explosive laughter, and as busy as they come.

When Edward Fox, former subaltern in the Loyal North Lancs, and no stranger to khaki, put on his sergeant's battle-dress and stood forth for our inspection, I thought he looked pretty good – but not good enough for ex-Paratrooper Badel, who fussed round him, tugging, straightening, and exhorting, while I, at Alan's insistence, manufactured a circlet of the little lead weights with which we used to make our trousers hang neatly over our anklets. Edward bore it with his usual patience, and I must admit that Badel had him looking fit to mount guard. He didn't stop there. Harrison Ford emerged from the unit barber looking slightly bemused; Alan, I gathered, had been supervising his haircut.

I have said he was likeable, with his happy enthusiasm and unfailing good humour; he was also a very hard man indeed. On the one hand, there was the brilliant classical actor, one of the great Romeos and for many the one and only Darcy in *Pride and Prejudice*, a splendid mimic who did a superb Gielgud and a truly cruel Olivier. "Larry would try to psych you out, you know. He quite upset Michael Redgrave, but when he tried it on with me, looking down his nose from a great height –" Alan was quite short, perhaps five-seven or -eight "– I fixed the bugger. I just stared at his fly buttons."

On the other hand, there was the man who told us straight-faced that when he had caught hooligans vandalising his car, he had broken their wrists – I can still see Edward Fox's look of horror at this revelation. For there was no doubt it was true; the war taught cold-blooded ruthlessness to a generation, and produced many walking paradoxes, trained killers who were also kind and sincere Christians. Alan was a devout Roman Catholic, and genuinely compassionate; I've no reason to doubt the story that he had spent an hour on the telephone using all his charm and tact (and probably his acting ability) to persuade a hysterical girl not to commit suicide; it was at the time of his Stratford Romeo, when he was being bombarded with worshipping messages and confidences from admiring females.

But the old Airborne man was never far from the surface, as William Dieterle, the German director, discovered on the Hollywood set of *Salome*, in which Alan appeared with Rita Hayworth and Charles Laughton. Dieterle was, in Alan's description, "a typical Hun", and when he slapped the face of an unfortunate gofer he found himself confronted by an icy Badel.

"I told him, 'Look, mate, I've just spent five years putting down your bloody countrymen, and I don't mind adding you to the list. You don't slap anyone while I'm around, see?' And he didn't." Which may explain why Alan's Hollywood career was comparatively brief – that and his spirited objection to changes made in the *Salome* script to the words of Christ as given in the New Testament; this ended in confrontation with the celebrated Harry Cohn and a writer who explained: "Well, you see, Alan, we thought Jesus sounded just a bit cocky in there."

With the script complete my job was effectively over, and I was able to spend time with Kathy and two of the children who had flown out to Zagreb. I rejoined the unit later, for the life of me I can't think why, for all that stays in memory is an argument with Robert Shaw about rugby – he had played at county level, for Cornwall, I think – and a rain-sodden afternoon on a bleak hillside watching him and Ford hitting German guards with shovels while Barbara Bach shot them with a tommy-gun.

I didn't see the film until many months afterwards, but in the meantime, near the end of shooting, I received a letter from a friend in the unit which read, in part: "Eddie as always is a delight, Barnsby grows on one, Shaw is competent when sober."

Poor Robert. He died only a year later, of a heart attack; he was only fifty-one. A multi-talented man, not only a fine actor but a gifted writer, and it is good to remember how he threw off his customary gruffness and became positively cheerful in telling me about his latest play, which was half-finished and, he believed, the best thing he'd ever written. But being Robert Shaw it was not long before he was giving tongue to his vexation at the mounting expense of the golf course he was having built on his estate in Ireland, and the cares of fatherhood – he had, I believe, ten children. "God, d'you have any idea of the cost of kids' shoes? Yes, of course you have." Brooding pause. "Not as much as I have, though."

I got no writing credit on *Force Ten* in Britain, which I thought a bit hard, since I'd contributed a fair amount, but I was given one in America, which was a consolation. Carl Foreman's typewriter, I'm afraid, is still somewhere on a hilltop in Yugoslavia.

Crime and Punishment

FEW THINGS infuriate the ordinary citizen more than liberal attitudes to crime and criminals. And not only infuriate, but offend against justice, common sense, and fair play. The ordinary citizen is neither a brute nor a sadist; he is humane (as most liberals are not), he is compassionate when it is called for, leans over backwards to be fair, and is ready to give a second chance. But he knows the difference between right and wrong, and has an instinctive sense of the difference between right and mere legality. He believes that wrongdoing should be punished with appropriate degrees of severity; deep in his understanding lies a feeling that eye for eye and tooth for tooth is not without merit, and that the punishment should fit the crime.

He is disturbed at the way in which liberal concern seems focused on the criminal rather than the victim. He grits his teeth when he reads of young offenders being sent on luxurious safaris which honest folk cannot afford, of derisory sentences handed down for heinous crimes, of criminals who hold the law and society in open contempt, of old, helpless folk battered and tortured and slain, and of little children raped and murdered – and knows that the law of his land decrees that not a finger must be laid on the perpetrator, assuming he is caught, which he probably won't be. He is justly furious when the vilest of criminals, the Bradys and Hindleys and Krays, are the subjects of campaigns for their release, when every decent instinct tells him that they should have been dead long ago.

He is tired, almost beyond anger and disgust, of liberals who insist that rehabilitation of the criminal must have priority, that he must be "understood" rather than punished, that our prisons are a "national disgrace" – which they are in that they are far too soft and shockingly run – and that he, the citizen, is some kind of vengeful monster when he suggests that a harsher way with criminals might be tried with advantage. He is tired of being called a barbarian, and uncivilised, when he knows that the true barbarians are the liberals who by their policies have turned Britain into an open sewer, have encouraged the criminal, and so undermined the forces of law and order that the citizen can no longer count on that protection which is the first duty of a civilised state.

He knows that those who brought about the abolition of the death penalty and corporal punishment (both, he notes, in defiance of the great majority of public opinion), who "reformed" the penal system so that hard labour became a thing of the past and prisoners were given sheets on their beds, television to watch, and recreational facilities denied to many outside prison – he knows that they are the criminal's friends, their aiders and abettors, and, it follows, the enemies of the law-abiding public.

This statement will be scoffed at, of course, but we, the public who do not believe in putting the criminal first and the victim second, know that it is true. We know that chatter about being tough on crime and the causes of crime is just a politician's silly lie, and that absolutely nothing will be done to combat crime until there is a return to common sense by treating the criminal as an enemy and dealing with him accordingly. But that, of course, is something that no politician would dare to say, even if he believed it, which most of them probably do not. Why should they? They're all right, Jack, and when a beleaguered householder shoots a burglar and, against all decency and reason, is sentenced to life imprisonment

143

the liberal lobby shake their heads censoriously and agree that he has no right to effective self-defence.

A thought occurs: Mr Blair and his kind presumably have armed security – so if, in the undoubtedly worthy cause of protecting Mr Blair, a security man were to kill an intruder, would the security man go to prison for life?

The failure of successive governments to deal with crime, their surrender to liberal pressure and flat refusal to do anything practical, is in itself the greatest crime of all. When any particularly appalling crime is committed – the murder of a child, usually – there is an immediate pious wail from the Left and an endless waffling of platitudes featuring the word "unacceptable", an earnest debate about the causes of crime, a hypocritical lip-service to "doing something", a laying of flowers and weeping for the cameras, a great shaking of fat heads on *Question Time*, perhaps a rushing through Parliament of cosmetic and totally useless measures to "crack down" which everyone, including the police and judiciary, regard with contempt, and a stern admonition from Downing Street that it is the responsibility of us all, because government can't tackle the problem on its own, and it is up to the public, etc., etc. – and it is all meaningless, and we know it, but it beats the hell out of doing anything. Government, of either party, talks about the public's responsibility while abdicating its own with a cowardice matched only by its callousness, and, failing to protect the public, refuses the public the right to defend themselves.

Ask the man or woman in the street what should be done about this disgraceful state of affairs, and they'll tell you, in simple terms which no politician would have the nerve to use, much less act upon. Easier by far to pontificate fatuously while the next victim is raped and strangled . . . and then the great mockery of inactivity and pretended concern can be gone through again.

We could discuss the failure to deal with crime at length, but there's no profit in that; better to say what should be done about it, and I am confident that what follows would command the support of a majority of Britons, if it were ever put to them in a referendum, which of course it never will be.

First, it is plain that no country can call itself civilised which does not have the death penalty for murder. That is not to say that it must be inflicted in every case; far from it. But it must be there. Since it was abolished, criminal killing and violent crime have rocketed, and only a fool or a liar would deny the obvious truth: the death penalty is a deterrent, and those abolitionists who deny it are lying. They've got to lie. To admit the truth that they know in their hearts, that the gallows deters, but that they still want none of it, would be to put themselves in the morally impossible position of saying that they would rather the innocent died than the guilty. So they must persist in their falsehood, flying blindly in the face of common sense, honesty, and human experience since time began.

What, in all our literature, in our very sense of being, is the ultimate sanction? Death. Not life imprisonment (which term is a lie also), not probation, not stern words from the bench, not even prison visits from the late Lord Longford, but death. (I am reminded of what a Glasgow police sergeant told me about his arrest of a villain: "He didn't say don't put me in jail, he didn't say don't send me to the psychiatrist, he said don't hit me, mister. So I hit him – blooter!" No doubt Lord Macpherson would say that this was institutional violence. The point is that the policeman knew what worked.)

Deterrence is not the only reason for capital punishment. Simple justice is another, equally strong. There is a human instinct that one who kills deliberately and unlawfully has forfeited the right to live. Not because anything less would leave him able to kill again, but because it is just and proper that he should die. There have, incidentally, been some seventy cases, since abolition, of murderers killing a second time after release, and even the most fervent abolitionist cannot deny that the death penalty, if applied, would have saved many innocent lives. (So would a true life sentence.) The abolitionist has no answer to this except the outworn claptrap about the sanctity of human life (the murderer's life, never mind the victim's), and the parrot-cry that the state has no right to end a human existence, no Christian conscience can condone it, and so on.

Therein lies the nub: conscience – of which, no doubt, the abolitionist is proud. The appalling fact is that he puts his conscience above the life of the victim. It is not too much to say that as long as he can go to bed thinking: "Thank God I hold the right, enlightened view on capital punishment, and live in a country where it doesn't exist", he couldn't care less how many children and old folk are butchered. They are expendable, but his conscience isn't. What it is to have a conscience, eh? To be able to live with the knowledge of the abominable tortures inflicted on children by Hindley and Brady, and yet maintain that the lives of those two bestial murderers must remain inviolate. Liberals have achieved abolition, and are proud of it, and the devil with those victims they have condemned to death as a result.

The stark truth, of course, is that they have not abolished the death penalty at all. They have merely transferred it from the guilty to the innocent – and incidentally ensured that many more violent deaths occur. They can live with that, apparently, shielding those ragged shreds of conscience behind the lie that the death penalty would have no effect on the murder rate. Well, we know of seventy cases where it would, and that is one hard fact that not all the twisting of truth and careful selection of statistics can explain away.

It can be objected, very properly, that the trouble with the death penalty is that you may execute the wrong man, and many abolitionists try to link this with the false pretence that people like me want every murderer to hang. Certainly not, and I remind them that *before* abolition only a minority of murderers were executed. My contention is that the death sentence should be applied only when the guilt of the accused is beyond doubt – not what is called reasonable doubt, but any doubt at all. There are such open and shut cases. Where a shadow of doubt attends a conviction, the sentence should be life imprisonment – meaning just that, not release after nine years. (It is a sign of the law's guilty conscience that it has to pretend that a few years in jail is "life". Why the silly and unnecessary lie, which only brings the law's integrity and intelligence into disrepute, and reflects no credit on those who administer it without protest?)

What is necessary is simply that the death penalty should exist, a permanent deterrent, and that would certainly be enough at least to give pause to the armed robber, the violent thug, and (dare one suggest it?) the domestic killer who pleads loss of control, provocation, drink, drugs, an abused childhood, and any other excuse that comes to mind. Thanks to the reformers, we are now used to the wife who murders her husband in his sleep, and the husband who bludgeons or stabs his wife to death – and both will plead that the dead spouse had made life hell for them, and all too often walk free with a sympathetic benediction from the idiot on the bench. It seems not to occur to anyone that they heard only one side of the case; that the dead victim, reviled from the witness box (and no doubt often deserving of vilification), has had no chance to put a case, being dead.

We are assured that such murders, usually committed in blind passion, would not be deterred by the death penalty, that penalties don't cross the minds of such killers. No? Could that be because the penalties don't exist – not real penalties to stay a murderous hand even in blind rage. Is it ridiculous to suggest that the knowledge, at the back of every mind, that the gallows is there, the ultimate sanction, might not prevent many domestic quarrels from becoming fatal ones?

No one would suggest for a moment that the deranged mother should face the death penalty for murdering her child in a frenzy of desperation – but again, is it not possible that even a deranged mother, knowing that she lived in a state that executed murderers, might out of that awful knowledge be moved to hold her hand? And if I am thought to be lacking in compassion and understanding even to cite such a case, let me point out that I do so out of concern not for the mother but for the infant victim.

Surely even liberals are not too obtuse to have learned the age-old lesson that when it comes to restraining the criminal, or imposing discipline (whether on the mob or in the classroom), a threat is sufficient nine times out of ten if it is understood that it is not an empty one. At present all the tough talk of "cracking down" and "three strikes and out" is seen for what it is: empty sound, and the criminal simply laughs at the fatuous politician and goes his lawless way in the sure knowledge that nothing can possibly happen to him except a short spell of what Solzhenitsyn called warm cells and white bread. With the enlightened lobby getting their bowels in an uproar about the prisoner's human rights, too.

But if the brute knows, as he puts the boot into the old lady's face, that he will be flogged extremely painfully, he will think twice; he will be less liable to throw people into rivers and laugh as they drown if he knows that his neck will be broken by way of retribution.

That paragraph should be enough to convince anyone of liberal tendencies that I am a vengeful sadist. I'm not, but if I were, would it matter if it saved an old lady from being battered to death, or a young life from being snuffed out by a true sadist?

There are many emotional arguments against the death penalty – the horror of execution, the cold-blooded extinction of life, the ghastly ritual of trapdoor and noose. Yes, it's horrible. It was equally horrible when the victim died. I have been asked, could I bear to carry out an execution. Yes, without hesitation. I was trained to kill, like my whole generation, and for the life of me I fail to understand how the liberal conscience can live with killing in war (blowing children to pieces in Kosovo, for example) but insist on the right to life of the Hindleys and Bradys and similar vermin.

The restoration of corporal punishment is also long overdue. If there is a deterrent to match the rope, it is the cat, as many old lags will testify. The birch should also be reintroduced for juvenile offenders. While we had it in the Isle of Man, this was a safe place; my teenage daughter and her friends could hitchhike home from dances in the middle of the night without fear; it was common to leave doors, and certainly cars, unlocked.

Then, under pressure from Westminster, birching was abolished, and girls no longer hitchhike home. The police, whose arrival at the scene of rowdyism used to send the offenders fleeing, now find the hooligans waiting for them. Violence has increased, assault is not uncommon, and murders have taken place in an island where unlawful killing used to be something that had happened in the distant past.

What a triumph for enlightened thought. What a vindication of the noble lord who contended that the permissive society is a civilised society. It probably seems so in the agreeable surroundings of High Table, or the Lords' dining room, with the civilised ones comfortably insulated by port and brandy and the certainty that no criminals are likely to break in and assault them. The view from the pavement, where the pensioner is having his face stamped on, is rather different.

It is worth mentioning that in the years I lived on Man before we were forced to abandon the birch, there was only one instance of an actual birching taking place, on a young thug who had used a broken glass on someone's face. Years later, when he committed another offence, a leading liberal newspaper in Britain crowed triumphantly that his birching had proved no deterrent. What they omitted to report, with typical dishonesty, was that the new offence had not been committed in the Isle of Man. Indeed, the culprit had taken care never to visit the island again.

Noose, cat, birch – horrible things, indeed, but less horrible than the murders, maimings, rapes, tortures, and uncountable lesser offences they would undoubtedly prevent. But that cannot be admitted; indeed, the very thought must be suppressed, and in this the government and its enlightened supporters are ably abetted by much of the media, especially the BBC. I do not for a moment believe that the grieving parents of a murdered child, on whom television intrudes with such ghoulish delight, have never expressed a wish to see the death penalty restored – and yet, *mirabile dictu*, their wish has never been reported in any news bulletin that I have seen. And we need not ask how long a senior policeman would last in his job if he had the temerity to call for capital punishment.

Suppression of opinion in the name of political correctness is, of course, absolutely necessary; censor a widely held view, and people will think it is not widely held at all. It is a lesson that Dr Goebbels and the Soviet commissars knew by heart, and how they would have admired the technique of the BBC anchorman who, on encountering a death penalty advocate, cut him off abruptly with the words: "Oh, we don't want to hear from *you*!"

No, indeed. Muzzle the majority and the majority will begin to doubt that it is a majority.

It will be argued, naturally, that the opinion of the majority is irrelevant. It may not be stated quite so bluntly, except by people like the politician quoted earlier, who believe, in his felicitous phrase, that grass-roots opinion is "a negation of political leadership". So there.

I am straying, sensibly you will agree, from my main thesis on the death penalty, but it is so patently right, and so widely supported, that I can leave it and touch for a moment on our penal system. It is my belief, borne of experience, that the best correctional policy is to make prisons unpleasant places to which criminals will be in no haste to return. I remember the military jails of my youth and, recalling the salutary effect they had on their unfortunate inmates, cannot suppress the thought that their discipline might with advantage be imposed on criminals today. They wouldn't know what had hit them, and they wouldn't like it. This is the psychological approach, you understand. Even less would they like the restoration of hard labour, prison uniform, and spartan living, with only limited recreation for those who had earned it.

Those foolish enough to break their way on to the roof and demonstrate by hurling down slates ... no, I am not going to advocate shooting them down, but simply that for every day they spend on the roof voluntarily, they should spend one compulsorily, without benefit of nourishment. It's a splendid, simple, politically incorrect old rule: behave, and do as you're told, or you don't eat. Now that does work, believe me.

Alas, none of these fine things will happen. The crime wave will continue to swell, the innocent will die and suffer, and our alleged leaders will wring their hands and talk about "addressing the problem" and monitoring everything in sight and tackling "root causes" such as poverty and disadvantage and lack of opportunity and social injustice and sunspots – everything, in fact, except human wickedness, greed, and cruelty, which are the most common causes, far and away.

The great and good, especially those who by their progressive policies have brought about the ruin of our education system, will probably not care to admit that a major root cause of crime is the breakdown of discipline in schools. Political correctness cannot face the glaring truth that a child who has no sanctions to fear, and therefore no restraints on his behaviour, is far more likely to grow into a man who respects no law, than the child who is properly disciplined – which means, on occasion, punished. But even mention of punishment will draw squeals of liberal indignation about "child abuse" – a truly weasel attempt to confuse disciplining a naughty child with paedophile activity. But what am I saying? Horror of horrors, I have used the word "naughty", which has been banned in case it upsets some little darling whose record of street crime and classroom assaults would scarify Al Capone.

We are told, repeatedly, that violence is no answer to the problem. This is nonsense. With children who attack teachers, bully and rob and enjoy using violence on their fellows, violence is the only answer. But rather than face the truth, government and our education pundits insist on suspensions, and expulsions, and special classes for disruptive pupils, with social workers and psychiatrists speculating aimlessly on the *reasons* for playground mayhem and vandalism and the culture of disobedience.

Well, we know what their conclusions will be, and no doubt poverty and broken homes and single-parent upbringing and child abuse can have something to do with it. Certainly the permissive society culture which promotes easy divorce and pays lip-service to family values while undermining them, makes for the kind of home which is a breeding-ground for juvenile delinquency. Government ministers have the impudence to prate about the need for proper behaviour to be instilled in the home, and go out of their way to make it impossible by prosecuting parents if they punish their children.

This rank hypocrisy extends to the schools, where the full rigour of the law is employed against a teacher who is alleged to have slapped a child threatening her with assault. Having denied the teacher the means of imposing discipline, government can only make pious noises when asked, what is the teacher to do? Punishment aside, is she not entitled to self-defence? Not in Cool Britannia, she isn't.

So we have suspension and expulsion, and the denial to children of a decent education. Even the worst behaved are still entitled to schooling, but the present banning of discipline (for that is what it is) ensures that most of them will leave school semi-literate and ripe for mischief and, eventually, crime. They have been taught that society is a soft mark, and that however they misbehave or offend there will be no real penalty.

The most effective penalty is corporal punishment, and before the p.c. brigade start accusing me of advocating the torture chamber for errant toddlers, let me say that as child and parent corporal punishment played little part in my life. My bottom was painfully smacked in infancy by my father, but I loved and respected him no whit the less; I was caned once (in England, two cuts, for reading the *Wizard* during a French lesson), and belted three or four times, usually for throwing knives (in Scotland, where the tawse was the instrument of punishment).

I will not claim blimpishly that it did me good or made a man of me. It didn't; it wasn't meant to. But my father's smacks discouraged bad behaviour, I was never detected reading the *Wizard* in class again, and I learned to practise my knife artistry outside school. The beatings were not severe; they were rather a reminder of the disciplinary machine that lay behind, a deterrent that exists no longer. Admittedly, sheer moral force was the main disciplinary instrument of society between the wars (a phenomenon impossible to explain today), but fear of physical punishment went hand in hand with it, and together they worked remarkably.

My own children seldom needed more than a withering look from their mother or me, but they knew that the possibility of sterner measures existed – and that is the key to controlling all human behaviour. If I seem to repeat myself it is because one tends to when an obvious, patent truth is being denied or ignored by fools. For example, bullying in schools seems to have reached epidemic proportions, yet nothing is easier to stop. Simply empower teachers to inflict corporal punishment; if the bully knows he is going to have his backside painfully thrashed, he will desist from bullying.

And how, scoffs the liberal, is a frail female teacher to chastise a hulking thug? She isn't; she is going to report him to the headmaster or mistress who will instruct a burly assistant janitor, paid out of the small fortune that will be saved from the abolition of special classes for disruptive pupils, to inflict the punishment. And any parent who comes round to the school seeking revenge will be liable, after due process, to a fine or worse. If a parent wishes to have a child's punishment investigated, that too must be properly carried out.

It's easy . . . and the bully doesn't have to be expelled or denied schooling, his victims will not suffer from his cruelty or, provided school discipline is properly organised and supervised, have to demean themselves by complaining to higher authority – the only remedy that "educationalists" seem able to think of. We have come to this, that what used to be looked on as the most contemptible thing a child could do, namely, telling tales, sneaking, clyping, grassing, ratting, peaching, narking, turning stool-pigeon (you can tell the odium in which it was held by the rich variety of synonyms) is now recommended behaviour. That is the depth to which children are being advised to sink, simply because our rulers are too spineless and stupid to tackle the evil head-on.*

How cruel they are to children; how they fail them by their neglect, not only the well-behaved pupil but the disruptive lout or young virago. They are being denied the good, untroubled education that is their birthright – one might say their human right, to use a phrase which should strike a chord in liberal minds. And all because the enlightened sneer at such folk wisdom as "Spare the rod and spoil the child", and never have the wit, apparently, to wonder how the saying came to be proverbial.

There still exists, of course, among such thinkers, the belief that a child is naturally good, and only some aberration of circumstance or upbringing causes bad behaviour. Believe that and you'll believe anything. It was my wife who pointed out to me, after careful observation of our own children and their playmates at the

* The most effective cure for bullying, as my generation know from experience, was that advocated in *Tom Brown's Schooldays*, where Tom and East ganged up on the bully Flashman and beat the stuffing out of him.

toddler stage, that you will see in the nursery every crime in the book except sexual assault: GBH, attempted murder, theft, blackmail, extortion, lying, fraud, false pretence, menacing, putting in fear, robbery with violence, conspiracy, mayhem – the whole Newgate Calendar is on show, and if sex and high treason are exceptions it is only because the little blighters haven't got round to them yet.

I have rambled somewhat, yet I hope I have at least illustrated the old truth that as the twig is bent so grows the tree. I hope, too, to have demonstrated that I and the majority who share most of my views – they tend to live in Crewe and Arbroath and Truro and Larne and Llandudno and similar places, rather than in Islington, Hampstead, the Palace of Westminster or Broadcasting House – are not really cruel or unfeeling or vindictive folk. We want crime prevented and properly punished, and our children and grandchildren safely and humanely schooled. That is all, and we are tired of those selfish and hard-hearted bigots who refuse to let us have these things, and will not face the obvious truth, that capital and corporal punishment should never have been abolished.

They won't be restored in my time. For one thing, we have the paradox that while a national majority favour the death penalty, p.c. has already had such an effect that juries would be reluctant to send even a proved serial murderer to the gallows. And the fury that would erupt if a non-white were hanged is not to be contemplated. If, or more probably when, so-called democracy fails, and totalitarianism triumphs, they will be re-imposed with a vengeance, either by communist or fascist dictators.

Meanwhile we must all suffer from the weakness of bad governments and the folly of permissive policies. And every time I hear of some defenceless old woman beaten to death by thugs, or a little child raped and strangled by a paedophile, I shall have to bite back the words: "Well done, congratulations, all you abolitionists and enlightened liberals and champions of the permissive society! That's another family who have a lot to thank you for."

A shameful thing to say? No, a shameful thing to *have* to say. At least I'm still capable of shame, even if the liberal establishment is not.

No One Did It Better

A T THE MUCH-ADMIRED opening ceremony of the Sydney Olympics in 2000 (which I thought rather vulgar), great emphasis was laid on the Aborigines, but there was virtually no acknowledgement that it was Britain that made modern Australia; a Captain Cook figure made a brief appearance, and that was it. A stranger, noting the amount of attention paid to Stone Age barbarians and to the arrival of the non-British immigrants in modern times, would never have guessed that Australia and its people are more British than anything else. Many of them may wish to cut the tie, but that's beside the point.

This deliberate down-playing of the British contribution is, of course, just another manifestation of the politically correct tendency to denigrate Britain (and especially England) and the Empire at every opportunity. Regrettably, there is no shortage of detractors in Britain itself. Many are sincere, half-educated liberals, or New Labour zealots who seem to detest British history (a prejudice which led them to neglect a heaven-sent opportunity for a patriotic celebration of the Millennium, and make themselves a laughing-stock with their ridiculous Dome), while others are simply dishonest, deliberately distorting history by selecting every item they can find to Britain's discredit, and carefully avoiding its virtues.

This happens on even the most trivial level, as witness such cinematic drivel as *Pocahontas, Braveheart* and *The Patriot*, all of which shamelessly presented a false picture of their subjects, with the apparent intention of vilifying the English as the ultimate arch-villains. Which wouldn't matter a hoot if it didn't damage the education of our children, as I'm afraid does much of the all-too-slanted history they are taught at school. The trouble with the big lie is that it works unless it is refuted, and I don't kid myself that my voice is big enough to stem the tide of revisionist propaganda. But I can state the truth as I know it, from study and observation, just for the record, and that at least will be something.

I write as a convinced Imperialist – which means that I believe that the case for the British Empire as one of the best things that ever happened to an undeserving world is proved, open and shut. Of course it had its faults, grievous ones; there are bad blots on our record – and what country since time began is blameless? We know that history is one long catalogue of theft, slaughter, and conquest, and no one can deny that Britain was better at these things than anyone else. We were, and still are at heart, a nation of pirates, and as a fine historian once said, let the world not reproach us with it, but be thankful.

Why? Because with all the greed and lust of dominion and bucca-neering zeal that drove our ancestors, the wondrous paradox is that they left the world better than they found it. If no other country was so rapacious and acquisitive and successful at doing down its competitors, no other country did half as much to spread freedom, law, good government and democratic principle around the globe; as a civilising force Britain and its Empire were unique, and if proof is required one need only compare the state of imperial lands when they were under the Union flag, with their present condition. At best, as in India and many smaller, usually insular, territories where British influence lingers most strongly, the peoples are no better governed than they were, to say the least; at worst, independence (laughably called freedom) has been a ghastly tragedy, as in those African countries which have been transformed from prosperous, law-abiding colonies into bankrupt bloody dictatorships under the tyranny of evil thugs like Mugabe and Amin and the butchers of Biafra.

It is liberal dogma that responsibility for the African horrors rests with the Imperialists who allegedly did not prepare the colonies for independence – conveniently overlooking the fact that it was the indecent haste of Attlee's Labour government in getting out of India that led to a carnage in which two million died.

The Empire had to end, but those who hurried its demise (including the United States, which short-sightedly lost no opportunity of twisting the lion's tail, and now wonders why places like the Middle East are in endless turmoil; it would make you weep) bear a heavy share of guilt for the ills which so often accompanied independence. I shan't forget a symbolic little notice pinned to the wall of a bungalow, far up a river in Borneo, which had once been a British resident's headquarters, recording the programme of inoculation against malaria: it stopped abruptly on the date of British withdrawal.

Ah, well, if you want to incur everlasting hostility, do someone a favour: they'll never forgive you. Perhaps that explains the anti-British feeling. Or perhaps we're just not very likeable. Who cares? We did what we did, and it was worth doing, and no one could have done it better – or half as well.

"Thirty Years in Hollywood and You Can still Learn Something New"

I KNEW THAT Burt Lancaster and I were never going to be soul-mates the moment he suddenly exclaimed: "What the hell d'you think we're paying you for?" Annoyed, I hesitated between "You're not paying enough to take that tone," and "Up yours, Lancaster!", but discarded both: I knew his knees were hurting him, we'd had a long hard session in which my ideas had risen farther and farther over the top, I didn't want to walk out on an excellent project on the spur of the moment, and even at the age of sixty-four he looked as though he might still be able (in his own words) to "throw Ernie Borgnine out the window."*

So I took my time and replied: "For ideas which you don't seem to like. So d'you want me to quit? I might as well if you're going to start talking that way." He growled: "Ah, for Christ's sake!" and we resumed our search for a plot for a sequel to *The Crimson Pirate*. Perfectly amiably, but with no intention on my side of prolonging

---

* Unfortunately I've forgotten the context of this remark, but I know it didn't imply any bad blood between them. They made several pictures together, and Lancaster's company produced Borgnine's greatest success, *Marty*, which won a clutch of Oscars, including best actor for Borgnine himself. Knowing how physically competitive actors can be, I rather think that Lancaster was just being macho. I'm by no means sure that he could have defenestrated Borgnine, a man of impressive physique and genial disposition whom I met only once, when Richard Fleischer introduced us in Chasen's restaurant. He lacked Lancaster's height, but made up for it in width; it was like shaking hands with a cheerful gorilla.

our association beyond the next few days, which he had paid handsomely for in advance. I was still prepared to write him a screenplay if our discussion went well and the price was right, but I wasn't going to commit myself to working with him on set and location for three months, which was what he wanted; that, I realised after the momentary exposure of his hairy heel, would inevitably end in strong language, explosion, and me on my way to the nearest airport.

It wasn't that we didn't get on; quite the reverse. In the time we had already spent discussing the project, I'd found myself closer to him where ideas were concerned than to his partners, Harold Hecht and Jim Hill. He was the one who really wanted to make that sequel, he was intelligent and well-read (surprising me by his admiration for Mervyn Peake) and was not only an anglophile but a romantic one: in childhood he had devoured Jeffery Farnol, "Lady Charmian and Black Bartlemy's Treasure, the whole lot. Used to buy 'em for ten cents from a stall in Little Italy, sell 'em back for seven, then buy another for ten."

It was easy to understand why, although he had built a reputation as a serious actor with an Oscar to his credit, he had made good old-fashioned over-the-top swashbucklers like *The Flame and the Arrow* and *The Crimson Pirate*, and having read *Flashman* he had decided that I was the man to write his sequel for him.

I was enthusiastic, but I guessed before we met that he would not be the easiest man in the world to work with. His screen persona suggested a formidable, probably overbearing character, and I recalled seeing a quote in which he had said: "If I'm working with frightened people, I tend to dominate them. I'm no doll, that's for sure." Never mind frightened people, he'd have tried to dominate the Duke of Wellington. Indeed, he'd given me a hint of this at our first meeting. "You fight your corner," were the words he used, stabbing a forefinger. "Don't mind me. It's your ideas we want, so you be a stubborn Scotsman, Georgie – a stubborn Scotsman, right?"

I assured him I would be – and prepared myself for script-conference brawls. They didn't happen, and he never "exuded the physical menace" which one writer discovered in him. His irritable demand to know what he was paying me for was the nearest we came to a quarrel, but that, my doubts about his partners' enthusiasm for the project, their apparent lack of agreement on how it should be developed, and Burt's own tendency to talk about a script's "kinetic values", gradually persuaded me that by and large I might be happier doing something else.

Which was a pity, for *Crimson Pirate* II could have been great fun on screen (if no doubt hell to make), and he was a most interesting man. For that matter, Hecht-Hill-Lancaster was a most interesting outfit, with a remarkable track record which included *Marty, Separate Tables, The Devil's Disciple, Vera Cruz, Sweet Smell of Success*, and several Academy Awards. Yet they operated out of a small office on Pico Boulevard, a most modest set-up by Hollywood standards, with only a single secretary so far as I could see, a quiet and efficient young lady who ruled the place and ferried me to and from my hotel in Lancaster's BMW. "Ah, you're a hard-working Jewish girl, Sandy," he would say. "We've got to find you a nice Jewish boy, with blue eyes."

The founding father of the group, credited with discovering Lancaster, bringing him to Hollywood, and helping him to become one of the first movie stars to break away from the studio system to form his own production company, in which James Hill later joined them, was Harold Hecht. He was a tiny dynamo, an elderly and ebullient Jew who met me at LA Airport, making contact in the crowded baggage area by climbing on a pile of someone else's luggage and bawling through cupped hands, "Mr Frayzhur! Mr Frayzhur!" (Frasers in America get used to hearing their name pronounced in the old Highland way imported long ago by Gaelic-speaking settlers, and now familiar world-wide through the *Frasier* TV show.) It was like being paged by a demented

Nibelung who seized my suitcase and used it to flail his way to the exit while he kept up a running fire of comment to me and passers-by.

He bounced about alarmingly in his seat as he drove me at frightening speed to my hotel in Pacific Palisades, of all places, cross-examining me on my movie c.v., and damning the director and producers of my last picture ("Journeyman work! Journeyman work!") It emerged that he was a showbiz jack-of-all-trades who had been with the Metropolitan Opera (as a dancer), worked with Boleslawski and stage-managed the first American production of Bernard Shaw's "western", *The Shewing up of Blanco Posnet*, been a film dance director, and produced many of Lancaster's pictures.

Once at the hotel he harried the manager and desk clerks with manic energy, insisted on accompanying me to my room, which he inspected critically while I inhaled the familiar musty smell of American hotels and noted that the water still came out of the taps as foam, and then he shot away, haranguing the bellhop all the way to the elevator, leaving me wondering what I'd got myself into this time.

Jim Hill, whom I met next morning, was a more sober and reassuring figure, a producer and writer who had been the fifth husband of Rita Hayworth (of whom he wrote a memoir). He was to play a leading role in our talks and was plagued by acute fibrositis in his neck and shoulders.

We drove to the office on Pico, and there I met Lancaster himself, large, grave, courteous, and the most precisely controlled man, I think, that I've ever seen. It was not only in his movements and body language which, as his fans well know, were careful and deft and rather mannered, but in his thoughts and speech, that this curious deliberate precision showed; he would not respond immediately in conversation, but wait for a second, studying the speaker (I almost said opponent) before replying quickly and directly to the point; it was all exact, without "ahs" and "ers" or incomplete and careless phrases, more like the written word than speech.

I've no doubt that this precision was a result of early professional training. He was an acrobat before he was an actor, and it showed in his disciplined physical skill. Hecht told me that, early in their acquaintance, while they were taking an evening stroll, they passed a tall building shrouded in iron scaffolding onto which Lancaster had suddenly leaped, swarming to the top at high speed and descending again in a series of swings, trapeze-fashion, from bar to bar, before resuming his walk. I didn't doubt it. During one of our talks my cigarette lighter ceased to function, and as I clicked unsuccessfully Burt, seated at his desk across the room, with his chair tilted back, flipped a book of matches casually in my direction. He was at least ten to twelve feet away; the match-book fell neatly into the empty ashtray beside me.

On that first meeting, after checking me into a new hotel, the Century Plaza, which was handier for his office, he took me to lunch at his club. I think it was called the Hillcrest, but I'm not certain; it had a splendid-looking golf course, was luxurious in the extreme, and was Jewish – whether it was the club which Hollywood Jews are alleged to have formed when they were barred from other clubs, I don't know, but Lancaster, the Anglo-Saxon gentile, was extremely proud to be one of the few non-Jewish members.

We had an excellent lunch (scrambled eggs and sausages for Burt, cold salmon for me) beside a picture window overlooking the golf course, and having ascertained that I played, he said we might fit in a game, adding rather hastily: "Not for money, of course." I was under no illusion that he thought I might bankrupt him; he looked and talked like a low-handicap man, and I'm sure his concern was that he would beat the blazes out of me, bad knees notwithstanding, and win back the expense money he was paying me, which would have been embarrassing for us both.

He had played in pro-celebrity events, one of them at Gleneagles, where he had encountered George C. Scott, a keen golfer and an even more dedicated drinker. On *Prince and Pauper* Scott had disposed single-handed of a bottle of highly expensive Highland single malt which I had given to Dick Fleischer, with the result that he'd been incapable of movement until the next day. Something similar had happened at Gleneagles, where on the morning of the event Scott had been discovered insensible on the floor of the hospitality room, where he had spent the night. He was eventually revived enough to speak, and was heard to mutter: "I gotta have a piss and I gotta get outa here." To which one of the hotel staff had made the classic rejoinder: "Yes, sir, but not in that order." After which they had poured Scott into a car which took him to Prestwick en route for home.

During lunch I indulged my uncontrollable urge to interview – once a reporter, always a reporter – and discovered that Lancaster was a good subject who, while pleasantly modest, had no objection to talking about himself. It was just a question of pressing a tactful button or two, and listening.

His name was Burton Stephen Lancaster, he had been born and brought up in the Italian district of New York, and his father's family were from Lancashire, but how far back he wasn't sure. He added, grinning, that there was a family tradition that they were descended from John of Gaunt which, taking into account the Lancaster name and the old Duke's prodigal begetting of descendants, is not entirely improbable. But he doubted if he could prove a claim to John of Gaunt's mythical treasure. His mother, whose name was Roberts, had come from Belfast. He was, by his own account, simply an Englishman, although I once heard him say to a fan who asked if he was of Italian descent: "No, English ... English-Irish."

His affection for Britain, no doubt fostered by Jeffery Farnol, was strong; the so-called special relationship he described as "solid", and he had conceived an immense admiration for the British infantry whom, as a soldier himself, he had encountered in Europe. "I remember these guys, Commandos – Jesus, great big hard men, you'd never find tougher, and it didn't matter what was happening, action, fighting, God knows what – they had to have their tea! I tell you, they were something to see. They lived on tea!"

It was his ambition to back-pack his way round England, along the minor roads and country lanes (he was *certainly* under the influence of Farnol), "but I guess I won't make it now; the legs aren't so good." He had developed knee trouble, a legacy of his acrobatics – which takes me off at a tangent to his faithful friend and helper, Nick Cravat, the dapper little Italian gymnast who appeared in many of his films and was my escort when we went to the studios. Nick was garrulous and extrovert, given to engaging perfect strangers in conversation, much of which would not bear repetition; I recall occasions, at lunch-counters and in coffee-shops, where I tried to look as though I weren't with him. He also held strong views on the admission of very young girls to gymnastics, and the harm they would come to – this was at a time when the East European children were dazzling the world with their acrobatics.

"It's just exploitation!" Nick would fume. "They'll be burned out, old women before their time! Goddamit, it's all wrong!" He may have been right; he was certainly deeply moved. His other preoccupation, from what I saw, was to be self-appointed caretaker to Lancaster, whom he would upbraid unmercifully over such things as the car key which Burt lost or mislaid on the afternoon when we drove to a viewing theatre on the old Fox lot for a screening of *The Three Musketeers*, which Burt wanted to see as an example of my screenwriting. When we came out, he couldn't find the key, and Cravat tore strips off him like a wife with a pub-crawling husband. Lancaster endured this in impassive silence, obviously waiting for the pay-off, which came when Nick, having rebuked his fill, dived under the BMW and emerged with the spare key which he had attached to the undercarriage.

"Why'd I do that, huh? Cos I knew you'd lose your key! You always do! Isn't it a good thing I put a spare underneath there, huh? Isn't it? I always put a spare there," he told me, "because he's the most absent-minded s.o.b. in town, that's why. You wouldn't believe the things he forgets . . ." etc. Lancaster bore this patiently as we drove back to the office with Nick parroting his reproofs from the back seat.

I never discovered whether Burt liked the *Musketeers* or not, for he watched with his customary silent concentration, and had only one comment to make afterwards. "You know your best line in that movie? It's when D'Artagnan won't accept Buckingham's friendship, and Buckingham presents him with a sword and holds out his hand and says: 'Will you take this – and this – from an enemy?' That's a great line."

I made a note that Burt Lancaster was not averse to a little manly sentiment.

We went to see one other movie, a cloak-and-sworder made not long before. I wasn't keen – the last thing you need before starting a script is to see something similar – but Burt had arranged a special screening; he didn't come himself, having seen it, and Nick slept soundly until halfway through, when I woke him up and said I'd seen enough. When we got back to the office, Burt asked me what I'd thought of it.

"Possibly it could have been worse," I said, "but I doubt it."

He nodded judicially. "That's what I thought. Now you know what we don't want."

Our working routine was simple. In the morning we conferred at the office, Burt, Hill, and I, and occasionally Harold; in the afternoon I would write up what we had talked over, sketching scenes, trying out dialogue, mulling over possible plot-lines and variations for next day. It went well at first, and a plot-line emerged;

the Crimson Pirate, grown old, becomes curator of a pirate museum in retirement (the museum would feature memorabilia of such "pirates" as Fairbanks Senior, Flynn, Power, Sanders, Rathbone, and others) but has to take up arms again to assist his son, who, thanks to the care father has lavished on his education, has become something big and respectable in the outposts of empire and got himself into trouble as yet unspecified.

The bare bones of the beginning, you understand; there would be father-son bother, with the lad despising the old fellow, and a corrupt Viceroy or Governor-General or whatever, to be played by Rex Harrison. The son would probably be Michael York, with whom we had both worked, I on the Musketeers, Burt on *The Island of Dr Moreau*, and I pushed hard for Christopher Lee as principal villain; not only was he the best heavy in the business, he had also appeared as a minor supporting villain in the original *Crimson Pirate*, a most exploitable point. For love interest we provided father with a buxom wealthy widow who would be forever pestering him to settle down, while York would be given a wilting young lady of fashion.

I seem to recall that we kicked around the idea of a kind of romantic chiasmus, the son becoming infatuated with the widow, and the languid little aristocrat setting her cap at the old man. I know I suggested a beautiful black female pirate (a character I used later in a novel, *The Pyrates*), and that Burt countered with a smouldering Latin villainess to partner Rex Harrison, someone like Katy Jurado.

If all this sounds random, inconclusive, and corny, well, to quote Munro Stahr: "I'm just making movies." That's how it's done, by chasing false trails, exchanging wild ideas, and gradually moving towards a coherent story-line. Well, fairly coherent.

We had got about halfway (and had our momentary tiff) when it dawned on me that this was as far as I wanted to go. It's a strange thing: on the face of it you're making good progress, the ideas are taking shape, your associates are cautiously enthusiastic, one part of you is eager to see the thing take off – and at the same time you know that it's not going to happen. I liked the project as well as ever; if we could have agreed a final rough outline, and I could have gone home and written it quietly and delivered it in the recommended Hemingway style (change down as you reach the studio gates, hurl your manuscript through them, and accelerate away) and never seen Pico Boulevard again, that would have been fine. But I knew when it came to contract that they'd want me there for the shoot and, as I said earlier, life was too short.

And yet . . . while your mind's made up, there is still a small voice saying, "Don't be too hasty. You may feel different in a week or two."

But you must play fair. I told Burt I thought we'd gone as far as we could for the moment; I'd like to go home and think about it for a day or two. I added that I wasn't sure that I wanted to go on with it. Naturally, he wanted to know why; I told him I wasn't keen on three months' filming in the Mediterranean or wherever, and he asked would I at least go ahead with the synopsis; Jim Hill would come across to the Isle of Man to work with me, if that would help . . . I am as persuadable as the next man, Lancaster when he turned on the charm was a difficult man to refuse, Hill seemed genuinely eager to continue, and Harold Hecht almost tipped the scale when he said: "We'd really like you to go on, but if you decide not to . . . well, I can say we've had our money's worth."

Whether it was the old Hollywood treatment or not, I don't know; I like to think not. One thing I did know: if I did agree to an extension of my services, and completed the synopsis, there was no way I could turn my back on the movie after that. I was going to have to make a clean break or carry on.

The time they had already paid for was up anyway, and it was arranged that Burt and I would fly together to Heathrow – he was going on to Rome (to see his daughter, I think), and then to Russia to make some programme about battlefields. On the eve of our flight we were in the office when it occurred to me that I still had five hundred dollars remaining of the expenses they had given me on my arrival; I said since I hadn't spent it, they should have it back.

"No, it's yours," said Burt. "We agreed a figure; whether you've spent it or not doesn't matter."

I told him it did. If I hadn't had to use it, I wasn't entitled to it. He demurred, I insisted, Hecht and Hill watched with interest, and I finally settled the matter by laying the greenbacks on Burt's desk. (I would guess that Hecht concluded then and there that I would not be going on with the project, but he was wrong. I wasn't making a gesture, or a signal; it was just pure Presbyterianism.)

Burt began to laugh, something he rarely did. Then he shrugged, dropped the bills in his desk drawer, and shook his head, regarding me with what I can only call interested amusement.

"Thirty years in Hollywood," he said, "and you can still learn something new."

We flew out of LA next day – the only time in my life that I've been in a VIP lounge, unless you count the fuss they used to make over Westerners at Russian airports. I arrived first and checked in. "You're the Mr Frayzhur travelling with Mr Lancaster?" the hostess asked with bated breath, and thereafter I was practically carried through to a luxurious lounge and plied with canapés, soft drinks, coffee, and the daily papers – I had the feeling that if I'd asked to have my toe-nails buffed they'd have drummed up a manicurist. That, presumably is what major stars and their companions get all the time, and I'm not sure that it's always welcome. Burt gave the impression that he'd rather have been anonymous; he arrived at the last minute before boarding-time, wearing a cloth cap, blue glasses, a curious fleecy sleeveless jacket, and carrying his best suit in a portable hanger. Once we were installed at the back of first class, where he asked apologetically if I would mind taking the aisle seat (I learned why presently), he drew my attention to the price of our tickets – several thousand dollars apiece, even in those days.

"Look at that! You'd think you could buy the goddam airplane for that kind of money." He looked about him and sighed. "You know, Frankie Sinatra would reserve this whole cabin, the whole of first class."

I said that presumably Sinatra could afford it.

"Yeah ... they think we all can, movie stars making fortunes. What d'you think I'm worth? Four million bucks. Okay, I'm not complaining, it beats the hell out of circus work, but it's no big deal by Hollywood standards." He paused. "It'll do, though."

It was my opening to start interviewing again, and since Sinatra had been mentioned I asked about *From Here to Eternity*, and learned that Sinatra, the untrained actor, had a talent for getting the speech or the move right first time. "He was a natural; it seemed to come easy, spontaneously. Now Monty Clift thought about it." He recalled an emotional scene with Clift in which it had been suggested that Lancaster should kiss him. "Monty was all for it – he would be." Sardonic snort. "I said, 'No thanks, I pass.'"* Deborah Kerr? "Great actress, great lady."

He had chosen the window seat, I discovered, to avoid the attentions of admirers. "I can walk around Hollywood, hardly be noticed, maybe one or two people calling, 'Hi, Burt Lancaster!' but anywhere else they want to talk to you. In Europe especially. Old German women out in the country even, no kidding!"

As it turned out, having me on the aisle was only a partial protection; in the first hour of the flight at least four people

---

* Montgomery Clift was said to be homosexual, and after Lancaster's death it was put about that he, too, was a pervert. For what my opinion is worth, I doubt it very much, and imagine it was the kind of slander that often circulates about stars (as with Power, Flynn, and others), when they are safely dead and unable to sue.

approached him for his autograph, which he gave with great good humour, listening politely to one California matron who wanted to tell him how terrific he'd been in . . . here there followed a fairly full list of his pictures, "and, oh my goodness, that Italian one . . . you know, *The Lion* . . . no, no, *The Leopard*, you were marvellous. Of course, you are Italian, aren't you? Oh, you're not? I thought you were." She seemed disappointed, but settled down in a kneeling position in the aisle to continue her monologue until Burt took advantage of a pause to say: "I haven't introduced my friend here. He writes novels. You've heard of Flashman, of course."

Of course she had not, but she made a polite noise, Burt moved smoothly into his crossword puzzle, and I was left to make what conversation I could. It culminated with her asking in a dispirited way for my autograph, and I was aware of Lancaster smiling cynically over his rimless reading glasses.

When she had gone, with Burt bowing beautifully from a sitting position, we did our respective crosswords until he suggested we change papers – his was one of those huge American things consisting mostly of three and four-letter words – not as simple as you might think. Mine was the *Guardian*, not tough by British standards, but gibberish to an American; he stared at it in disgust, removed his glasses, and said "Okay, let's talk."

So we did, about everything except the project. He was what I can only call a liberal reactionary, or reactionary liberal, given to all the fashionable causes but with that deeply ingrained respect for traditional values typical of Americans of his race and generation. Obviously I don't remember it as a coherent conversation, but isolated things stay in memory: he was thinking of investing in a soccer club – the game looked like taking off in the US at that time – and talked knowledgeably of "Georgie Best"; he never went to Hollywood parties, his idea of a happy evening being to have Nick Cravat and a few friends over to his modest apartment and eat spaghetti; he had given up smoking, but the sight of me puffing away was too much for him, and he accounted for half my cigarettes on the flight.

As to his career, he was immensely proud of his performance in *The Leopard*, and of the praise it had received from Laurence Olivier when they met; he greatly admired Paul Scofield, with whom he'd appeared in *The Train*, and Mickey Rooney, whom we watched briefly in the in-flight movie ("Boy! what an actor!"); he had little to say of his best-known pictures, but dwelt rather on the lesser ones, like *Valdez is Coming*, and a violent prison drama early in his career, *Brute Force*, in which he had learned much from fellow-actors Hume Cronyn and Charles Bickford, and from that under-rated supporting player, John Hoyt, a notable Decius Brutus in Mankiewicz's *Julius Caesar*.

Valdez is Coming, in which he had played a downtrodden Mexican who eventually turns on his persecutors, he recalled for two reasons: one, it has no ending, the titles coming up with the final shoot-out not taking place, and two, because of an acting trick he had learned. The director had told him to keep his eyes lowered until the point in the film when the worm finally turned against his oppressor, and on the line: "Tell him Valdez is coming", to look up into camera for the first time. It worked; I've seen it.

He confessed to an ambition to work on the West End stage, as James Stewart and Henry Fonda had done, and wondered how London audiences would react to a play in which he and Kirk Douglas played Huckleberry Finn and Tom Sawyer grown old; he plainly had his doubts not only as to how it would be received, but whether he could get backing to put it on. I suggested he take it to the Edinburgh Festival, the "fringe" if necessary; all he need do, I assured him, was hire a hall and go to it; if it was a success, it would transfer to London without difficulty; if it flopped, well, they'd have lost nothing.

"Would the Edinburgh audiences come to see us?" He actually asked the question, frowning.

"For Kirk Douglas and Burt Lancaster?" I said. "Oh, I dare say you might get one or two ... dear God, man, you'd be a sell-out!"

But he was not convinced, and the play never reached Edinburgh. What it was like, I don't know, but unless it was one of the most frightful stinkers of all time I don't see how it could have failed, with those two.

We reached Heathrow at some godless hour, and as we walked along the interminable corridors he returned to the *Crimson Pirate* sequel. He wanted me to go on; we'd reach a good contract, we could have a terrific picture. "I hope you'll do it," he said. "I really do."

I was hugely flattered, as who wouldn't be, and murmured something grateful and non-committal. At this point we were met by a young man who seemed to be some kind of official airport greeter, and who bade Burt welcome at considerable length without saying a single useful or relevant thing. Burt bore him with exemplary patience, got rid of him politely, and repeated his hope that I'd carry on. We shook hands and parted, I to go to Terminal One, he to catch his Rome connection, walking briskly away with that slightly splay-footed gait, his good suit hung on one finger. An unusual man, even by Hollywood standards; tough, talented, straightforward, courteously aggressive (or aggressively courteous), and a lot deeper than your average film actor. If there was a quality that came across it was seriousness; he was not a man who took life lightly.

I can't say he was my favourite acquaintance in the film world – but then I'm dam' sure I wasn't his, for after talking the thing over with Kathy and Douglas Rae* I simply found my decision was firmer than ever, and packed the project in; in spite of Harold Hecht's kind words, it had been time and thought wasted all round, and the sequel to *The Crimson Pirate* was yet another of those

* Film agent

174

countless movies that are planned, discussed, enthused over, magnificently cast, envisioned in splendour, and never get made. I can regret never seeing it on screen, but not my decision to walk away from it. I just have to think of those "kinetic values".

Pictures of Russia

Whoever said that Russia was an enigma inside a some-thing-or-other inside something else, was dead right. I don't understand the place yet. When my precious, battered copy of the works of Shakespeare (bought for eleven rupees in Bangalore in 1946) went missing in the Metropole Hotel, Moscow, I addressed the light fixture in scathing terms, on the assumption that that was where the bug would be planted, and the NKVD would know what I thought of them. I then complained to the manager, forcefully, and he was appalled.

"*William* Shakespeare?" he exclaimed, and I fought back the urge to cry: "No, Mad Jack Shakespeare, and it's my belief that some light-fingered Commie has made off with him." Which was as well, for Russians are a sensitive lot, and I have to admit they took my loss seriously, turning the hotel upside down before I remembered I'd left the book in the Intourist office.

You'd have thought they'd have taken a dim view of the Frasers after that, but when we returned to the hotel a fortnight later after a sweep through Leningrad, Kiev, Tashkent, and Samarkand, we were astonished to be accommodated not in the kind of modest room we'd had previously, but in a magnificent white and gold suite straight out of a Fred Astaire musical of the thirties. It was like a fly in amber: high ornate ceiling, magnificent double doors through which you expected to see Edward Everett Horton hurrying in, a piano, splendid period furniture for Ginger to recline on in a feathery white dress, and bare electric wires sticking out of the skirting-board – but that was Russia, 1972 style.

What we had done to deserve such VIP treatment we never discovered. We were undistinguished travellers, quite apart from my Shakespeare explosion, and all I can think is that we asked so many journalistic questions that the authorities became wary of us, and it was either a suite at the Metropole or the Gulag. Yes, we were inquisitive, in areas where tourists are probably not supposed to tread.

We quite upset our fair young Intourist lady in Samarkand, for example, by quizzing her on race discrimination – indeed, it was apartheid, with the white Russians and the Asiatics as segregated as you could imagine, in districts, schools, and so forth – and I'll never forget dinner in the hotel with oriental beggars staring through the plate glass wall at the Russian smart set in their just-out-of-date finery, the men with string ties and the women with the inevitable hennaed hair.

We may also have disturbed the orthodoxy of a clever, intense little Jewish official at Tashkent who took us aside for a conversation which turned into a mutual grilling; that he was intelligence I've no doubt, I've seen the type too often. We talked of Israel and Ireland and the state of the world, and the novels of John Updike, which he admired, and my desire to visit Kashgar at the back of beyond. Kathy said, why didn't we just hop a plane there, and the little Jew looked thoughtfully into the distance and said: "You make it sound so easy." I hope he's in Israel now, where I'm sure he wanted to be.

Kathy and I were unusual, I suppose, in being among the few Britons to visit Russia at that time. We were on our own, with no accompaniment except the Intourist guides, smart, bright, educated and decorative young ladies who took their work seriously. I think we won the heart of the blonde ice-maiden in Moscow by intervening to deflect the snideries aimed at her by a party of Americans, who evidently couldn't forget the Cold War; at the other end of the scale was the imperious young lady in Kiev who informed us that she was an officer's daughter and proved it by striding around like Catherine the Great, barking orders at the peasantry, treating them like dirt, and giving the impression that she would produce a knout at any moment. They cringed, too, and it occurred to us that Lenin had failed not only to eliminate nationalities, but to do away with class distinction.

Looking back, Russia is a series of snapshots:

The little old women sweeping the snowy streets of Leningrad; the grizzled doorman with his row of medals, swelling with pride when I noticed them; the female lift attendant in her worn shabby clothes and a beautiful Hermès scarf, the gift of some American matron; the black-clad *babushkas* trudging through the snow with their string bags of oranges . . .

The two little close-cropped Russian boys staring entranced at the two small American girls behaving disgracefully at the next table, one of them crying her depravity aloud: "I was *so* bad!"; the cold-eyed Russian officers viewing tourist hippies in the *chayanya*, and thinking (as I was) how they'd like to get them on the parade ground . . .

The Tsarskoye Selo palace, with its wonderful Cameron gallery, where craftsmen were meticulously restoring the beautiful building wrecked by Hitler's invaders – whom our guide began by calling "Nazis" until she got carried away by her tale and they became most emphatically "Germans!" . . .

Our airport bus driving through a snowstorm at Kiev airport among the parked planes, with our driver shouting hopefully: "Tashkent?"; the flight itself with Genghis Khan in person sitting bald-headed and fearsome across the aisle restraining a hospitable Uzbek who was offering us a drink from his bottle, while in the seats behind us a trio of gleefully drunken Mongols, whom we christened the Filthistan Trio, kept changing places, usually on take-off or landing . . .

The party of Soviet working men visiting the great cathedral at Leningrad, viewing the wonders of its splendid nave with atheistical indifference . . . and then gradually, one after another, the hats coming off in instinctive reverence; huge snow-covered Mongol boots tramping over priceless carpets in a Tashkent hotel; the Berlin businessman offering sweets to the Moscow Intourist girls, boasting "German chocolates!" and the pert little Georgian remarking: "That's why they're called After Eights"; the discovery that if you want to find someone in Russia who is sure to speak English, look for a black face; walking home from the circus through the darkened streets of Moscow, where in the days before *glasnost* and *perestroika* and (ha!) democracy, there were no gangsters or muggers, no one needed a bodyguard, and young girls could stroll in safety – and how ironic that the Russia for which we both feel such nostalgia should be the "Evil Empire" of communism . . .

Standing in Samarkand market, looking down the Golden Road to the distant snowy peaks of Afghanistan, seeing the hawk faces go by, and thinking "Oh, I know you from a long time ago on the other side of those mountains"; eating "white partridge and jam" in Moscow, and the wonderful bread of Central Asia in Tashkent (but avoiding at all costs Chicken Kiev in Kiev); drinking caravan tea, and wondering if there was ever such a cold, melancholy, magical land with such kindly people in it.

The Defeat of the British Army

WOMEN HAVE no place in the Army, Navy, or RAF. They served magnificently in the old ATS, WRNS and WAAF, and the war effort would have been useless without them and the nursing services and those dauntless ladies who brought their tea and wads to the front line. Our armed forces are the poorer for the passing of the women's auxiliaries, and they should be revived. But mixing men and women on the same footing is mad, bad, and damned dangerous.

I am not principally concerned with the obvious folly of putting the sexes together in ships or camps, with the inevitable consequences, or with those enterprising women who join up, get pregnant, and soak the taxpayer for compensation when they are properly dismissed the service; only an institution as traditionally brainless as the Ministry of Defence would permit this.* But I am positively alarmed at the folly of those who, without thinking the thing through, advocated the admission of women to those arms of the service where they may be involved in battle. Ignorant folk may suppose that they can be allowed into the sappers or the signals or the artillery in safety, but this is nonsense, as every old soldier knows.†

---

* Or the ridiculous case in which a female sailor was given compensation for "sexual harassment" and the alleged "harasser" was subsequently cleared by court martial.
† It was distressing to hear of a very high-ranking officer actually suggesting that in the Royal Artillery roles could be apportioned according to strength, so that the strongest gunner could lift the shells while others with greater firing skills would concentrate on launching the weapons.

All those branches of the service find themselves frequently in close combat, and that is where women simply do not belong.

Few, if any, of the advocates for women in the forces have any experience of war, but that never stopped a zealous, uninformed idiot from demanding female integration, blundering blindly along the politically correct path, no doubt delighting feminists and giving soldiers the horrors.

Admission of women to the corps was foolish enough, but the ultimate wicked and cowardly lunacy was the campaign for them as front-line infantry, now abandoned (for the moment, anyway) because tests have shown (*mirabile dictu)* that women aren't as robust as men, and that using them in the front line would undermine Army efficiency. What kind of moron thought that tests were necessary to reach this staggering conclusion, we are not told, nor what kind of sick mind could even contemplate the employment of female infantry and tank troops in the first place.

In case anyone still thinks that women have a place in the front line (and because I'm sure the dingbats and feminists will resume their disgraceful campaign eventually), I shall restate the case, though God knows in a sane world it should not be necessary. I emphasise that I am talking not only about the infantry and tanks, but about the corps – indeed, about any military duty that may take a woman into contact with an armed enemy.

That women are physically weaker than men (as even a New Labour minister might have deduced from their absence from the England rugby team and their failure to win the Wimbledon men's singles or the world heavyweight title) is only the first of their military handicaps. They cannot march as far or as fast as men, or

---

Setting aside the optimistic assumption that the weakest (women, presumably) would have the greater firing skills, what happens when the gun position is overrun by the enemy? ("Quick, Private Samson, lift that shell! Private Mildred, pull the lanyard – oh, dear, that horrid great German brute has trampled on her! And she did so well in training . . .") Oh, for the days when the top soldier was a Montgomery or a Slim, who knew what close-quarter fighting meant. Which prompts the disturbing question: would either of them, or any officer who did not hold politically correct views, be considered for high command in today's forces?

endure the front-line ordeal as well, or drive a bayonet into an enemy with the same force, or tackle bare-handed an opponent far more muscular and brutal than they are. Some may be trained to shoot as well, but whether they will do so in action with male callousness (and eagerness) is doubtful. Courage doesn't come into it. Women are if anything braver than men, but the notion of a female teenager fighting hand-to-hand with a Panzer Grenadier or a Japanese White Tiger – or a Royal Marine – is ludicrous.*

Soldiers have to do all these things, do them well, and keep on doing them. Modern enlightened opinion prefers not to dwell on the realities of war, but thinks of peace-keeping and policing and protecting helpless civilians, or at worst in terms of "smart bombs" and air strikes against some vague, distant enemy (preferably one of the Kosovan or Afghan variety, who can't hit back), and of press conferences at which defence spokesmen point at maps and talk (and frequently lie) in official jargon.

War isn't like that. War is men killing each other, often at close quarters, and doing their damnedest to stay alive. And until you have done that, against a capable enemy, you don't have any idea of what it's like, honestly. Mr Spielberg may splash the screen with gore, and publicists may declare: "You are there!", but you're not. You're snug in a cinema watching a load of crap performed by actors. Hand-to-hand fighting is different, and it's no place for a woman. (It's no place for anyone, including me, but for a woman least of all.)

And not only for the obvious reason that she is more likely, by reason of physical weakness, to get killed. I say nothing of supposed feminine delicacy or squeamishness, which would handicap some, if not all; there are some tough, callous bitches around – but they

* The folly of the female-fighter campaign was perfectly illustrated in the film comedy, *The Great Race*, in which Natalie Wood, having boasted of winning the women's international fencing championship, was easily disarmed by Tony Curtis, who observed: "Now, if it had been the *men's* international fencing championship . . ."

are still not as tough or prone to slaughter as men. Their instinct is different, and anyone who doubts this might have learned something from the sight of two of my grandsons rushing about blasting imaginary targets with their space-guns, while my tiny granddaughter raced ahead of them scooping up her dolls and crying: "Save dee babees!"

Another excellent reason for not allowing women anywhere near the front line is that they will certainly get men killed; they will cause casualties by their very presence. This is the opinion of one who, from personal experience shared by millions of his generation, knows what he is talking about. The feminists don't, the government don't. Not all that many senior officers do, for that matter. I do, and concern for the lives of British soldiers who would undoubtedly die for the selfish vanity of feminists and the wilful folly of ignorant politicians, commands me to say so.

You see, it's a question of male instinct. When you're in there, with the shot flying and grenades exploding, and ruthless and valiant enemies trying to shoot, stab, disembowel, or blow you up, you have to concentrate something wonderful, with as few distractions as possible. Certainly you have a care for the safety and survival of your comrades, but you know they can look after themselves, and can devote yourself to your own immediate concerns. The point is that you don't have to worry unduly about them. They are as capable as you are.

But if one of them is a woman, however well trained and fit and fierce and formidable, you are going to worry about her whether you like it or not, just because she's female, and it's ingrained in you since the Stone Age that it's up to you to look out for her and protect her. And if you do – if you give that split second to her which you wouldn't give to a man, it's like taking your eye off the ball if only for an instant, and you're liable to end up dead. "Is she okay?" is always going to be in your mind, and it's a question you can't afford when survival is on a knife edge. And it isn't fair that a soldier should have to carry that extra, unnecessary burden just because a pack of cranks got imbecile ideas about equality and "women's rights". The right to get killed? And to get their male comrades killed?

Feminist fools and their supporters will say that men must be "educated" out of their protective attitude,* and trained to regard a woman as one of the boys (who needs privacy, and has a monthly period, and is liable to cystitis in cold and wet). How childish can you get? Men are the way they are, and you can no more train them not to have a care of women (or train women not to *expect* masculine care, maybe?) than you can train the sun not to rise. You can't change that, and anyone fool enough to try knows as little of human nature as Hoon and Robertson do of war.

But the whole business is too stupid for words. I think back to Burma, and the filth and the ghastly country, the leeches and malaria and dysentery and jungle sores, the ceaseless downpour of the monsoon, the permanent sodden state of clothing and gear and puckered skin, the blistered feet and the sheer pain of trying to stay awake, or keep going when every muscle seemed to be on fire – and I haven't got to the bloody Japanese yet, with their poisoned stakes and booby traps and nasty habit of using prisoners for bayonet practice and no-surrender valour and fighting ability to match our own . . . almost.

Take that as an honest description of infantry campaigning, and ask yourself: do you really want women going through that? Or

* The Equal Opportunities Commission said that very thing to a Commons committee, who reported: "Their (the E.O.C.) view was that proper training equips personnel to deal with any (sic) crisis . . . personnel would respond in combat in the way in which they had been trained to respond, and if this involved working in a mixed team of men and women, they could be trained in that way."

For crass optimism this deserved some kind of prize, but of course the committee wouldn't have dared contradict the E.O.C. who, incidentally, felt that women should be allowed to fight for no better reason than that they want "to have a go at doing it." (Only a bounder would recall Gilbert's line about the lady "who doesn't think she waltzes, but would rather like to try.") It should be noted that the committee, like their battle-hardened E.O.C. advisers, hadn't the foggiest idea of what crises can arise in close combat, beyond what they'd learned from John Wayne movies.

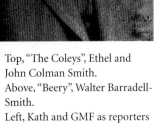

Top, "The Coleys", Ethel and
John Colman Smith.
Above, "Beery", Walter Barradell-
Smith.
Left, Kath and GMF as reporters
in Regina, Saskatchewan, 1949.

Malcolm McDowell (Flashman) with Britt Ekland (Duchess Irma) in *Royal Flash*. Right, Oliver Reed (Bismarck) squares up to Henry Cooper (John Gully); below, "Not a bad Bismarck" – Oliver Reed as the young Iron Chancellor; below right, Alan Bates (Rudi von Starnberg).

Overleaf, the members of *Force Ten from Navarone*. From left, Franco Nero, Harrison Ford, Robert Shaw, Edward Fox, and Carl Weathers.

Above, Burt Lancaster with Nick Cravat in *The Crimson Pirate*;
right, Brigitte Nielsen and Arnold Schwarzenegger in *Red Sonja*.

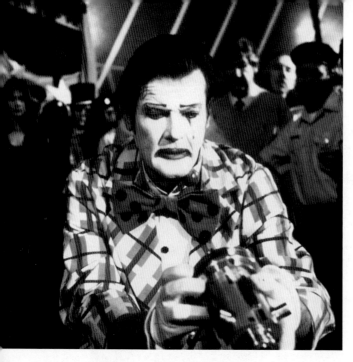

Above, Roger Moore in clown makeup in *Octopussy*, and below,
making the presentation to Cubby Broccoli at the Academy Awards.

have you swallowed the tale told by the women-into-battle brigade (who know nothing of war, remember) that it can never happen again, that a soldier's function is now limited to feeding hungry refugees and keeping a fatherly eye on piccaninnies, because the "smart bombs" and technical wizardry have changed the ultimate face of war, and the rifle and bayonet and grenade are things of the past?

That lie has been nailed in Afghanistan, where we see that when all the vaunted sophisticated weaponry has been hurled at the enemy, and his territory is a smoking ruin, he is still there, as he has been since Caesar's day and will be in the future, in the cellar or the bunker or the cave, and has to be winkled out, which is a bloody horrible, dangerous, often fatal business. Do you want your daughter or sister or sweetheart doing it – or rather, trying to do it? She may look smashing on parade – but do you really want her coming home in a body bag? Can you live with the thought of her falling prisoner to some of the less civilised Balkan guerrillas, or to an African simba who may be HIV positive? That's what putting women in the front line means, and I have to ask: have British men, at Westminster and elsewhere, so degenerated that they would be content to sit safe at home while their womenfolk did their fighting for them? Would Mr Blair really be prepared to do a Queen Victoria and wave our young women off to war?

I think, I hope, that British men would think twice. The feminists I'm not sure of, because they're so bloody irrational in their crazed quest for what they think is equality (when the silly cows have got the upper hand to start with, as their non-feminist sisters know full well) that one cannot read their minds with confidence. I'm appealing to the sane, humane majority when I say: "Don't send your daughter up the line, Mrs Worthington." It's no place for her.

Unfortunately some young women, deceived by propaganda, will think it is, and learn their dreadful error only when they find themselves in the thick of it, as I pray to God they never do. They may believe the nonsense that exercises on Salisbury Plain and careful testing have indicated that women are fit to be, if not infantry, at least sappers and gunners and signallers. Well, I've been to battle school and done more assault courses than I can count, and I can assure them beyond peradventure that training exercises bear no meaningful relation to battle, and are absolutely no test of anyone's fitness for combat, male or female. And that the young lady who blithely supposed that "anyone can learn to fire a rifle, can't they?" as though that were all there is to it, has much to learn.

Nor should they be taken in by the argument that the Russians and Vietcong used fighting women. Of course women *can* fight, and do, magnificently, when their country's back is to the wall; one of my earliest lessons in Border history told how the women of Carlisle had fought hand to hand with Bruce's besiegers seven hundred years ago. But a fight for sheer survival is one thing; a politically correct policy inspired by the ignorant is quite another. Yes, women can fight; the point is, should they, and I think I have advanced unanswerable reasons why they should not. It is worth noting that Israel, whose history is one long struggle for existence, and which needs every fighter it can get, does not use its female soldiers in the front line.

There is a note of despair in the cry that women are needed because of a shortage of male recruits. When the real need arises men will join up, and if meanwhile the shortage becomes desperate, the old policy of offering convicted felons the choice between jail and the Army (which has been seriously suggested) can be revived. I speak once more from experience: criminals can make good soldiers.

But the most curious argument I have seen aired is that while opposition to female soldiers is common among us old sweats, young officers of today, who have served with women and, being mostly graduates, have been educated in an atmosphere of liberal, progressive tolerance, etc., are all for them. I'll bet, but the point is that they haven't served with them in battle, and the obvious attractions of shepherding some pretty miss through a firing exercise or over an assault course will vanish altogether when she's lying alongside, shot in the stomach or bleeding to death with a severed artery. Sorry to be brutal, but that is the end result of a policy which is just sheer cruel bloody madness.

How curious, that a liberal intelligentsia who are usually so critical of the military, should be perfectly prepared to do for Jane and Jill, as well as Harry and Jack, with their plan of attack.

If it were not so certain to lead to tragedy, there would be a richly comic side to female soldiering. Some of the changes recommended and already made as a result of turning the fair sex into brutal if not licentious soldiery are simply beyond sanity; they read like a send-up even as I write them, but I'm assured that they are true.

For example, no male soldier may touch a female soldier without first saying: "I am going to touch you." One female soldier has been quoted as saying she fell about laughing, as well she might. "It's more sexual than saying nothing," was her comment – and indeed one can imagine what it would sound like when spoken in the smooth murmur of a Leslie Phillips or the lecherous chuckle of a Sid James. In the Army of fifty years ago, incidentally, touching a soldier, even tapping a finger on a dirty button, was forbidden, taboo, for the obvious reason that the difference between a casual touch and a stronger one which may be anything from a shove to an assaulting blow, is a matter of degree – and opinion. I shall not soon forget the outraged scream of RSM Bradley, Coldstream Guards, when a drill sergeant grasped a soldier's arm to correct the slope of a rifle. The Army of the forties took no chances.

Today, an instructor may touch a recruit "if he's feeling the creases in your trousers to see how sharp they are". If he can't tell by looking at them, he must be a borderline case – and anyway, by today's bizarre standards, doesn't all this touching amount to sexual harassment?

Again, female recruits were ordered to say "Zero" instead of "Oh!", presumably because "Oh!" might sound sexy. I fancy that Marlene Dietrich or Mae West could have loaded the word "Zero" with enough wanton sensuality to start a riot, but let that go.

Plainly the lunatics have taken over the asylum. Not content with trying to get women killed in action, the politically correct brigade have agitated for the disabled to be admitted to the forces, a campaign supported by an MP who accused the military of still living in the days of rifles and bayonets, as though these were things of the past. Tosh was talked about such distinguished disabled fighting men as Nelson and Bader, overlooking the fact that they entered the service as whole men who became expert in their trade before losing limbs, and remained expert afterwards.

No doubt someone confined to a wheelchair could do a pay-clerk's job (although how he would cope if his office were attacked by the enemy is another matter), but it would be a dangerous precedent; we have seen enough of the p.c. brigade to know that it would be only a matter of time before the disabled clerk would be suing the army for denying him promotion.

It has been proposed in all seriousness that soldiers should be able to sue their officers for giving "bad" orders, a novel idea which would have bankrupted most officers of my acquaintance, myself included, to say nothing of such military blunderers as Napoleon, whose performance in Russia would have kept half the lawyers in Europe in gainful employment.

The list of insanities is endless: we read of plans to make assault courses easier, of banning the use of barbed wire in training, and of a European directive to reduce the decibel level of military bands and even words of command – it may be hard to apply it during an artillery barrage, but doubtless the experts will want the troops to operate in ear-muffs, so that they can die through not hearing orders. Europe, which is behind most of these lunacies, has ordained that male soldiers must be trained to react correctly to their female comrades, and I have read with disbelief that NCOs must guard against using harsh language to recruits, who must be given time to recover if they are upset. Thus are heroes made.

All these follies are presumably part of the policy of creating what some idiot has called "a humanitarian, responsible new army". You can picture him lost in a dreamworld where the military's only role will be "peace-keeping", and that never again will they be called on to do nasty things like shooting enemies or sticking bayonets in them. It is significant that the American military academy, West Point, has banned the word "kill" from its cadets' vocabulary; no doubt some crank will call for a similar prohibition at Sandhurst.

This is bad enough, but there are other signs which must worry anyone concerned for the country's martial efficiency. I haven't been close to the Army for some years, but you don't have to be close to realise that all is not as it should be.

There is, it seems, bullying, and there have been courts martial as a result. I served four years in war and post-wartime as a private soldier, junior NCO, and commissioned officer, and never knew a case of bullying. As a recruit in the Durham Light Infantry, I saw it *tried*, and I also saw the would-be bullies dealt with drastically by their comrades. Later I commanded a platoon of aggressive and volatile Glaswegians and hard-handed Aberdonians: the notion of anyone bullying in that company would have been laughable, and if anyone had tried it his feet wouldn't have touched.

So when I hear of bullying in the Army today, I know that there are junior officers and senior NCOs who aren't fit for their jobs. And that is disturbing.

I hear also of racial harassment. I've served with coloured soldiers, and had one in the platoon I commanded. No one harassed him, or discriminated against him; it simply wasn't done. Those Glasgow hard men (and they were hard beyond the comprehension of nowadays) would have thought it shameful; it would have offended their ingrained sense of good manners and proper behaviour.

Maybe I was lucky, serving in such splendid regiments as the DLI, the Border, and the Gordons. One of the misfortunes that has befallen the Army is that they no longer exist, for the simplest of reasons. The Empire's gone, and the money with it. We no longer police the ends of the earth or have to fight for survival against superpowers like Germany and Japan. The Army, like the other services, must be smaller, so the powers-that-be make a complete balls-up of reducing it in size, continuing to waste vast sums on defence establishments, unnecessary auxiliaries, and manic adventures like Afghanistan and Yugoslavia, while destroying the regiments which, when it comes to the bit, have to defend the realm against its enemies.

They need not have been amalgamated out of their old existence. An eminently practical alternative offered itself – not entirely politically correct, perhaps, but sound and simple. Take my old regiment, the Gordons, described by Churchill as the finest in the world; rather than amalgamate they could have hired out as mercenaries in the old Scottish tradition of the Gardes Ecossaises, the first great free lances more than a thousand years ago. God knows there's no lack of employment around the world; they would have made money and kept themselves in excellent training against the day when Britain needed them again. It would have been worth suggesting if only to hear the scream that would have gone up from the wimps at Westminster – and it wouldn't have been any sillier an idea than sending wee lassies into action against the West Side Boys, and a sight less wicked.

But the amalgamation scandal is a bee in my busily-buzzing bonnet, so I leave it for other anxieties which plague the old soldier as he wonders if the Army is as good as it was. He consoles himself with the thought that this has been a worry since Xenophon got his ticket, and that the new boys proved themselves splendidly in the Falklands, and later in Sierra Leone – an operation which I honestly believe no other army could have carried out so well. But he frets at the suspicion that Private Atkins is not getting the care and material and intelligent organisation he deserves.

Tiny things jar on him because, in his book, they smack of poor thinking, even amateurism, on high. In his day, infantry were streamlined to the belt for fast movement; now he sees them cumbered with enough gear to outfit a brigade, a certain handicap in sudden crisis – how do they swim a river or scramble through a hedge in that lot? He marvels at TV pictures of an infantry leader with an enormous shovel strapped to his back – what for? Why isn't it back with the stores instead of hampering him in an ambush? Was it really necessary to patrol in Belfast with full kit, automatic weapons, and camouflage paint? And are the Army authorities content with all these things?

Perhaps my criticism is out of date and unjustified . . . but not when I hear of faulty weaponry, failing communications gear, soldiers improvising to cover incompetence on high, and, most scandalous of all, being exposed to radiation and chemical harm because the M.o.D. thought there was "little risk" – and never a word of the criminal blunderers being called to account. Or when I hear of such nonsense as "counselling" after active service. Certainly warfare can have dreadful traumatic effects, needing careful treatment, but such cases are the exception. They won't be if the "counselling" fanatics succeed in their aim of undermining morale – tell a man he needs "counselling", and he'll be first in the queue on sick parade, bawling for the psychiatrist, because that's human nature.

A distinguished general who once commanded the SAS told me that after the Gulf War forms were issued to all soldiers advising them that they might need "counselling", even although, as my informant said, "many of them had done no more than walk from the hotel to the swimming pool and back". I put this to General de la Billiere, and his response was "No one gave *me* a form." Come to think of it, it would have been a foolhardy psychiatrist who did.

"Counselling", bullying, racism, p.c. follies without number – no, all is not well in the Army. I see on television a group of recruits (including women) being made to eat grubs as part of "survival training", a nasty stupidity (you don't need to eat insects when there's vegetation) plainly designed simply to impress the recruits with the toughness of Army training. It's part of the macho culture which leads to men dying of exhaustion on exercises, a culture that arises whenever people want to prove themselves and have to invent dangers and hardships because there isn't a real war to give them the opportunity. And the M.o.D. claptrap is pumped out about the Army being better trained than ever before, and the reductions and neglect are glossed over with lying clichés such as "leaner and better" and "paring away surplus fat to create a more efficient fighting machine".

To use a military vulgarism . . . balls. It's not true, chiefly because successive governments have treated the forces negligently and bowed down abjectly before p.c. campaigners who have already done incalculable harm. Their hatred of all things military expresses itself in such a concentrated drive against morale and discipline that one is forced to conclude that it is not simply misguided, but a deliberate attempt to destroy our military capacity. Of one thing I'm certain: if I were a hostile power bent on destroying Britain's ability to defend herself or fight a real campaign, I couldn't have done a better job than our rulers, Tory and Labour, have done over the past twenty years.

These, of course, are just the paranoid ravings of a blood-lusting blimp, as any liberal can tell. They are also the heartfelt concerns of one of a generation of confirmed pacifists. Ours is not the pacifism of a military-hating Leftist establishment which pays lip-service to national defence while plunging recklessly into foreign adventures which are no concern of ours; we care deeply for the safety of our country, and of our successors in uniform. We despair of a government which not only pitches us unnecessarily into an Afghan war, but at the same time seems bent on aligning us with European "allies" who show no sign of having our interests at heart and have proved broken reeds (and deadly enemies) in the past. Afghanistan may prove to be a less perilous folly in the long run than the move to make us part of a European army, a so-called Rapid Reaction Force – dear God, their idea of rapid reaction is sixty days! Saddam Hussein could conquer half the Middle East in that time. Participation with a European force, almost certainly German-led and German-dominated, is the last thing we need, and all the Europhile claptrap cannot make a case for it.

Consider: quite apart from the unreliability of the other European powers, Germany is not, on her record, as I have pointed out elsewhere, to be trusted. Aggressive expansionism has always been her trade, and one may ask, if the day comes, as well it may, when she decides to try conclusions with Russia again, will a Britain committed to European union and alliance be able to keep out? I don't know; unlike the experts who *know* there is never going to be another great war, I cannot read the future.

One thing I do know, though. I have four grandsons, four "valiant young Britons" in Churchill's words, and over my dead body will they ever be drafted into a war, or any military action whatsoever, at the behest of Europe. Blair and other Europhiles may crawl to their Continental friends, and clothe in high-sounding lies their readiness to sacrifice British lives in Europe's quarrels. Very well, let them fill a pit. That'll be the day.

Special Relationship

SPECULATION ... that a hundred years from now the United States will have split into three – a Hispanic and Asiatic state in the West and Southwest, a black state in the Southeast, and a white state in the North, including Canada. Another possibility: that the Southwest will have gone back to Mexico.

Americans will scoff at this as crazy. It is the habit of great countries of imperial pretensions to take the future for granted, as the Romans no doubt did in Trajan's day, and as Britons, with a few far-sighted exceptions, did at Victoria's jubilees, and Americans do now. They envisage their country going on forever, one and indivisible, more or less as it is now – or if not forever, at least into the age of Captain Kirk, who is a reflection of America, so that's all right.

It is difficult for young countries on the crest of the wave, and for young people for that matter, to realise that Today, far from being permanent, is already almost Yesterday, and as for Tomorrow, God alone knows. But why should I even entertain the possibility of the USA fragmenting? She is the richest, strongest, most materially advanced country on earth, proud of herself and her polity, confident of the future; she has never (not even in 1942) been seriously menaced with invasion, she will repel the terrorist menace, and she survived in the 1860s the one real threat to her unity – but that is the point. The danger then came from internal dissension, and that,

I believe, is where it will lie henceforth. But I shan't be here to see it. Neither will those who call me crackers.

I sincerely hope I'm wrong, for a strong, united America is the hope of the world, and while I disapprove strongly of her assault on Afghanistan, and think we should have looked to our own interests first, I have to admit that Blair's present action (however much it may cost us in blood and treasure) has strengthened the special relationship as nothing else has done since the 1940s. He was rash and wrong, but at least that much good has come of it.

Of course the relationship, however warm it may be at the very highest level, has less to do with politics than with the social, cultural, and even spiritual ties between us. At its simplest, we are *interested* in America, and they in us, and it matters little who occupies the White House and Number 10 so long as we read each other's books, watch each other's films and plays, laugh at each other's jokes, and feel at home in each other's countries – all of which sprang originally from blood kinship and shared history, and continues with our shared language and laws and community of ideas.

We *know* each other in a way that sets us apart from Europe, despite America's huge immigration from the Continent, and the Euromania which affects some of Britain's dimmer politicians. What interest do the great mass of Britons and Americans take in French or German elections? None, and who in either country could name the French, German, or Italian head of state? Precious few – but every sentient Briton knows George W. Bush (and followed his entertaining election, and the lurid scandal of his predecessor, with avid interest). Likewise no foreign story in the last few years excited more interest in the US than the glittering rise and tragic fall of the Princess of Wales. And every American knows the Queen. All of that is what goes to the making of the "special relationship", and it will endure as long as both countries continue to speak the tongue that Shakespeare spake (more or less), and hold the faith that Milton held.

As to that tongue of Shakespeare's, an eccentric American has advised me that it is high time we stopped calling it "English", and substituted "Anglo-American". Actually, he thinks it should simply be "American", since the United States is the only remaining super-power (a fascinating piece of reasoning, this) but for sentimental reasons he is prepared, jolly decently, to stick "Anglo" in front. In support of this remarkable claim he quotes H. L. Mencken, a well-regarded American pundit who had a most colossal bee in his bonnet on the subject, and even wrote a book about it.

Mencken's case was that the "American form of the English language" departed from the parent stem and began "to drag English with it". He held that "the Englishman has yielded so much to American example . . . that what he speaks promises to become . . . a kind of dialect of American."

As an example of the fly sitting on the chariot wheel and compli-menting itself on the dust it raises, this is a beauty. It apparently escaped Mencken's attention that in the whole passage of his from which I have quoted, a passage of around three hundred words, there is not one of American origin; all were coined in England, as were the grammar, syntax, and form of the language. What he and my correspondent failed to understand is that American English is just another group of dialects of the mother tongue, and no more a separate "language" than Australian, South African, Canadian, Scots, sub-continental Indian, and all the other dialects of English spoken world-wide. Of course vocabularies differ, but very slightly when one considers the colossal bank of words common to all, and what is spoken in Britain (again, a great variety of dialects) has certainly been enriched (some might say polluted) by American words and usages, but the root and being of the language have not altered. English is English still, overwhelmingly so.

What is at work in Mencken and others, of course, is a manifes-tation of that mutual envy and rivalry which have existed since 1776, and even earlier. We envy American power and wealth and pre-eminence (which they like to call leadership, bless 'em); America envies British culture and self-satisfaction, and has an inferiority complex about them which is expressed in braggadocio, of which Menckenitis is simply an expression. It has even been claimed in the United States (and echoed by the ignorant here) that America is responsible for English being the world language. American films, TV and pop culture are advanced in support of this claim, and it seems almost cruel to point out that long before there was such a thing as an American sound movie, let alone US TV programmes and pop, English was already the official language of one-quarter of the human race who inhabited the British Empire, which had spread the English tongue over the Orient, Africa, and, incidentally, North America.

I should add that I hold America and its people in an affection and admiration amounting almost to love. (I love my children and grandchildren, too, but that doesn't stop me correcting their wilder flights when necessary.) To conclude, I can only adapt the words of the American poet Alice Duer Miller when she wrote of her love for England, and say that in a world where there is no United States I do not wish to live.

Everywhere but Hong Kong

GEORGES-ALAIN VUILLE was Swiss, short, stout, excitable, and great fun. On occasion I wondered if he might not be certifiably mad, but I feel I owe him a great debt, not only because he commissioned (and paid for) a fortune's worth of screenplays, but because he entertained Kathy and me in a Riviera villa once used by John F. Kennedy, paid for first-class travel and hotels in all kinds of exotic places (Hollywood, Madrid, Cannes, Gstaad, Sicily, etc.) where he lavished hospitality like a Greek tycoon, and kept us and many others entertained with his constant enthusiastic chatter, his high spirits, and his mania for telephoning in public at the top of his voice and in several languages.

"'Oo we phone now?" was his war-cry. "I know – we get Kirk Dooglass!" And he would start shouting into the phone, often interrupting himself to repeat aloud what the other party was saying. I have heard him pursue Douglas, William Holden, Rex Harrison, and some nameless unfortunate at Warner Brothers whom he roundly abused in Italian, all within the course of a couple of hours. He was trying, with mounting frenzy, to cast a picture which was already well into production, and since Holden and Harrison finished up in supporting roles, his energy paid off.

That bout of phoning ended with his slamming down the receiver with a cry of "Telly Savalas, bah!" followed by a torrent of words which I didn't understand, a bellowed instruction to his cook that he wanted steak *bleu* for dinner, and a heated discussion with his lady, whom he was reluctant to take flamenco dancing after midnight.

That was Georges-Alain, who for a brief hectic hour was the talk of the film world (c. 1977–79), the boy wonder who was going to be the new DeMille ... and then it all faded away.

I had never heard of him when Dick Fleischer phoned me shortly after *Prince and Pauper*. Vuille had the rights to James Clavell's novel, *Taipan*, and wanted Fleischer to direct a mega-budget film of it; Fleischer had stipulated that I should do the screenplay "and I was prepared to be obnoxious if he wanted a different writer." Which was kind and flattering, but I would have jumped at the project anyway. I knew *Taipan* was a massive best-selling historical novel, I'd have worked with Fleischer on anything, and from the sound of it Vuille had the drive and the bankroll to make the film a blockbuster. Douglas Rae negotiated my deal, and I sat down to read the paperback, several hundred pages long.

It was a wonderful atrocity. I'll never say of a man "He can't write", because it has been said by lofty critics of authors who are read by countless millions – Ian Fleming, Conan Doyle, and Edgar Rice Burroughs (who may be no Stevenson as a stylist, but made enough to found a university, which not many authors do, and won the grudging respect of my English teacher, as we shall see). But I must be honest and say that Clavell's book struck me as supremely dreadful ... and yet ...

Much of it I found turgid and corny, and it bore some of the worst marks of the American historical fiction-writer (Clavell was actually a very British Australian) adrift in a non-American subject. There were enough trivial inaccuracies to worry me, and a romantic misconception of how early Victorians spoke, thought, and behaved.

For example, Brock, the heavy, talked a bizarre kind of English in which he said things like "Thee be a bagful o' farts," but the tone and style of the whole thing were so wrong that I began to wonder how far the Chinese background, of which I knew little, was to be trusted. It was fairly bursting with colourful Oriental stuff, social and cultural, and I was far from sure whether it was authentic or the product of Clavell's fertile imagination.

In fact, it was a great hodge-podge, and certainly not literary – but it contained what used to be called a rattling good yarn, with highlights which would translate spectacularly to the screen.

It is set in Hong Kong in the early 1840s, where Britain has just taken possession, and bears some passing resemblance to historic fact. Since the great entrepreneurs of the island, Jardine Matheson, were Scots, Clavell had made his central character a Scottish adventurer, Dirk Struan, a sort of Rhett Butler figure, half-merchant, half-pirate, and all swashbuckler, locked in deadly feud with a fellow-adventurer, Tyler Brock. They play out their rivalry against a background of imperial expansion, opium-running, piracy, sex, skulduggery, and general turmoil; there is intrigue, escape, betrayal, love pure and profane by the bucket, duelling, sea battles, ships exploding, and Manchu bannermen tramping by the thousands. I have to salute Clavell for his Chinese pirate with a Cockney accent who wants to send his son to a public school, and for his device of binding Struan to do favours for the bearers of special silver coins, which are produced in the most unexpected places – but for some reason the author leaves half of them unused, which is frustrating.

In short, whatever its literary merits, it had everything necessary for a big-screen epic, concluding with a colossal typhoon, and was going to cost a bomb.

It would obviously have to be considerably cut and condensed, and given a stronger narrative form than it had in the novel; characters would have to be reshaped, incidents changed, the dialogue translated from Hollywood-speak into early Victorian – but from a scriptwriter's viewpoint it was a bloody gold-mine. Clavell might not be able to "write" a story, but by gum he could "see" it.

I flew to Nice and the Villa Nelleric, a palatial edifice of marble and glass and luxurious furnishings, where I met Vuille for the first time, and, more immediately important for me, Clavell himself, a burly heavyweight who looked more like a business tycoon than the screenwriter, director, and producer he was, in addition to being a successful novelist. He had an impressive track record, including *The Great Escape, 633 Squadron,* and *To Sir, with Love*; when we walked out on the terrace looking down on the rocky cliffs dropping to the Mediterranean, I asked why he hadn't written the script himself.

"I did," he said. "Twice. Didn't work." He paused. "It's got to be Sean, hasn't it?"

"Connery – for Struan? I don't see how Vuille could go past him. He's made for it."

Unfortunately, Vuille could, and did, but I'll come to that. In the meantime I talked the thing over with Clavell and Vuille and Maud Spector, the casting expert – how far we discussed possible actors at this point, I don't remember; as far as I was concerned, Connery was essential, and I pushed for Robert Shaw, with whom I'd worked on *Force Ten*, for Brock (alas, he died soon afterwards), but I don't think it was until later that Edward Fox, David Niven, John Gielgud, Shirley Maclaine, Alan Badel, and Telly Savalas were pencilled in for various parts – probably without their knowledge. Possible Brocks included George C. Scott, Anthony Quinn, and Rod Steiger, but it was agreed then, and was wrestled over all through pre-production, that the vital casting would be Struan's Chinese mistress – a big part for which an unknown Chinese girl was essential.

"There aren't any around, and we can't use a non-Chinese in make-up," Fleischer was adamant. "They'd picket the theatres. We've just got to find her."

That wasn't my business. I went home and started writing. It was to be a three-hour epic, which meant about 180 of my typed pages – or more probably, knowing me, 200 and cut left right and centre afterwards. Fleischer had told me that various attempts, apart from Clavell's, had already been made at a script, but I refused to look at them, and he agreed. Starting from scratch is the only way to ensure yourself a sole screen credit; work on another man's draft, and he'll claim a share, naturally enough – and it doesn't matter if you've rewritten him entire, his agent will still be in there hollering.

Whereby hangs an interesting tale. I had met Carl Foreman a few times – at an award ceremony, in the White Elephant, and once, as I've already related, in his London office when I was on my way to Yugoslavia to work on *Force Ten from Navarone*, and we had discussed his Phileas Fogg, Junior, idea, in which I'd expressed guarded interest – not expecting anything to come of it, and it hadn't. That was all my acquaintance with Carl Foreman.

Now, just as I was getting down to work, he came on the phone to my home. "I hear you're rewriting my *Taipan* script," said he. I said I wasn't; I didn't know he'd done a script, but anyway, I was starting from scratch. (The alarm bells were tinkling.)

"Why don't I send it to you, anyway?" he said.

"Because I don't want to see it," I said.

"Why not?"

"Are you kidding?"

"I'll send it anyway."

"Sorry . . . what was that? I'm not hearing you – there's something wrong with the line . . . oh, blast!" Etc, etc.

He sent the script, too, the crafty brute, and I promptly shot it off to Douglas Rae unopened, with instructions to return it forthwith.

If I seem to have been unduly cautious, I wasn't. For self-protection it was necessary that I shouldn't see Carl's draft – for one thing, it might colour my view of the project, but far more importantly, it might cost me a sole credit if he could claim that I had in any way used or adapted his material. It would be tricky;

since both his script and mine would be based on the same novel, there were bound to be resemblances, but if it could be argued that there were resemblances which had *no basis in the book* (in other words, if Carl had put in original stuff of his own, and my script contained roughly similar material), it would look as though I'd got it from him, and he would have a fair case for demanding a share of the credit.

Carl's offer to show me his script was fair enough – he'd done work, and he hoped to get credit for it – but I was being equally fair in refusing to look at it: I wanted it to be my movie based on my script, alone and unaided. He was just a wee bit naughty in trying to force his script on me when I'd made it plain I didn't want it.

I've still not seen his script, but if Carl were alive I'd never be able to convince him of that. By one of those coincidences, we had both invented identical closing scenes for which there was absolutely no basis in the book. So Dick Fleischer tells me. Mind you, the scene is one which might well occur to any scriptwriter; it involves a shot of the Hong Kong beach in 1841, suddenly pulling back in a colossal zoom to show Hong Kong as it is today. We thought of it independently, which is something that happens more often than you'd think.

I finished my first draft, thinking Connery throughout – and Shaw, even though I knew now that he would never play it. I sent it off – and got the best reaction to a script I've ever had in my life. Fleischer was enthusiastic, Scott liked it, especially the part for the Chinese girl (but didn't want to play Brock, who reminded him of Long John Silver), and as for Georges-Alain: "Oh, Georges, I cried! It is so beautiful! I am reading it in the car, and I cry, believe me! I cried and cried!"

When you get that kind of response you prepare to write the second draft to take care of all the changes they'll want when they've come down off Cloud Nine. Sure enough, a week later found me chopping and changing – I can't remember what, now, but it didn't take long, and the script was ready to try out on the big names Georges-Alain had in his sights.

Connery was not among them. I got quite stroppy about it, so did Fleischer, but Georges-Alain was adamant. He wanted the biggest in the business, which admittedly Connery wasn't at that time – as if that mattered, when he fitted the part like a glove. So the script went to Hollywood, but who turned it down or couldn't come to terms with Georges-Alain, I don't know: Clint Eastwood was mentioned, and Dick Fleischer told me that Paul Newman had been complimentary but said that he was "a twentieth-century man", which was true; Westerns aside, he's never been at his best in costume. Anyway, casting is not a writer's affair, but when I heard that Georges-Alain was thinking of offering Connery the part of *Brock*, I came pretty close to apoplexy.

And then, out of a blue sky, he came up with Steve McQueen, for $10 million, the highest price in cinema history up to that time.

All this took some months, and while my memory of events is sharp enough, it isn't coherent. No reason why it should be, since with the script complete I was involved only intermittently. We made at least two visits to the Villa Nelleric, Kathy and I and the Fleischers, conferring with Georges-Alain and generally living the Riviera life, eating at the Eden Roc and having tea at the Hotel du Cap, which was so damned exclusive that guests were expected to pay in raw cash, to the chagrin of wealthy Americans. The Cannes Film Festival was on during one of our visits, and Georges-Alain improved the shining hour with an enormous banner proclaiming "Taipan" to the lobby of the Carlton Hotel, where he kept an office full of telephones for shouting into. He dragged me to a lunch on the beach, where we ate at long trestle tables under awnings, up to our calves in the powder that passes for sand at Cannes; like everything to do with the Festival, it was noisy, frenzied, tacky, and generally hell on earth, a view shared by a tall, weary-looking man opposite me who looked familiar and turned out to be Yves Montand.

I suppose Kathy and I and the Fleischers weren't really what you'd call Cannes Festival people; no one in his right mind could be. We avoided the hysterics of the Croisette, keeping together for protection, lazing in the villa garden, teaching Georges-Alain's delightful little son, Jonathan, to recite "This little piggy went to market" in French, cruising gently to the shops, and dining quietly together at a respectable hour – unlike Georges-Alain and his lady who seemed to like dinner at midnight, followed, in spite of Georges-Alain's protests, by (guess what?) flamenco dancing.

How out of step I was, I realised when an American journalist, brimming with Riviera *joie de vivre*, asked what I was doing that evening; I said, "Reading Macaulay's *History of England*", at which he stared, before scribbling in his notebook, muttering: "Jesus, that's gotta be a first for the Cannes Festival!"

At this time Vuille had another film in production, *Ashanti*, about a black American woman doctor, wife to Michael Caine, who is kidnapped by slave-trader Peter Ustinov and carried across Africa to be sold to an Arab prince, with Caine and Kabir Bedi in pursuit – this was the movie for which Georges-Alain's telephone heroics had secured the services of Rex Harrison and William Holden. Late in the day Omar Sharif was cast as the Arab prince, and since they wanted his part expanded without delay, and I was convenient, they made me an offer I couldn't refuse.

Georges-Alain had shifted his base of operations to Gstaad, so I found myself bucketing over the Alps in a plane so tiny it must have been made from a kit; I was slightly reassured by the phlegmatic calm of the only other passenger, Georges-Alain's brother John, a large, quiet young man who was the temperamental opposite of his sibling, although he evidently had his share of the family's eccentricity – later that year I received a Christmas card from him, from beyond the Arctic Circle in the Canadian north, where he had moved house; the following year his card came from Central Africa, where he was doing relief work. I regret not hearing from him since, from wherever.

I've no idea what I was meant to be doing in Gstaad. I certainly did no work, and my only memories are of spending two nights of extreme discomfort at Georges-Alain's chalet, in a wooden bed designed for a dwarf, and being introduced, at dinner in the Palace Hotel, to Turtle Soup Lady Curzon, one of those gastronomic treats which linger in the memory, like Toast Rothschild in the Normandie Grill in Bangkok, or game pie at the Castletown Golf Links Hotel, Isle of Man.

In Palermo it was raw beef, ordered at the suggestion of Peter Ustinov, and I've tasted worse. Fleischer, Vuille and I had flown there because that was where the next lot of shooting was to happen; Omar Sharif was expected, so I pounded the typewriter into the small hours; whether it got into the film I don't know. But no trip is wasted if it includes Mr Ustinov; he won my heart at our first meeting by impersonating the Isle of Man – this is done by sitting in a chair and using your limbs to represent the Manx three-legged symbol, and probably only Ustinov can do it. We talked tennis and old movies and our Army service, and he reminisced about Stewart Granger's caravan, where the seats were covered with the skins of Granger's big-game trophies, and Ustinov sat on a settee and rose again with fur all over him and bald hide where he had been sitting.

Around this time we went to Madrid, for no good reason that I can remember; it must have been to do with *Ashanti*, for I recall the leading lady, Beverly Johnson, and Kabir Bedi being relentlessly photographed by yelling paparazzi, and I should remember the works of Velasquez at the Prado also, but philistine that I am what sticks in my mind is that the Villa Magna was one of the best hotels Kathy and I had ever struck.

All this time, pre-production of *Taipan* was apparently going ahead, and Georges-Alain was so bullish that he demanded I write a sequel without delay. I thought it would be a good idea to get the first film into production at least, but it was another offer I couldn't refuse, and a few weeks later I had finished *Taipan II*. And then – this is true, and Fleischer and others will bear me out – damned if Vuille didn't ask for a *third* script, a prequel to the original.

It was my fault for inventing, in *Taipan I*, a reference to Struan and Brock having served together at Trafalgar, where I suggested their rivalry had begun. This grabbed Vuille, and if I had been a scoundrel I would have accepted a contract (and, to me, an enormous fee) for a third movie. But fair's fair; I assumed that *Taipan I* would get made, and with McQueen in the lead it would probably be a smash – but you never know, and I wasn't going to take his money for a third movie when he still hadn't shot a foot of the first one. I don't regret it; some things you can't do.

Presbyterian conscience is a hell of a note; it cost me that commission, and the chance to work with David Lean, who at that time was preparing *The Bounty*, and asked me, through his producer, my friend Eddie Fowlie, who had worked on *Prince and Pauper*, if I was interested in doing a script. I'd have given my right arm to accept; apart from the privilege of working with Lean, I'd been defending Bligh in print for years – but although I had legally fulfilled my contract to Vuille, I had said (as I always do) that I was with the movie to the finish, and since I knew it would need more work eventually, I had to pass *The Bounty*, not without some gnashing of teeth.

Lean sent me his outline notes, and we talked at length on the phone. God, that man was a genius. He described shots and set-ups that I can see in my mind's eye yet; it was all visual stuff, little plot or dialogue, although we touched on the great mystery: why did the mutiny take place? What got into Christian? Bligh was no tyrant, but he had a vicious tongue – was it just that? And so forth. We agreed firmly on one point, which I offer for *Bounty* historians to consider: the joker in the pack was Midshipman Young.

I can't regret that job, either, since the script was finally done by Robert Bolt, and I know when I'm outclassed.

And the Taipan story was entering its final phase. Kathy and I flew again to LA, and Fleischer, Vuille and I took the elevator to the top floor of the Beverly Wilshire, where Steve McQueen had a penthouse. He opened the door to us, a slighter figure than I'd expected, neatly bearded, but looking rather tired. I knew he hadn't been well, and that it was more than two years since he'd made a picture, the last being Ibsen's *An Enemy of the People*, which had flopped, although he had acquitted himself well, holding his own with the likes of Charles Durning.

He surveyed us closely, not unlike a sentry, and then invited us into the kitchen where he was brewing coffee – the best I've ever tasted outside Turkey, very black and sweetened with honey. He explained that his girl-friend (whom he didn't name) had forbidden him sugar, but he had successfully concealed the honey jar. It didn't quite fit with Thomas Crown and Bullitt, nor did his slightly defensive reference to Ravel's *Bolero* which he was playing "to put me in the mood for an action movie". He would have preferred some rousing sea music; I suggested Korngold's *Sea-Hawk* or *Captain Blood*, and he scribbled a note on his kitchen pad.

He had set four chairs round a small table in the living-room, on which there were scripts and pencils, and I realised that this was a methodical man. He put on a pair of glasses (rimless, I think), flipped open a script, and looked inquiringly at me.

Now, usually, an actor on first acquaintance will say something complimentary about your work: Malcolm McDowell, Rex Harrison, Roger Moore, Heston, York, Badel, Fox, Lee, and others were meticulous about this. McQueen looked in silence, and it struck me that while he'd been courteous, he hadn't given us any glad hand in welcome. But it was up to me, and I was making some explanatory remark or other about the story when he interrupted.

"You're from Scotland, aren't you?"

I said I was – and I wish I had a picture of him as he smiled for the first time, with a tilt of his chin, and said with supreme satisfaction: "I'm Scotch."

I might have known it, from his appearance and manner; I asked when his people had come over, but he didn't know; several generations back, according to his grandmother. But the ice was broken from that moment, and I blessed the Scottish mafia of Hollywood; it isn't as vocal as the Irish or as evident as the Jewish, but it's there all right.

It took us two days, word by word and look by look, to go through the script, and I don't remember any actor as intent and painstaking as he was. He wanted to know the why and wherefore of every detail; for instance, the script opened with two tall ships racing, then cut to Brock and his son on their deck, then cut to Struan's officers – but no sign of Struan. It was a tense sequence, both sides determined to win; McQueen wondered why he wasn't to be visible. I explained that I'd been inspired by *The Sea Hawk*, in which Errol Flynn is not seen but his voice is heard while a group of officers register his presence. It doesn't read particularly effectively, but McQueen saw at once how well it could work on screen, with his voice quiet and assured amid all the hubbub, and his first appearance in a moment of crisis an almost casual drifting into shot, authoritative and calm.

"Okay," he said. "That's Struan."

From my point of view it was a good read-through; he had no major objections, and those he had were mainly technical, as when he asked me to change a scene in which he was up to the knees in water in a ship's hold, shifting boxes of silver: could I fix it so that he didn't get his feet wet? He was still recuperating, and didn't want to take any chances.

We had occasional brushes. I don't remember why we disagreed,

209

but I got rather testy and he gave me the blue-eyed stare and said bleakly: "Gee, you're attractive when you're mad." Again, when I suggested Oliver Reed would be good as Brock's son, he shook his head firmly. "No, sir. No way. Not him."

I didn't know, then, the reason for their mutual dislike, which I've described earlier, but I could see there was no point in pushing for Oliver, so I let it drop.

How good an actor he was he demonstrated on two occasions when he was unhappy with dialogue. He didn't want to call someone a rascal ("Too European, George"), and when I assured him his grandmother wouldn't have thought so, he shook his head. "Don't have to say it. I can *look* it." Which he did, very effectively, but later, when he suggested that he could go through a sequence of talk without saying a word, I had to protest. Struan's Chinese mistress had to give him information, and Struan had to reply; there was no way round it. Steve sat silent, thinking. Then:

"Go ahead, you say the girl's lines."

So I did. She had three brief speeches, and to each one he simply responded with an appropriate look. I had to admit he was right, Fleischer smiled, and Vuille laughed in admiration.

Steve worried a little about his accent ("I'm American. I can't play British") until I assured him that a Scots adventurer in the 1840s who had been footloose since childhood might well have acquired an American accent. Anyway, it was a state of mind as much as anything; we would have him saying "Aye" and "Uh-huh" and "Away!" occasionally, and that would do it.

Our final difference came towards the finish, when Struan and Brock, preparing to fight it out, realise that they can't because their children are going to marry each other, and you can't kill someone's father as a wedding present. So their angry confrontation gets nowhere, but it doesn't matter since that's when the typhoon strikes.

That didn't suit Steve. He wanted to beat the stuffing out of

Brock. "Top o' the hill!" he exclaimed, pointing to an imaginary duelling ground, so I said I'd work on it and see what could be done. He suggested that he run me in his pickup truck to his ranch in Idaho, where I could revise in peace, but I declined with thanks.

Between sessions we talked at random, about motor-cycles and the Clan McQueen and his time in China when he had stayed with a Chinese of sinister reputation ("I guess he killed a few people") and the potplants outside the door of his penthouse which he feared were deteriorating. "I think Lee Marvin's peeing on them." Whether Lee Marvin lived along the corridor, where there were potplants in profusion, I didn't inquire.

At last we were done. I had smoked several packets of cigarettes, Steve had chewed a plug of tobacco, Georges-Alain had said little, and Fleischer had presided in his avuncular way, targeting the essentials every time. McQueen showed him great respect, referring to him as "my director".

"Well, what does my director think?" he said as he closed the script. Fleischer said he thought we had a movie, a good movie, a big movie.

"Know what I think?" Steve tapped the script and paid me the biggest compliment I've ever had as a screenwriter. "I think we've got *Gone with the Wind* here." God bless him.

It never happened, of course. What went wrong between Vuille and McQueen I never discovered, except that money, that astronomical fee, was involved. Not long after I was watching the Parkinson show, and was astonished to hear Roger Moore say that he was polishing up his Scots accent for *Taipan*; that too fell through, and Moore and I discussed Georges-Alain some months later. Fleischer left the project, and I lost interest, and then came the news that Steve McQueen had died in Mexico, and *Taipan* faded into the limbo of movies that never got made. A production did take place years later, but not with my script, and I never saw it.

You get used to writing outlines and synopses and full screenplays for pictures that never reach the screen, usually because some optimist has run out of money. I regret *Taipan* more than most, but console myself with the belief that it got me *Octopussy*.

How to Encourage Race Hatred

IT DEPENDS ENTIRELY what you mean by "racist". The word is used indiscriminately, frequently as a term of abuse, and is highly emotive, often deliberately so. At worst it implies bitter hatred, a deep-seated rancour and active hostility towards those of a different colour or racial origin. At the top of the scale one can put Adolf Hitler, who showed his detestation of Jews by slaughtering millions of them. On a different level we have Simon Legree, who regarded black people as animals and treated them accordingly, but did not hate them in a Hitlerian way. He and Hitler may certainly be bracketed together as racists in the fullest sense, but one must recognise that they are racists in different degrees within their category.

At quite the other end of the scale are those who are often called racists for no better reason than that they feel an instinctive preference for their own kind. They are not Hitlers or Legrees, they may not even voice or indicate their preference, and indeed to call them racists is all too often an attempt to confuse the situation, and to imply that the commuter who sits beside a white passenger rather than a black one is taking the first step towards the gas chamber. It isn't true, and we know it, but this is what bedevils the whole race question – the attempt to tar all so-called "racists" with the same brush, and pretend that the man who simply likes his own folk best is a concentration camp guard in the making.

Now, if this preference is a sin, it is widespread, and to be found in areas where political correctness decrees that racism cannot exist. It cannot be denied that the preference is widely held in the black community; indeed, if what is called "institutionalised racism" exists in Britain, it is among blacks. They plainly feel a unity based on colour, a kinship and a sense of common experience – and there is absolutely nothing wrong with this provided it is not translated into discriminatory action against non-blacks. They are free to voice their sense of black unity, and frequently do – but white people do not have the same freedom. Let them give expression to their white identity, and they are condemned as racists. It comes down to this lamentable fact, that in our politically correct Western societies, only whites can be racist; black racism is an impossibility.

To take a simple example which demonstrates this – there exists in the US an organisation called the National Association for the Advancement of Coloured People; its existence is acceptable to the American public. But suppose someone proposed a similar association to promote the interest of white people – the screams of indignation would echo worldwide, and the proposer would be assailed with the most extreme abuse and probably end up in court, if not in jail. A leader of black opinion can say bluntly (and they usually do) that he puts black interest first, and plainly feels that he is entitled to discriminate against non-blacks; he will meet with no contradiction, and would be indignant if he did. But no white person would dare to speak as his black counterpart does.

Many years ago a black tennis player, Arthur Ashe, won the men's title at Wimbledon. A commentator (not Maskell, I hasten to say) announced afterwards that he was glad the black man had won. It passed unremarked. What would the harvest have been if Ashe's opponent, Jimmy Connors, had won, and a commentator had expressed delight that the white man had triumphed? The commentator would have been hounded out of his job amid roars of condemnation.

This may seem trivial; it isn't. It is the heart of the matter. It is a denial of equal treatment of black and white, a discrimination based on skin colour, and until this is recognised, and it is acknowledged that prejudice has two edges, and that racism is no more rooted or, to use the foolish and inaccurate term of the Macpherson report, "institutionalised", in the white community than it is in the black, there will be no improvement in race relations in this country.

Since I have probably said enough to convince the more obtuse or prejudiced that I keep a Ku Klux Klan uniform in my wardrobe, I should make my position clear. I am what I would call a racist in the sense that everyone in the world is a racist (for you are, you know), in preferring my own kind, by and large, to those of a different kind or culture. It's no big deal; it's a question of feeling more at home with those whom I know, and with whom I share a common culture and folk-experience.

I was happier in a North Country English regiment during the war, among fellow-Cumbrians, than I would have been in a Welsh or London regiment, and happier still when I went to a Highland regiment. I am no sports fanatic, but I feel pleasure when Scotland's soccer or rugby teams win (especially against England, I admit, and I have a distinct impression, from the sporting press and the TV images of stout fellows with St George's crosses painted on their faces, that there is some similar national feeling south of the Tweed, especially against Germany).

This is perfectly natural, and insofar as it shows a race-preference, it is surely racist, but in no sinister sense. I am happier among Britons than among foreigners, but that does not imply hostility to Chileans or Syrians, and I would certainly not discriminate actively against them, or treat them unfairly because they happened to be of a different race, creed, colour, etc. I simply like "my ain folk", and if there is anyone who does not share this feeling (or says he doesn't), and maintains that every human being is of equal value to him, regardless of kinship, colour, race, and so forth, I would ask him to consider the following question.

He is standing on a riverbank with his infant grandchild, and close by is another infant whom he has never seen. Both children fall in, and are in equal danger of drowning. Which one does he try to save first – his own or the stranger?

The answer is obvious, to me at any rate. You go for your own, you racist, you. Why racist? Because the race is simply an extension of the family. In my own case, I cleave first to my wife, children, and grandchildren; thereafter to my clan, the Frasers, and the folk of Cumberland among whom I grew up, thereafter the Britons, and so on. This is not, surely, to "discriminate against" the Australian aborigine or the American or Italian – or the African. Some fool (and he was a university lecturer, too) to whom I propounded my question, said "Ah, now, if one of the grandchildren were *black*, it would be an interesting question."

"You great balloon," I retorted, "can't you see that would be irrelevant? You would save *your own*, black, white, or khaki." But he couldn't see it.

As it happens, and possibly this is irrelevant, too, although I don't think so, I owe my life, indeed my existence, to a black African. He was a Kikuyu warrior named Wakibi, and when my father was wounded and had to be abandoned by his comrades in East Africa (it was that sort of war), Wakibi, who was his orderly, refused to leave him, tried to dress his wound, and finally carried him unconscious to safety. So I have an unpayable debt to that wild shield-and-spear hero not only for my father and myself, but for my children and grandchildren. Without Wakibi they wouldn't be here. *Bayete* Wakibi.

It follows that the view of race relations with which I was brought up was slightly unusual for the time. The word "nigger", which was not uncommon then (though less common than moderns may think) was simply anathema in the Fraser household, and I got into trouble at school for rounding on a classmate who, perfectly innocently, described an African child as "a little nigger boy". The acceptable term at that time, incidentally, was negro or coloured; black became beautiful later, and now I gather America has adopted Afro-American, which is as clumsy and daft an expression as I can conceive. It is a sign of the times that one has to be careful in choosing words; lack of intention to offend is no excuse, as the tyrants of the race relations industry have made clear. They have shown themselves eager to exploit race sensitivity, taking offence where none is meant, and trying to make mischief where none exists. They belong to all races, and do immense harm while pretending the purest of motives. Most of them I would call arrant racists, not in the Hitler sense, but not in the commuter sense either. Somewhere between and truly dangerous.

It has long been evident that the Race Relations Act was one of the most foolish and pernicious ever enacted by Parliament, and that the Commission for Racial Equality has proved itself to be a bad and unnecessary institution whose activities have been, to put it charitably, quite deplorable. If these seem unduly harsh and sweeping words, I employ them because, unlike some race activists, I care very much about racial harmony, and far from bringing it about, both the Act and the Commission seem to me to have done immense damage to race relations, and consequently to the social fabric of the country, which is probably beyond repair. They have bred resentment, suspicion, and hatred. We must assume that they were the product of good intentions; well, they have failed, tragically, for the fact is that no one intent on stirring up racial trouble could have done a better job.

The Commission have been openly pro-black, as has the BBC. How low the corporation's standards have sunk was seen when a black so-called comedian called the Queen a bitch. In an incredible display of race bias, the Broadcasting Standards Commission decided that this disgusting insult was permissible *since the speaker was black*. They ruled that "bitch" was acceptable "street slang" for a woman, and the BBC supported this with the feeble excuse that the speaker "was using the term as it is used in 'rap' music, to mean 'woman' and not as a term of abuse."

Would the BBC be equally tolerant if a white person called the offending comedian "a nigger", possibly advancing the excuse that the term was inoffensive because it was acceptable in certain white circles? Of course not; the BBC's racist bias aside, such an excuse would be false and hypocritical, as it was in the case of the black comedian (who, to do him justice, expressed regret for his ill manners). Words in the English language are not to be redefined by an immigrant minority in a way which they know perfectly well will give gross offence to those who speak the language properly, especially when the insult is directed at the Queen. A broadcasting authority with any sense of fitness would have banned the offender for life instead of trying to pretend that such despicable behaviour can be condoned in an unpleasant vulgarian simply because he is black.

This insistence on viewing the race question through dark glasses has become virtually an official policy which, while it fails to satisfy the black community who continue to nourish an understandable historic resentment, helps to build a similar – if usually unspoken – resentment in a white community which has been brainwashed into feeling guilty, and is thoroughly fed up with being made the scapegoat for problems which the race relations industry has created.* The race propaganda is, to use modern jargon, counter-productive; the parrot-cry that we are a multi-racial society, when we are not (London and many large centres of population are, but the greater part of the country is not, as yet), the nakedly racist demand that there should be quotas of blacks in Parliament (and Welsh, Scots, Cornish, Jewish, why not?), and the apparently

* An example of the kind of case that causes justified white anger and demonstrates how lunatic the race relations "system" can be, was that of the Asian who, having sued successfully for racial discrimination, sued again several years later after he had been promoted, his complaint being that he had apparently been given preferential treatment, and this had damaged his standing and caused him to lose the respect of his colleagues.

disproportionate number of black and brown faces among television presenters – all these things sow in the mind of the white population a feeling that they are being unfairly dealt with, that the dice are loaded against them – but by God they'd better not say so.*

But if it is largely fear of being called Nazis that keeps them quiet, there is also at work in them the instinctive tolerance and sense of fair play that distinguishes the island race, for which they are given little credit. They know too that the most militant and abusive black leaders no more represent the black population than the National Front does the white, and that the huge majority of blacks want nothing more than fair treatment and opportunity. I'm not pretending that the worst kind of white racists don't exist; we know they do. But they are a tiny minority. What I have called racial preference is universal, among all ethnic groups, but it's harmless, and only the race relations industry, in their untiring search for alleged offence, however trivial, would deny this.

We have not yet sunk to the point reached in the USA where the bigots demanded and got an apology for the use of the word "niggardly" (comment on the ignorance or stupidity of the complainant is superfluous – and would probably be described as racist anyway), but it is sometimes a near thing. The radio commentator who implied that black athletes were good runners because they were used to being chased by lions, was admittedly making a reference to their ethnic background, but could it be called seriously racist, and would any intelligent person take offence at what was obviously meant to be no more than a joke, albeit a pretty feeble

* At the time when Greg Dyke, the Director General, made his notorious remark about the BBC being "hideously white", the actual fact was that the proportion of non-whites employed by the Corporation was greater than the proportion of non-whites in the population as a whole. I also note, before anyone points it out to me, that the imposition of a realistic quota system in Parliament would entail the *reduction* of the number of Scottish M.P.s and, possibly, although I haven't counted, the number of Jewish ones. It would be interesting to see if the proportion of white English M.P.s is at present a fair one.

one? Yet there came the knee-jerk blare of protest from the race relations lobby, the commentator had to apologise, and race relations had taken another knock, not so much from the thoughtless comment as from the over-reaction which gave the incident so much publicity. The accounts I read, incidentally, contained no complaints from black athletes.

Racial jokes of this kind are as old as time. People have been finding humour in the traits, real or imagined, and the idiosyncrasies, habits, faults, and preferences of different races, since Stone Age man first noticed that the folk in the next cave were, by his lights, eccentric. Irish jokes, Scotch jokes, Polish jokes, Flemish jokes, Welsh jokes, American and English jokes, sub-continental Indian jokes ... we know them, and nobody really minds. Why not black jokes, provided they are told without intent to offend? I don't know, and I can't imagine what reason the Commission for Racial Equality would give. I can only be sure it wouldn't be the true one, for the true one is buried deep in the black consciousness, and no one dare speak its name. It is to do with slavery, and centuries of perceived racial inferiority, and that is all too recent to be got rid of easily. If it has bred in black people a race-consciousness, a resentment, even a hatred, that is not surprising. I'm not black, but if I were, I would feel it, by God I would, and it would take a great effort of will to realise that only time, and toleration, and a refusal to be offended, and institutionalised kindness and good manners, can hope eventually to consign race hatred and prejudice, if not recognition of racial difference, to the dustbin of history.

It is taken for granted, by all parties, that the task of bringing about this happy state of affairs rests squarely on the white community. I am not so sure; it is going to take some effort on the part of blacks, too. There was a black lady academic lecturing in this country not long ago, who said, in a reproachful tone, that whenever she met white people, she was aware that they were registering her skin colour. It didn't occur to her, apparently, that she was doing exactly the same thing about them. When she does understand that, she will have done something to improve race relations.

Reverting to the matter of inter-racial humour, I'm reminded of an encounter I had in Beverly Hills with a very old, plainly very rich gentleman named Marx. (He looked extremely like Groucho, but wasn't, and I like to think he was either Zeppo or Gummo, but he probably wasn't one of them either.) He used to take breakfast in the Pink Turtle café of the Beverly Wilshire every day, as I did. One morning I needed an extra cent to pay my bill, and to my surprise Mr Marx, whom I had never met, rose and offered me a copper; I accepted gratefully, and next morning laid a cent on his table as repayment. He fell about laughing, crying "A Scotchman and a Jew!" The point being, of course, that Scots and Jews are notoriously careful of money, and this is a constant subject of jokes – to which we don't take exception *because we don't mind*; in fact, we're rather proud of our tight-fisted reputation; it's a virtue, in a way.

I'd like to think that the black athlete/lion joke would be received in the same way. For one thing, it recognises a sporting phenomenon – that black athletes, on the whole, far outclass their white rivals in track events. Watching the skill of black footballers, I foresee the day when the premiership teams will be largely black: they are that good, and living proof of an obvious truth which is invariably denied by the politically correct: that there are such things as racial characteristics and special racial skills. Black boxers have long dominated a sport in which supremacy belonged successively to the English, the Irish, the Jews, the Italians, and the Hispanics; the Chinese can murder the world at table tennis; the Iroquois are famously immune to vertigo at great heights; illiterate Madrasis, they say, can tell you the square root of a number by some mysterious mental process; children of Southeast Asian origin have startled educationalists by their brilliance – and these things have nothing to do with immediate environment; they are in the creature to begin with.

This, to be sure, is heresy to the politically correct; they deny the evidence manifest all around us, in the human and animal kingdoms. Exactly why they do, is a mystery; presumably they fear that to recognise racial differences will lead to racial discrimination – and that is precisely the fear that must be eroded if racial harmony is ever to be achieved.

There are hopeful signs. I have alluded to racial jokes, and there is no more powerful tool in the destruction of race prejudice than humour, as witness such comedians as Sammy Davis Junior and Charlie Williams, who have found race funny; that excellent television programme, *The Fresh Prince of Bel Air*, is forever sending up racial attitudes, showing the other side of the coin exploited by Alf Garnett. This is a healthy sign, and perhaps a portent, if only an infinitesimal one to set against the evils that beset the races – the National Front, the Paki-bashing, the abuse shouted and scrawled on walls, the shameful exploitation of cases like the Stephen Lawrence murder, the naked anti-police prejudice fuelled by asinine inquiry findings, and worst of all, I say again, the damage done by the bigots of the race relations industry – who, of course, have a vested interest in mischief-making, since the biased exaggeration of race problems can be used to justify their existence and the waste of public money on their salaries.

Sometimes I wonder if the pendulum is beginning to swing, and the public is awakening to the sheer dishonesty of the campaign to burden them with guilt. The race bigots do tend to overreach themselves, as with the ridiculous report of Mr Straw's costly and unnecessary inquiry which reached the incredible conclusion that the words "British" and "English" carried harmful racist connotations, and indeed that "Britishness" did not exist; they cited their own garbled version of an imperial history which they plainly did not understand, or want to understand, to support their case. It would be comic if it were not deadly serious.

It may be, for all I know, that the substantial minority of the inquiry body who were not of white British extraction, and who presumably were from recently arrived families, did not find "British" a desirable, or even understandable, word. Why should they? An ethnic minority, of whatever colour or race, are seldom in tune with the majority, and are certainly not the most authoritative commentators on the country's identity. One can imagine the scorn that would be poured, very properly, on a second-generation British immigrant to, say, modern India or South Africa or the USA, who pontificated on the very essence of those countries. Yet the nonentities (I'm sorry, but they are no more) of the Runnymede Trust (and there's a mind-boggling misappropriation for you), do not hesitate to tell us that our entity is a lie, that Britain is racist, and the empire a thoroughly bad thing. Impudence is far too mild a word.

It is possible, I suppose, that the non-white members of the inquiry tended to feel uncomfortable or excluded in Britain, perhaps even resentful, and that this distorted their view. Sometimes such views seem to carry an undertone of simple hatred, and that the attitude of the inquiry to Britain and the British was hostile is beyond a doubt. But that was in tune with New Labour, who set out, quite deliberately, to undermine the traditional values on which the United Kingdom was founded, and which served as an example to the world.

Whatever the emotions and motives of the inquiry, it is a pity that it reached such fatuous conclusions, entirely at odds with the beliefs of the rest of the population, including that vast majority of non-white citizens who are glad and proud to be British, and are aware that, with all their admitted faults, the island people are far more racially tolerant than most, and that this, ironically, is a legacy of that imperial past which is an object of such loathing to the politically correct.

It is not a past understood, obviously, by Mr Straw who, although he had the belated sense to reject the mischievous report on which he had squandered a small fortune over three years, has a most curious view of British history. He spoke, at one time, of the "English propensity to violence" which he believed was used to "subjugate" the Scots, Irish, and Welsh "who've been over the centuries under the cosh of the English". Really, one doesn't know where to begin in the face of such monumental ignorance, and can only lament that Student Straw must have spent less time at lectures than he did on street-corner agitation.

I've delivered myself on the race question, and the longer I ponder it the more insoluble it seems – to me, at any rate. There is so much misunderstanding, so much hypocrisy, so much contradiction and inconsistency and, alas, so much dishonesty and ill will, that the subject begins to resemble an enormous Gordian knot, and contemplating it I can see no happy issue until the whole of mankind is khaki-coloured, which I suppose is inevitable unless the human species wipes itself out with Aids, or drugs, or racial and religious war, or a combination of all three. But not in my time, with luck.

In the meantime, it might help if the understanding and tolerance expected of the white community towards the non-white were reciprocated. This never seems to crop up in discussions on race, but it is perhaps something for the black community, the young of all races, the politically correct, and those who work in race relations, to bear in mind. We old white crumblies grew up in a virtually all-white Britain, and adjustment to a society which has become about 12 per cent coloured in the past half-century, has not been a simple matter of course. In my childhood a black or brown face was a rarity; practically everyone, policemen, magistrates, politicians, teachers, bus conductors, footballers (excepting Frank Soo, a Chinese who played for Stoke), shopkeepers, soldiers, labourers, peers of the realm, etc., was white. I was about to add doctors, until I remembered that in my native city of Carlisle there were four non-white GPs, referred to, without a suggestion of "racism", as the Black Doctors, and highly regarded, but for the rest, black and brown people were unusual, distant, and rather exotic (Paul Robeson, Sabu, Joe Louis, Duke Ellington, West Indian cricketers, and all those talented black Hollywood comedians like Willie Best and Rochester who are now frowned on as the depths of political incorrectness).

It changed with the war, with black GIs and the Ink Spots and Lena Horne and the Rev. Henry ("Homicide Hank") Armstrong, but the new racial mix in the population, which began with the Empire Windrush, has taken some getting used to, like television and mobile phones and e-mail and pizzas and yellow lines on the streets. We've had to get acclimatised, just as the immigrants have had to, as one does to all changes. We had to accept from the first that the old adage "When in Rome do as Rome does" was a dead letter, and that Rome was expected to adapt to suit the newcomers rather than the other way around. Integration was the watchword until it was seen that white resistance, and black reluctance based on a desire to hold on to ethnic cultures, militated against it, and that the best that could be hoped for was acceptance and tolerance by both sides. Perhaps it is happening at long last, and the old resistance and reluctance are fading away. They will vanish all the sooner if the race relations industry stop deliberately fomenting racial strife.

I conclude with a few points for which there was no convenient place in this piece, but which may be worth a moment's thought.

1. The infantry section in which I served in Burma were, by today's lights, racists to a man, in speech and deed and outlook. It is impossible to explain to the twenty-first century, with all its preconceptions resulting from revisionist propaganda, just what the British soldier's attitude towards India and the Indians was, fifty–sixty years ago, but looking back I have the impression that it was

as much social as racial. For centuries the British had been masters of India, with inevitable consequences; they (we) considered themselves superior to the Indian civilians, but not only because of colour; the British swaddy, looking at the teeming slums of Bombay and Calcutta, at the beggars, at the half-clad natives in their shanties, the swarming crowds of the cities, and the primitive peasants of the countryside, couldn't *help* feeling he was superior to *that*, and in this respect his views were exactly those of every Indian above the level of the Untouchables. And show me the Western liberal of today, faced with the squalor of the lower reaches of the sub-continent, who says he doesn't feel superior, and I'll show you a liar. But is his feeling racial or social? Let him work it out for himself.

But whatever superiority the swaddy may have felt, it stopped abruptly at the level of the Indian military. That, too, was inevitable; no one who had gone into action alongside the Baluch or the Gurkha or the Sikh could feel anything but unalloyed admiration, respect, and gratitude. I know I felt it, and no race relations expert need waste his time trying to find tell-tale traces of "superiority" in me and my comrades, because they aren't there, mate. And that is why so many of us love the sub-continent and its people still, and feel only disgust and contempt for those who would try to stir up strife between us.

2. It was announced recently that the state of California no longer had a white majority. The Hispanics, it was said, now outnumbered them – which left me bewildered and asking of no one in particular: when in God's name did Spaniards and Mexicans cease to be white?

3. Why should any trace of black ancestry automatically render a person black in the eyes of the world, even if most of his ancestors are white? Why should Muhammad Ali, who is obviously of European as well as African extraction, be considered black rather than white? I know it's an elementary question, perhaps even a childish

one; I'd just like to hear it answered honestly. Which reminds me that when I was asked to write a piece for a national daily paper on Alex Haley's celebrated account of his family's transition from Africa to America, *Roots*, and I wondered why he had dealt only with his black ancestors, and neglected his white ones, that part of my article was carefully cut out. I still don't know why; it seemed to me to be a not unimportant point.

4. I have made clear what I think of offensive racial epithets, and note the double standard under which I can be called a Scotch bastard, or some other choice noun (as has happened on occasion), without any outcry from the racially sensitive, who would run screaming in circles if a similar insult was offered to a coloured person. But this it seems is an acceptable inconsistency nowadays: a young journalist of my acquaintance actually told me that he felt it would be worse in him to call a black man a black bastard, than it would be for a black man to call him a white (or honky) bastard. I found this appalling and patronising, no doubt for the same reason that I think positive discrimination is abominable, and a sure recipe for race hatred.

5. I simply do not know what to make of the successful black American (I think he was an academic) who said he thanked God for the Atlantic slave trade, because without it he would still have been in the jungle instead of enjoying an affluent lifestyle in the US.

6. But I know exactly what to think when I see black athletes at the Olympic Games, draped in Union Jacks on the medal podium and fairly bursting with pride. They're not the only ones – and I don't expect the politically correct to understand this, but I thank God for the British Empire.

7. Anyone who wants to get an insight into the dramatic change that has taken place in American racial attitudes should hunt down a clip of film made for the instruction of GIs in war-time Britain. The presenter is that distinguished actor, the late Burgess Meredith,

wearing US uniform, and addressing the camera from a railway platform somewhere in England. He is drawing the audience's attention to an elderly British woman who is bidding farewell to a black GI; she has had him to tea, and remarks that she comes from Birmingham, England, while he comes from Birmingham, Alabama.

Meredith turns back to the camera with a concerned expression, and the purport of his comment is that while Americans know that such black-white socialising is unacceptable, GIs must realise that this is Britain, where there is no such colour bar. I wish I could remember the actual words, or that the BBC would screen the clip as a historic document. I have no doubt that in later years poor Burgess Meredith broke into a cold sweat whenever he remembered it.

Which reminds me, for no good reason, of my father's experience in a war-time train, when he, a douce Scots doctor, found himself in a compartment with exuberant black American soldiers who taught him to sing "Pistol-packin' Momma", to his great delight. Knowing him, I'll bet he tried his Swahili on them.

7. Finally, I recall a conversation from half a century ago, at the Officers Training School, Bangalore, in which I took part with a couple of British cadets, a Pathan, a Sikh nobleman, and a worldly Bengali. (I remark in passing that until you have seen racial and social discrimination by Indians, you haven't lived.)* It was a fairly alcoholic discussion, in which we put the world thoroughly to rights, dealing among other things with the race question. We did it with a freedom and lack of inhibition and embarrassment which I doubt would be possible for today's hung-up generation, and at the conclusion, while a quartet consisting of the two Britons (Scots Presbyterians), the Sikh, and the Pathan, were singing "The Sash My Father Wore" for the benefit of two Liverpool Irishmen across the

* It is called the caste system, which I'm reliably informed shows no signs of decay, and which truly can be called "institutionalised".

corridor (it's true, so help me), the Bengali put an arm round my neck and sobbed drunkenly:

"Oh, Jock, you are white and I am brown, and that is okay absolutely. It's these chee-chee bastards I cannot stand."

A chee-chee is an Anglo-Indian half-caste. I thought then, and I think now, this is too big a problem for you, George.

You note, by the way, that he said "brown", not "black", which he would have regarded as offensive. I'm reminded of this every time I hear a race relations pundit lumping all coloured people under the "black" heading. Some Indian and Pakistani community leaders may pretend to go along with this, for political reasons, but (unless I learned absolutely nothing during my time in India) they don't believe it for a moment. Asians regard themselves as different from Africans, and vice versa, and they're both right.

Which brings me to a related subject, the flood of refugees into Britain which has lately risen to unimagined proportions, and excited passions on all sides. The Right wishes to restrict immigration, and polls have indicated that two-thirds of the public agree. I dare say that the majority is even greater, and includes many of the old guard of the Labour Party, but that they know better, much better, than to say so.* But there is a liberal element which seems hell-bent on swamping the country with foreign fugitives, heaven knows why. Whether their motives are altruistic, or simply spring from hatred of the Right, or they want to repopulate Britain for some mysterious reason of their own, is not clear. What is manifest, however, is their doctrine, which is based on

* If they did, they would be reviled as racists, like the Tory M.P. who spoke of the "destruction" of "our homogeneous Anglo-Saxon society by massive immigration"; he was rebuked even by his own party leader. It mattered not that he was telling a plain, obvious truth; it had sinister implications in liberal eyes, and therefore must never be mentioned. Poor Alexander Pope, when he wrote that "to speak his thought is every freeman's right", could not foresee Cool Britannia.

the curious notion that any foreigner wishing to settle in Britain should be welcomed with open arms, given money, clothing, accommodation, and protection, and absorbed into the community with all possible speed. Anyone who questions this is a xenophobe, a racist, probably a fascist, and certainly an unmitigated swine. This is the current wisdom, and the result is that we are besieged by hordes of alien scroungers, bums, criminals, layabouts, and riff-raff – and I refer to the majority of "asylum seekers"; no doubt there are a few worthy and persecuted souls who find it best to flee their own countries – although exactly how they made those countries too hot to hold them is seldom reliably revealed, nor is it explained why this should entitle them to sanctuary in Britain.

Much is made of the British tradition of welcoming refugees, and where these are genuine, like the Jews escaping from Germany and the Nazi-occupied countries in the thirties and forties, it is a tradition to be proud of.* But that is a long way from the Afghans who arrived in a hi-jacked aircraft with no claim whatever to asylum, and who should have been deported immediately, since no assessment of their cases was necessary. The same applies to the Balkan and Asian moochers and loafers who, it seems, must be kept at the public charges and treated as honoured guests until their cases have been examined, at vast expense to the British tax-payer, while the bleeding-heart lobby demand that they be given asylum, the refugees themselves complain and even demonstrate if they are not housed in a style far exceeding anything they knew at home, and the cry of "Human rights!" is used as an indiscriminate bludgeon on the long-suffering citizenry.

It is undoubtedly true that some refugees will become decent, if

---

* Liberals invariably cite the Jews, Flemings, and Huguenots as proof of the benefits to Britain of immigration, but omit to mention that none of these groups expected to be given free money, clothing, food, and accommodation, like the Balkan refugees, nor did they demand that British society change its ways to suit them, like the post-war immigrant activists.

largely unwanted, members of the community, and equally true that others will remain mere burdens on the public weal.

At the moment we are ridiculously lax. No foreign refugee, asylum seeker, or would-be immigrant should be allowed into Britain unless (a) they are entitled to British citizenship as natives of the Commonwealth, or (b) it can be shown beyond doubt that their admission will be of benefit to Britain, or (c) in exceptional circumstances only, it can be shown that they are decent folk in real danger of serious *and undeserved* persecution in the lands from which they have fled. We should not be in the business of giving sanctuary to criminals or revolutionaries simply because the penalties they may incur in their own countries are more severe than would be applied in Britain, nor should we automatically accept anyone fleeing a country whose government is deemed politically incorrect by the chattering classes.

Anyone caught entering the country illegally should be deported without ado or appeal, and anyone resident in Britain who is not a British citizen, and is convicted of a felony, should be deported either at once or on completion of a prison sentence if one is imposed.

Do I seem extreme? Possibly, to liberals, but not to the sensible majority; and certainly no more extreme than those who were so unscrupulous and dishonest as to accuse William Hague of "playing the race card" simply because he questioned the wisdom of government policy. There is something far wrong with a country in which the needs and welfare of deserving Britons can be neglected while illegal immigrants receive sympathy and assistance beyond the bounds of sanity, and can even be compensated with five-figure sums after being jailed for entering the country on fake passports; a country in which citizenship was granted with indecent haste to Indians whose characters have been questioned but who just happened to have contributed lavishly to the Labour government's great white elephant, the Dome – while a Rhodesian with four

British grandparents was refused a passport, as were Gurkhas whose loyal service to Britain is unmatched. Hardly a country to be proud of.

Not According to
Lady Bracknell

I KNEW Marks and Spencer were in trouble when I bought a salmon and cucumber sandwich and discovered that the cucumber had been added in small chunks *with the rind still on*. Aunt Augusta would have gone berserk, assuming that Lane had been depraved (or drunk) enough to serve up such abominations. Mind you, even the best places can err: the Peninsula Hotel in Hong Kong once presented me with smoked salmon sandwiches garnished with raw onion rings. No wonder the place fell into the hands of the Communists.

Which reminds me, the modern craze for garlic and peppers is symptomatic of Britain's decline. Time was when both were unknown here, and the atmosphere was not rendered hideous by a stench reminiscent of an inferior Paraguayan bordello. (I have never been in Paraguay; I merely surmise.)

"You Want to put Bond in a Gorilla Suit?"

THERE MAY HAVE BEEN nicer people in Hollywood than Albert "Cubby" Broccoli, but I never met them. As his nickname implies, he was plump and cuddly and gentle; he was also generous and considerate, and his staff and colleagues regarded him with an affection which I suspect was unique towards a movie tycoon. He had a modesty and an innocence and an air of vulnerability which seemed to inspire a protective feeling in those around him. They showed him a respect that had nothing to do with fear of a man who controlled the most successful series of films in the history of the cinema; it was simply that they liked him, and Cubby knew it, and was touchingly grateful for it.

I remember when he received a special award at an Oscar ceremony (presented appropriately by Roger Moore) and I doubt if there was a more nervous man in California that night. But he made a gracious, careful acceptance speech, and because he was Cubby, and for no other reason, I made a point of congratulating him in his office next morning. His response astonished me by its earnestness, almost as though he were relieved.

"Was it all right? Really, I mean, was it okay? Well, thank you, George, thank you very much. I'm glad you thought it was all right. It was kind of a ... you know ... Roger was great, wasn't he? Thanks, George, I appreciate it ... God bless."

If I'd been an old friend or close relative I might not have been surprised at such evident sincerity, but I was merely his screenwriter of the moment, whose opinion didn't matter zilch, and of no importance in his scheme of things – but that was Cubby all over. He was a man of deep feeling, and where another might have nodded acknowledgement, Cubby felt real gratitude and showed it. I was impressed, and went straight to my typewriter to record his words while they were still fresh. The foregoing paragraph is Cubby Broccoli verbatim.

For a brilliant producer who had built the James Bond operation into a huge continuing blockbuster and international household word, he was strangely anxious and defensive where his product was concerned. Let anyone infringe, or even appear to infringe, on Bond, and Cubby would fret about it; when someone advertised a toy pistol with a drawing vaguely resembling the famous shot of 007 seen down a gun barrel at the start of the credits, Cubby showed it to me more in sorrow than in anger; how, he wondered, could anyone do a thing like that? I doubt if he did anything about it, but it upset him for an hour or two.

I have a picture of him looking unhappy during a discussion in his London office at South Audley Street. Roger Moore had been offered what I think was a cameo appearance in someone else's thriller, and Cubby didn't want him to take it; I think he felt it would somehow tarnish the Bond image. Roger listened politely, and then said gently: "But Cubby, I've got to keep the cars filled up," which seemed an eminently reasonable answer to me – indeed, it has passed into my family's language. Cubby continued to look reproachful, but I don't know whether Roger eventually took the role or not. I've a feeling he didn't.

When I worked on *Octopussy* I couldn't be sure whether Cubby approved of my participation or not. I've an idea – and I may well be wrong – that I had been imposed on him, possibly by David Begelman, then head man at MGM-UA. After the *Taipan* episode

I had worked on an MGM project about General Stilwell, the celebrated "Vinegar Joe" of the Burma campaign; Martin Ritt wanted to do it with Paul Newman, and since I had served in Burma and was available, Ritt had asked me to write it. To cut a long story short, difficulties arose, not with Ritt, but on the production side. I was adamant that Madam Chiang Kai-shek, who was still alive, must be treated with absolute accuracy in the script, for two reasons: I won't falsify history, and if Madam were portrayed unfairly she could sue us stupid. The view of some (not, I repeat, Ritt) was that she could sue and welcome, it would all be publicity. At this point I had withdrawn, and my lawyer, the late Nicholas Baker, MP, had fought a gruelling but successful battle with MGM's legal department before I was shot of the project, with my money intact.

I can regret it, for it could have been a splendid role for Newman as Stilwell (with Timothy West, for my money, as Slim), but I rather think there would have been ructions eventually, since Ritt regarded Stilwell as something of a hero while I looked on him as an unpleasant, self-promoting creep. Quite. As it was, Ritt and I parted friends, the MGM legal eagles learned a considerable respect for Lincoln's Inn Fields, Begelman liked what I'd done, and I *think* had proposed me for *Octopussy*.

I may have been imagining that Cubby had misgivings about me; possibly he was wary of writers, unpredictable creatures who might not treat 007 with the deference Cubby thought he deserved. I may have seemed unduly casual and flippant, as when I had Bond assuming the costume of a circus clown, and absolutely horrifying Cubby by later proposing an even more bizarre disguise for his hero; I can still hear his cry of outraged disbelief: "You want to put Bond in a *gorilla suit*?"

I did, Cubby was persuaded, and it worked to general satisfaction, but I believe that deep down Cubby still regarded me as a bit of a loose cannon. Perhaps he sensed that I, too, had my reservations; I'd thought hard before taking the *Octopussy* assignment, partly because I wasn't sure that I wanted to be involved in such a high-profile notoriously popular entertainment, partly because I was scared stiff of working on the biggest of big pictures which was totally different from anything I'd ever done. On the other hand, was I going to pass up a Bond movie? The chance to be part of cinema history?

I swithered, and compromised by asking Douglas Rae to name a price that I thought (hoped?) might well be turned down. It wasn't, and in due course I found myself mounting the steps of the celebrated Iron Lung, once I believe the writers' building but now the main office in the great MGM lot at Culver City, to begin a long and intensive series of round-table discussions with the principals of the Bond production team.

Now I am bound not to go into details, but I can at least say that a Bond screenplay (in my experience at least) resembles a Dumas novel insofar as both emerge from a consultative process, after which the author goes home and writes the thing. That is what I did, and afterwards the executive producer and writer Michael G. Wilson, and the doyen of Bond scripters, Richard Maibaum, added and subtracted and amended, hence the shared screen credit. But I can't leave the subject without paying a deserved tribute to Cubby, an avuncular chairman, to Michael Wilson, an inspired ideas man, and to John Glen, the director, who brought a wealth of editing and directing experience. And to the rest of Cubby's team: when you've worked with them, you've worked with the best in the business.

It was a tough, exhausting process, but from the writer's point of view it had immense advantages all too rare in the film world: you knew it was going to get made, that no expense would be spared, that you would have no problems about money, hotels, transport, or expenses, all of which were cut and dried, that the whole operation would be managed with a professionalism second to none, that it would be a happy ship (Roger Moore gleefully crying "Commiserations!" when I was introduced as the writer), and that it was simply the most important thing in Hollywood.

This was brought home when Michael Wilson joined Kathy and me at breakfast in our hotel on the first morning. The coffee shop was full of young Hollywood bravos talking deals, exchanging gossip, butchering characters, and generally acting like Sammy Glick, "taking meetings", "doing lunch" (I won't swear they didn't call it "lunchee"), and bandying big names – until Wilson got to his feet and said: "Well, we mustn't keep Cubby waiting." Silence descended like a great blanket; heads turned at the magic name; and then the whispering started and continued until we had left, followed by respectful stares, and an echo of the magic word "Bond".

Culver City is the only studio where they've given me a slot in the VIP car park, where the gate guard greeted me with a respectful nod and my name, and where I was treated to the sight of Walter Matthau uncoiling himself from a car too small for him, prowling towards the office with the cares of the world on his shoulders and a tiny pork-pie hat on his head, stopping for a lugubrious word with the guard, and generally behaving like . . . Walter Matthau.

My car, like Matthau's, was a modest saloon, a poor relation to the Caddies and Bentleys and Begelman's beautiful green Rolls, and had been hired from a counter in the studio on the first day. I emphasise day, because by the time I drove back to our hotel on Rodeo Drive, several miles north in Beverly Hills, night had fallen, and I had discovered that my headlights were on full, and I couldn't find how to dip them.

This can be embarrassing at the best of times; on Wilshire or Beverly Boulevard, with God knows how many lanes of traffic, massive automobiles sweeping past blasting their horns, strange lights flashing everywhere, and having to remember to drive on the right, it's an absolute nightmare. I began to panic; for one thing, I couldn't get into the proper lane for Rodeo Drive, oncoming drivers were swearing and honking at me, and I could see myself mounting the pavement (sorry, sidewalk) and bursting into tears – when there, parked outside the Beverly Wilshire with its roof-lights flashing, was an undoubted police car. I pulled in behind it, got out, approached a stalwart member of Beverly Hills' finest standing on the offside, and said: "Excuse me, officer, I'm British, and I can't get my headlights dipped . . ."

They tell me that in New York I'd either have been arrested or shot, but they order things far otherwise in Tinseltown. Without turning his head the policeman said: "There's a little levver under the steering column" – and my thanks died on my lips as I realised that he was gun in hand, covering an enormous black man dressed in spangled leather and a pirate head-scarf who was spread-eagled against the side of the police car. I managed at last to say "Thank you, officer," and as he frisked his prisoner with a practised hand and cuffed his wrists, he replied affably: "You're welcome. Have a nice evening."

I know our policemen are wonderful, but for calm, competence, and courtesy, commend me to a Beverly Hills cop.

The Rodeo Hotel, where Kathy and I lived before we moved to the Beverly Hilton, was bang in the middle of what is probably the most astronomically expensive shopping area on earth. Hard by were all the ritzy establishments: Van Cleef and Arpels, Hermès, Gucci, and the rest, and I gaped in disbelief at the price ticket of several hundred dollars on a cardigan I could have bought for £20 in Hawick (where it was made). It is an area held in enormous respect by the tour bus operators and their passengers; Kathy and I took a Beverly Hills tour from downtown, simply out of interest, and the driver, having warned passengers at the outset to put away their "wacky terbacky", waxed absolutely lyrical about the Homes of the Stars and the sheer impossibility of surviving in the Golden Triangle unless you had a seven-figure income. The tourists loved it, and I realised that our supposedly class-ridden British society simply isn't in it compared to the dollar-measured status of that strange area between Wilshire and Sunset reaching to the coast. You want snobbery and social distinction, you've got it.

It has to be seen to be believed, let alone understood. There was a magazine, which I studied goggle-eyed, dealing with the doings of Beverly Hills Society and "the Desert Set" and others; it was crammed with pictures of celebrities at parties, with a text that would have entranced Henry James: "Then the action shifted to the Rumpus Room of the Hotel Sheets, where after a mouth-watering feast of Beef Wellington with stone-ground English mustard, the younger set went poolside while their elders turned dance-happy . . ."

There was another side to the film capital which I used to see each day as I drove from Rodeo down Beverly Boulevard and other thoroughfares (including one which the natives pronounced "Kinker-dyne" but we would call Kincardine) to Culver City. At one point I had to cross Venice Boulevard, and took immense care to time my arrival to the green light, for the street corners were peopled by the most alarming thugs of all colours, nightmare beings in black leather and chains and beards and Boris Karloff boots, balefully regarding the drivers as they accelerated across Venice sighing with relief. You wouldn't want to be held up at that inter-section by a red light, believe me. (In nightmares, I sometimes stop at the Venice lights to ask someone the time, or the way to Malibu.)

We stayed modestly north of Wilshire, taking our meals at the less expensive restaurants and coffee rooms like the Pink Turtle, and only occasionally at the upmarket places, the Bella Fontana, Chasens with the Fleischers, L'Orangerie, and one astonishing estab-lishment whose atmosphere I find difficult to describe; it was exclu-sive, luxuriously appointed, and had Greg Bautzer dining at a corner table, but there was an affectation about the place which I can only say chimed perfectly with finger-bowls and stone-ground English mustard.

There was grouse on the menu, and it was as tough as an Army boot. I complained, and presently the proprietor arrived, to assure me that grouse were naturally tough birds, as a result of flying through the heather with a vigorous wing action which developed their breast muscles, hence the toughness. I don't know if a visitor from Hoosier Falls, Indiana, would have accepted this, but I suspect he might; the proprietor's attitude suggested that he thought I would buy it until one of the waiters nudged him and muttered: "He's from Scotland, for Christ's sake!" This gave the proprietor pause, as he realised that I did know what a grouse was, and was not to be deluded by fine talk of vigorous wing actions. He weighed his words.

"Sir," he said at last, "allow me to offer you some lobster. And a glass of Napoleon brandy. On the house."

And in spite of my protests, he insisted, and even parked himself at our table for the rest of the meal, a sure sign of embarrassment in an American restaurateur. I was reminded of an incident in Colorado Springs when, having ordered, we were awaiting our meal, there was a crash as of shipwreck from the kitchen, and presently the manager arrived, seated himself, and said cheerily: "Hi, there! That was your dinner . . ."

Say what you will, our American cousins have got style.

At the studio we either ate in the Walnut Room, the exclusive part of the commissary where the top people had their MGM Chicken Noodle soup and matzos, or at Ships, a popular eating-house outside, where Cubby worked the toaster (there was one at each table) and ordered for everyone. ("Chicken pot pie for George, Mabel. George *always* has chicken pot pie." So I did.) It was cosier, and better food, but Cubby had a permanent table in the Walnut Room, and felt obliged to mingle with the other big wheels from time to time.

Among these was Joe Fischer, head of the studio, who would stride through with his entourage, like a liner attended by tugs. He was moustached and imposing and, above all, audible. Cubby introduced me as the new Bond writer, upon which Fischer cried: "He's not writing! He's eating!" at which sally his henchmen fell about, and the party passed on, chortling. "Funny guy," said Cubby, sighing. Next day I was lunching alone, for some reason, and Fischer again hove in view with his gaggle in tow, caught sight of me, bellowed "He's *still* eating!" and strode on, with his minions having fits. No one else took the slightest notice; Joe Fischer was just another studio boss, after all – indeed, only once did I see heads turn in the commissary, when a tall, bronzed, silver-haired man slipped unobtrusively down the side of the great room to the door, and the whisper went round: "Cary Grant!" Hollywood isn't usually a star-struck place, but there are exceptions.

As to *Octopussy* . . . very seldom does a writer contribute anything to a film apart from his screenplay, but this was to be an exception; I was the one who decided that the film would be set in India. At the outset Cubby had reeled off the places Bond had been in the series so far; India was conspicuously absent, and since I'd soldiered there, and knew that for once "great locations" would have real meaning, I fastened on it, Cubby agreed, that was that, and, whatever its other merits, I think that *Octopussy* is by far the most exotic-looking of all the Bond pictures.

I was also able to do something that I'd never achieved before: get an actor a part. On the Musketeers I'd tried to wangle a job for one of the great swashbucklers, Louis Hayward, but no one was listening; on *Octopussy*, when they were looking for an Indian assistant villain, I was able to suggest Kabir Bedi, whom I'd met on *Ashanti*, and he was cast, most successfully.

There were counterbalancing disappointments. For the opening sequence before the credits, I tried to sell the TT motor-cycle race (which I've mentioned in the introduction). It is one of the great sporting spectacles, the world has never had the chance to see it, and it was made for a duel-to-the-death sidecar race between Bond and a heavy. The sidecars in those days were simply flat boards to which the passenger clung as the bikes hurtled along at sickening speeds, and for passengers we would have two Bond dollies, heroine and villainess, built on the lines of the gorgeous Swedish and German girls who used to prowl the TT in their black leathers, looking like blonde Emma Peels.

It would have made a terrific sequence, but it never got to the consideration stage, for it could only have been filmed during the actual races, when the island is awash with bikes and riders – and that happens in June, while we were in autumn, and couldn't hang about. Incidentally, it would have been wonderful publicity for my adopted home.

The other thing that didn't happen was a scene in which Bond, frantic to get change for the phone at a critical moment, would accost a passer-by . . . cut to Close Shot of Gert Froebe saying: "Sorry, I have only gold." Oh, well, it was an idea; you can't win them all.

Hollywood is full of extraordinary experts, and on this picture I encountered two of them, quiet unassuming young men named B. J. Worth and Rande Deluca, who for sheer cold nerve and brilliance at their trade are in a class by themselves. Bond films often feature aerial sequences, including sky-diving and the like, and in my ignorance I had assumed that these were done in the studio. So when Rande and B.J. were to double for Roger and Kabir Bedi in a fight on top of a plane, I was appalled to learn that this would be done not in a studio, but at God knows how many thousand feet, with the plane bucking all over the place. B.J., being bearded, was to double for Kabir, and would have a parachute under his jacket; Rande, as Bond, would have no parachute.

What, I asked Rande, would happen if he fell? "That's okay," he said, "B.J. will catch me." In other words, B.J. would hurl himself off the plane in a sky-dive, catch up with the plummeting Rande and seize him, open the chute, and drift with him to earth.

Words failed me, even after they had shown me a film sequence in which B.J. was seen piloting a light plane with Rande as passenger, Rande flinging himself out, B.J. diving the plane, overtaking Rande, who manoeuvred his sky-dive to bring himself alongside the plane and clamber aboard again. Mad as hatters, the pair of them, but they made that final aerial struggle in *Octopussy* a masterpiece of action cinema. The last time I saw them, Rande was limping; he had hurt his ankle getting out of a car.

With my writing duties done, I paid a final visit to Hollywood – I can't remember why, but presumably in case tidying was needed. I was glad the job was over at last, and I dare say Cubby was too. We had dealt well together, especially at our solitary Ships lunches when the others were out somewhere working, and he had reminisced entertainingly about Ian Fleming and Harry Saltzman and Sean Connery and that whole astonishing saga that is like nothing else in the cinema. He was seriously interested in a Flashman series of films, but it would have entailed all sorts of unscrambling of contracts, and he also thought it might prove even more expensive to make than Bond.

I date the end of our association from the moment when Louis Jourdan, that smoothest of Bond villains, asked me if I would be on hand for the shooting; I said I thought not, Cubby cried on a rising note "We can't afford him!", and M. Jourdan, who is charm and tact personified, steered the conversation effortlessly into other channels.

Octopussy had a gala opening attended by the Prince and Princess of Wales (she making the Bond dollies look like also-rans), and to Cubby's delight in the ensuing weeks we wiped the box-office floor with the competing *Never Say Never Again*. My own satisfaction was, and is, that I worked on a Bond picture. I've watched it since, and when it comes to the gorilla suit bit I feel slightly guilty as I hear in memory that anguished cry of incredulity. Sorry, Cubby . . . and thank you a thousand times.

*

It was only when I saw a documentary about MGM twenty years later that I realised how lucky I'd been, seeing the very last of the great film empire. At the time of *Octopussy*, MGM had just merged with United Artists, and that was really the end of it. Now all that is left are some of the buildings, I suppose, but of vastly greater importance, all those wonderful films which with luck will last forever.

I used to wander round the corridors of the huge headquarters building, once the home of Louis B. Mayer and Irving Thalberg, where Cubby now occupied the main suite of offices, first on the left after you got through the reception area where two pleasant but eagle-eyed young ladies screened visitors. The corridors were MGM's last will and testament, the walls covered with blow-ups of stills from past productions, star portraits, enormous group photographs with all the famous faces ranged in alphabetical order, so that you got Clark Gable and Errol Flynn side by side, for example, all making an extraordinary record presided over by an aged janitor-type who lived in a distant cubbyhole which, like the corridors, was plastered with star photos – but these were all autographed to the old man himself: Tracy, Lombard, Gable, Hepburn, the Barrymores, Powell, Loy, you name it, every big Metro name seemed to be there, and I wonder if there is a collection like it anywhere.

And not only MGM people. He had worked at various studios since the silent days over fifty years earlier, but Warners had been his favourite, and his gallery included Cagney and Raft and Bette Davis and Ann Sheridan. Sometimes, he confided, he would sneak a "foreign" portrait on to the corridor walls among all the MGM ones, "Eddie Robinson, maybe, he was a real gentleman." I got the impression that he was doing this to spite the shade of Louis B. Mayer.

I don't remember his name, or what function he had apart from taking care of his beloved pictures. Looking back, he seems like some Phantom of the Opera flitting along the passages of MGM, mysterious, watchful, jealous of his domain. I remember him saying something ever so corny, ever so Hollywood, and yet ever so moving as he surveyed his gallery of stars. "All my friends," he said. "Every one."

He'll be long gone now, like Metro-Goldwyn-Mayer.

Dumbing Down, Down, Down . . .

JOURNALISM, WRITTEN AND BROADCAST, has sunk to a shockingly low ebb, for several reasons. The first, of course, is the decline in education, brought about by the politically motivated reformers who wrecked a splendid system, especially that foul-mouthed Labour Minister who vowed "to destroy all those –ing grammar schools". Just the man for the education portfolio, obviously. He and his Socialist fellow-theoreticians did a terrific job in degrading scholastic standards in the name of equality, which meant dragging down the good to the level of the mediocre. The war has been waged against private and selective education – and I have lost count of the number of Socialists of my acquaintance who, while lauding the State system, have taken damned good care to get their children into private schools – or, the ultimate hypocrisy, into schools which are State-run but private in all that matters.

A frequent excuse is that their children have "special needs", but more often than not the loyal Labourite makes no bones about admitting that he (and especially she) couldn't care less about party policy, their kids are going to be all right, Jack, and get the best affordable, and sod the workers.

But we must not digress into the fascinating reaches of the Socialist conscience. The point is that the decline in educational standards is manifest in our national newspapers and magazines, and in the broadcast media. Our national press appears to be staffed by people who don't know "may" from "might", "he" from "him", "who" from "whom" (the latter word seems to have vanished from the popular papers altogether), "like" from "as", "enormity" from "enormous", "compunction" from "compulsion" (this in a leading "quality" broadsheet), and have no idea of the meaning of "decimate" and "oblivious". Worse still, modern editors don't spot these errors – or more probably don't recognise them as such.

This is not mere pedantry; I hope I'm not a nit-picker, and bottle up my emotions about a related subject, the sloppy use of jargon and clichés. I am tired of those who pursue a strategy in search of a solution within broad parameters on a level playing field while singing from the same hymn-sheet, and who use "summit" instead of "meeting", "loved ones" meaning "relatives", "monitoring" meaning "watching", and "task force" meaning "pack of official clowns", to say nothing of the dumber Americanisms, such as "free up", "meet with", "check out", "lose out", and "state of the art". I think if I see "vibrant", "dynamic" or "former glory" again I shall feel it is "time to move on", or possibly even "move forward". All right, I shall desist; I'd never get to the end of them. I return to simple grammar, and wonder where it went. Not to the Fourth Estate, that's certain.

I first became aware of this as deputy editor of the *Glasgow Herald*, a paper which fifty years ago was second to none in its journalistic standards, the training ground of Alastair Hetherington, Peregrine Worsthorne, Alastair Burnet, and many other distinguished newspapermen. We had a policy of recruiting university graduates, and I was alarmed at the poor quality of education, general knowledge, spelling, grammar, and general literacy of many, but by no means all, of the applicants I interviewed in the 1960s, when compared to that older generation of journalists, many of them largely self-educated, who had been the backbone of newspapers when I entered journalism after the war.

I must be careful about this, or I shall be accused of envious prejudice, not having been to a university myself, but those interviews and my general observation led me to question whether a university education is the best springboard for a journalistic career. It depends, of course, on the individual; no doubt there are many distinguished graduate journalists to stack against the Kiplings and Shaws and those wonderful editors who came out of the North, especially Dundee; no university could compare to training with D. C. Thomson.

Graduates laboured under a certain disadvantage: many tended to condescend to journalism rather than aspiring to it, assuming that they were fit simply by virtue of their academic training, and that they had little to learn, especially about writing, which was their goal rather than the mundane business of reporting and sub-editing. The production of elegantly phrased and trenchant "pieces" was what they had in mind – and many of them eventually became competent leader-writers, after an apprenticeship at the subs' tables, where they learned the hard way how to condense five hundred words into fifty and cut Alistair Cooke to half a column. (It wasn't really fair to give them Cooke; quite apart from the fact that cutting him was a crime, it was also damnably difficult, thanks to his almost narrative style.)

Some university men, by the way, made first-class subs; the best stone-sub I ever knew was a Strathclyde University drop-out who later managed a great publishing house.

And most of them turned into good newspapermen and women, once they had learned the basics and been educated out of some of the more bizarre notions they had picked up in academe – one aspirant told me that university had taught him to *think*, and I forbore to tell him that I could see no sign of it. Another spoke of "three years' exposure to excellence" and I was reminded of Peacock's Dr Foliot who spoke of a well-balanced sconce polished without and picked clean within; to do the lad justice, three weeks' exposure to an acid-tongued chief sub-editor wrought a wonderful change; he was made to understand that what-who-where-when (and if possible how-why) must be given priority in a news story, and that the first paragraph of almost any leader or "think-piece" is almost always expendable (try it on your own morning paper). He also developed a fine dirty mind, which is absolutely essential in a journalist.*

If I seem to harp on about graduates it is probably because I got my adult education in the Army and in that wonderful world of weekly newspapers and police courts, council meetings, garden fêtes, funerals (get the initials right), sporting events, fires, accidents, and Acts of God. I always feel a glow of comradeship when I hear a media interviewer or chat-show host remarking, invariably with pride, that he began on the Heckmondwyke Sentinel or the Tillicoultry Reminder; I know that he too has thrust his foot into doors, importuned impatient officials, wheedled policemen, and fought defensive rearguard actions against citizens outraged at having their privacy invaded. Incidentally, it's the finest training imaginable for a writer, especially at the subs' table, as Graham Greene, former sub on The Times, has testified.

It was a good newspaper generation that came up in the forties and fifties, trained by wise and wonderfully informed old hands who knew the works of Dickens and Hardy and Scott and Trollope backwards, as well as every personality and concern and scrap of gossip for thirty miles around and forty years back. Perhaps they're still there; I hope so, but I see little sign of it in our national press, popular or "quality".

I've spoken of the falling-off in basic education; even more worrying is the decline in what I can only call newspaper ethics. It used to be that news and comment had a great gulf betwixt them; you never, never mixed fact with opinion. No longer; front pages carry hopelessly loaded "news stories", and fair, objective reporting seems

---

* Journalist: a term despised by true newspaper folk who define it as a reporter looking for a job.

to be a thing of the past. On the *Herald*, as on all the great provincial newspapers of fifty years ago – *Scotsman, Yorkshire Post, Manchester Guardian* (before it got ideas beneath its station), *Birmingham Post, Western Mail, Liverpool Echo*, and all the rest – fairness was gospel. We were a Tory paper, and our leader columns were sometimes to the right of Genghis Khan, but our news pages were sacrosanct: I've seen the chief sub lay his rule on proofs to make sure that a Labour candidate got exactly the same space as his Conservative opponent.

Does that happen now? I doubt it, although I'm sure the provincial press still maintains higher standards than the nationals. Some of the distortion and dirty tricks that I see in the so-called quality nationals today make me ashamed of my old profession: I am no fan of Tony Blair, but he deserves a fair shake, and the paper which ran a phoney picture of him on Buckingham Palace balcony apparently upstaging the Queen was guilty of deplorable behaviour. No doubt the defence would be that it was an obvious fake; well, this old hack was taken in until he saw the tiny word "montage" above it, and I'm sure that many readers took it as genuine.

That is a bad case, but no worse than many others. The entrapment of the Countess of Wessex by a tabloid reporter disguised as an Arab sheikh was cheap and disgusting, but the depth was plumbed at the time of Princess Diana's death, when part of the nation went collectively mad, and sections of the press behaved disgracefully. I'm sure I am in a minority here, but I was appalled at the near-hysterical reaction of the crowds who strewed their floral tributes and metaphorically speaking beat their breasts in a display of lower-deck emotion which was as distasteful as it was exaggerated. I suppose many felt, to use the fashionable jargon, devastated, but was the tragic victim, however beautiful and bewitching, worth the kind of outpouring of grief that no other figure in living memory has received? I wondered at the time, what had happened to the moral fibre of the island race – the stiff upper lip, if you like – to make them behave like professional mourners howling for hire. The Prime Minister was proud. I was ashamed.

But deplorable as the public reaction was, that of the press and broadcast media was worse. They fuelled and stoked the campaign relentlessly, and with unprecedented yobbish bad manners black-mailed the Royal Family not merely into mourning, but into mourning in the way the gutter press dictated. "Show Us That You Care", or words to that effect, ran one headline: would the writer have dreamed of saying such a thing to a bereaved neighbour? And is the Royal Family not entitled to the same civility, the same decent treatment, as anyone else? Not in Cool Britannia, evidently.

To turn to a less distressing fault of modern journalism, there are increasing signs of amateurishness in production and presentation. Possibly the new computerisation of newspapers has something to do with it; my own experience began and ended with hot metal, so I can't tell; I know only that the end result is inferior. Design and layout are forgotten arts, and we have the choice of pages which are dogs' breakfasts in the populars and Saharas of type in the broadsheets. Plainly it has been forgotten that the first essential is to communicate with the reader, and that for this visual clarity is essential – I am thinking, as one example, of the maddeningly inexpert use of the overprint on colour pages, where text and back-ground are so similar in shade that the result is unreadable. But if the appearance is poor, the content is frequently worse; apart from the grammatical lapses which would shame a ten-year-old, there is an increasing sloppiness in the use of language, a lack of precision, a tendency to jargon, and often a quite wonderful ignorance and carelessness.

To give a trivial example: a headline said that the Pope had "refused" to apologise for the Vatican's attitude to the Holocaust; in fact, as the story which followed made clear, he had merely *failed* to apologise – and any so-called journalist who asks "What's the difference?" would be well advised to quit the media and resume his pick and shovel.

I mustn't be too censorious. Standards in journalism are still as high as those in most other callings, and superior to many (e.g., politics). But I do detect a worrying falling-off – show me a paper, any paper, and before I'm halfway through it I'll be grinding my teeth over several appalling gaffes. I spot them the more easily because I've committed them all myself (though not as a matter of course), and that does nothing for my temper. (I must have been like a dyspeptic Attila to work for.)

Thank God, incidentally, that my newspaper days are over – I hope. Not long ago I looked in on an evening paper where I'd once done Saturday afternoon sport, and it was like a ghastly futuristic sci-fi movie, with pallid slaves pecking away at their flickering green screens in near silence, and no clatter of typewriters, no choking reek of tobacco smoke, and not a laugh or an oath or a roar of rage to be heard. It was curiously lifeless, somehow, and lacking in that element which used to fill newspaper offices, a sort of crazy neurotic joy. Maybe I'm just getting old, and remember a time when everyone seemed to find life more fun.

We were lucky in my day: our newspapers did not suffer from obesity, there were no ridiculously swollen, multi-page, advertise-ment-crammed monstrosities with acres of space to be filled some-how. We didn't know when we were well off, writing stories a paragraph long for a four-page paper; even with twelve or sixteen the editorial was fighting a constant battle for space with the ads – and invariably losing.

But with today's mammoth papers the poor boobs have to write at ten times the length their subject is worth, and apart from over-padded news we have the curse of modern journalism, the prolifera-tion of the commentary, the background exposition, the in-depth analysis, the "think-piece", all adding up to an indigestible stream of crap which no one wants to read, and no one, to judge by the mechanical repetition and weary rambling, wants to write either. Oh, for the days when people knew what "two sticks" meant, sub-editors were ruthless destroyers, editors actually read their papers, and John Gordon and Hannen Swaffer and Ian Mackay and James Agate could say it all in a few good paragraphs.

Note, too, that the men I have just mentioned did not suffer from the delusion that journalism is interesting in itself, or that the public was fascinated by journalistic feuding carried on ad nauseam. One exchange of broadsides, fine, but the childish serial sniping of some modern writers is just a bore.

To conclude, I confess to a slight worry about press freedom. When I was a young reporter you could report anything in a court of law except the evidence in divorce cases (you had to rely on the judge's summing up), and the names of juveniles; I'm pretty sure you couldn't give the name of the accuser in a rape case either; anyway, you didn't. But today there seem to be all kinds of censorship: we hear of "reporting restrictions", and that names have been suppressed for "legal reasons"; in local government the closed meeting which prevents the electors knowing what the elected are doing, is commonplace. These are bad things in themselves, and a sign of times when it is possible for a Home Secretary (admittedly an unusually clownish one) to propose interference with the jury system, and it is suggested that in certain cases an accused shall have no right to confront his accuser.

It is also possible that some government will be so misguided as to try to bring in a "privacy" law. Now, in spite of politicians' babble about the "last chance saloon" there is no way in which this can be imposed in a free society, except in marginal prohibitions on photographic intrusion in certain circumstances. But there it must end. Press freedom was dearly bought in Britain, and any government short-sighted enough to let their civil servants tamper with it (assuming they had the intelligence to frame legislation through which any competent barrister couldn't drive a horse and cart) would just find themselves defied. You can't impose bad law on the *Sun* and the *News of the World* unless you assume totalitarian powers. And we are still some distance from that.

In the long run, one has to hope for a sense of decency and responsibility in journalists, but when it is lacking – as it sometimes is – there's nothing to be done but put up with it. God knows there is plenty wrong with our press, and always has been (even in the halcyon days of which I prattle so proudly); its standards have slipped, and it can be intrusive and beastly, but we must console ourselves with the words of A. P. Herbert: "Just be thankful that it's there."

P.S. I can't end without pointing out a distinction which politicians love to ignore and confuse, and about which the average reader may not have thought much. "Of public interest" and "in the public interest" are two entirely different things, as is plain if one looks at them closely. The first refers to something in which the public are interested, and will be happy to know; the second refers to something which, in the opinion of authority, it may or may not be good for the public to know. So when you hear either phrase used, correctly or not, pay very careful attention, because the bastards are probably up to something.

The sight of a pig urinating may seem an odd accompaniment to an observation on Montaigne, but that's British television for you. Gone are the days when it could claim to be the best in the world; now, in addition to the decline in programme quality, it seems to be suffering from a curious desire among producers to shock and disgust the viewers. The Montaigne-pig juxtaposition was unpleasant, unnecessary, and the product of a mind insensitive to the point of coarseness, a gratuitous vulgarity certain to offend normal sensibility while appealing to the laddish element whom the producers presumably regard as the norm. This leaning towards the ugly and distasteful is likewise seen in the close-ups of abdominal operations and carnivores tearing their prey to bloody shreds; the camera dwells on them even more lovingly than it does on stag beetles disembowelling each other, frogs and stick-insects copulating (along with the rest of the animal kingdom), and piles of festering rubbish featured in a programme about people whose occupation is cleaning up filth. (Muggeridge was right; you couldn't make it up.)

But while one would rather not have such things sprung on one out of the screen, and wonders occasionally what kind of mind plainly revels in showing them, they are infinitely preferable to the late-night obscenities, the foul-mouthed "comedians", the leering, filthy-minded chat show hosts of dubious sexual orientation mugging for their audiences of braying morons who think four-letter words the height of wit, the interminable explicit sex scenes, the sniggering innuendos of scruffy yobs on panel games, and the truly pathetic full-frontal displays by young idiots who think themselves ever so liberated and daring and haven't the brain or imagination to wonder how they'll feel when their grandchildren download the old fools' shameful antics from the internet fifty years hence. Or perhaps they don't give a dam.

Now, I know that I and my generation look prissy, prudish, and fuddy-duddy to a degree in Cool Britannia, being in thrall to those derided "Victorian values" which are such a hoot in the "in-yer-face" age. Of course we're old, but even in our youth we wouldn't have shared the modern delight in obscenity and ugliness and vicariously enjoyed suffering. We were squeamish that way, although no strangers to stark horror, death and disfigurement and pain and cruelty, and we committed and condoned deeds which are regarded as atrocious crimes today – but paradoxically, while our language was frequently foul and our sense of humour scabrous, and our behaviour uncouth, we did not care to have our maiden aunts offended, we cleaned up our language in public, we treated women as ladies and they responded in kind, we had a strong sense of privacy and decent reticence, we knew what was "done" and what was "not done". (Gad, how pompously antique can you get?)

Which probably looks like arrant hypocrisy to the youth of today. I don't think so, but even if we were, a bit of judicious hypocrisy never hurt anyone in civilised society.

We had just as many faults as the young today, but they were different faults; we were of our age just as moderns are of theirs (God help them). And being of our time, we wonder why so much television is frankly godawful, and even horrible and disgusting – to us, that is. Can it be that the teenagers and twenty-somethings of today are simply unaware of how revolting some of their entertainments look to their elders – and would look to every previous age since time began? Possibly; it's what they have been conditioned to accept and enjoy; they know no better.

But the children of the swinging sixties do, for they grew up in the twilight of a time when the old-fashioned values and ideals still lingered on in their parents, and one cannot help suspecting that resentment of that time and those people and values, a desire to raise two fingers to the past, and a rather unworthy intent to put the boot into the crumblies' sensibilities, is at work in the broadcast media, particular in TV.

It is as though they had taken as their watchword the execrable dictum of an odious BBC director-general of their time, who said that there were some people whom one would be glad to offend. What an odd ambition, and what a curious state of mind. Some people one might reasonably be glad to kill or banish, perhaps . . . but to offend? How ill-mannered. But his outlook is plainly reflected by those in television who lose no opportunity of rubbing the viewer's nose in filth, sparing no pains, apparently, to find new ways to upset and distress those who do not share their taste for the obnoxious.

There was a Scottish comedian whose declared ambition it was to see how far he could go with his adult material. I've worked with him, and he is genial and charming; he is also one of the funniest men I've ever seen, a natural comedian who epitomises that delight in the ridiculous, that sense that life is essentially one tremendous joke, so characteristic of the Glaswegian. That is what can infuriate me: the man doesn't *need* to be filthy. But he is internationally famous, and filth is the flavour of the time. A pity, when he has shown that he can be so much funnier without it.

I suppose it's all part of the permissive society, and can be traced back to the Lady Chatterley case, which had the literary trendies dancing in the streets, and to the late Kenneth Tynan who, in uttering his notorious four-letter first, coined his own appropriate epitaph. The tragedy is that when the floodgates are opened only slightly, and possibly with the best of intentions, it's only a matter of time before they're torn off their hinges by the torrent. And eventually we have the diverting spectacle of those ultra-liberals who rejoiced at the Chatterley decision, pursing their lips and wondering if things haven't gone a bit too far . . .

It is not only the eagerness to offend, so reminiscent of the third-former gleefully scrawling indecencies on the lavatory wall, that is deplorable in television; there is a morbid, garment-rending, often almost ghoulish quality about so much on our screens, a constant harping on disease and disability, on poverty and squalor, on social problems and alleged injustices and deprivations, on gloom and doom and all those fashionable obsessions which can be used to make the viewer feel thoroughly miserable – and, whenever possible, guilty. During the war, there was a prohibition against "spreading alarm and despondency"; with modern television it's a fine art.

Could any viewer, listener, or broadcaster fifty years ago have dreamed of a time when an evening's TV fare (and I have picked it entirely at random) would include *Vets in the Wild, Children's Hospital*, an episode of *The Bill* in which "Hollis uncovers strange goings-on at a crematorium", a report from South Africa on disabled athletes, an episode of *Brookside* in which "Mick is outraged at Gemma's school for their harsh approach to drug-taking", and on radio a report on brutalities by prison staff, plus life on three psychiatric wards?

Well, thank you, Noel Coward. I know I and my kind are trivial and light-minded, and that the modern media take their duties seriously, but really . . . I'm surprised the evening's spot of homely fun didn't include a programme on depression, or the victims of religious persecution in Lower Slobovia, or the endangered state of the great crested gob-stopper, or lingering coverage of emaciated beggars crawling with flies, presented by a reproachful TV commentator. Why not? We have already been given a series on Embarrassing Illnesses ("socially sensitive medical disorders") with a riveting segment about piles.

I am not being heartless. I know it is considered proper and even essential that we be shown all these things, and feel care, concern, and compassion – but there's a difference between presenting a balanced picture of the world's activities and obsession with the unhealthy and unhappy. In my time I've seen enough of the world's miseries close to, and I don't need them shoved in my face night after night.

The depressive tendency in news and documentaries spills over into soaps and dramas, with the emphasis on the sordid and violent in series about the police, hospitals, women's prisons, and just about every subject that lends itself to tragedy, enacted by coarse, unpleasant plebeians whose mode of communication is all too often an aggressive snarl or a hysterical scream, usually in a Cockney accent. Possibly this is some sort of therapy for the real-life Royle families (who I'm sure are legion), but it brings no comfort to those who see it for what it is: a shocking example, a picture of society, especially working-class society, that is neither attractive nor healthy, accompanied by a steady, persistent dumbing down, a reduction to the lowest common denominator, a presentation of the worst kind of model for impressionable minds, especially in children. Nature has a habit of imitating art, and television is doing nothing to instil good behaviour, good manners, or good nature, to say nothing of morality or decency. Indeed, quite the opposite.

It is contended, frequently by purveyors of pornography and violence, that their programmes have no corrupting effect on the young. This is a wicked lie. The power of TV is acknowledged, even by the lunatic fringe, when it's a question of discouraging excessive dieting in thin women, or helping to stamp out smoking, or promote safe sex. If TV had no influence, what would be the point of banning cigarette advertising? No, there is ample evidence of the effect of pornography and violence on the immature. What is less obvious is the slow, steady erosion of values, and the gradual deterioration of behaviour.

I cannot measure the effect on juveniles of programmes which show teenagers, plainly stoned out of their minds, raving under psychedelic lights, or flailing the air like religious fanatics in adulation of some squealing blonde or dreadlocked caterwauler, or being encouraged to talk smut by a frenzied slattern with a microphone, but I doubt if it's good. I confess I even worry about such seemingly unimportant things as the sheer ugliness of teen fashions, of mere children with studs in their noses and tongues and navels, of their manipulation by a media which worships false gods like the appalling national lottery, and of their lack of ambition to improve themselves socially and culturally.

Once it was the ambition of young people to speak well (affected posh it would be considered nowadays), to talk like, say, the old BBC news readers or Alec Guinness or Valerie Hobson. Not now; the broadcast media have entered on a deliberate policy of encouraging regional accents – which are perfectly acceptable so long as they remain *universally* intelligible and are backed by a decent education. All too often they are neither; the dreadful Estuary English, especially jarring in the quacking female, has replaced received pronunciation, and decent enunciation has followed good diction through the floor.

Naturally I have noticed most of all the deterioration in Scottish accents. Whether it is thought to be worthy and robustly Caledonian to talk like a Gorbals news vendor, I cannot say, but many Scots do who would once have aspired, if not to the mincing tones of Kelvinside and Morningside, at least to a pleasant articulation free of glottal stops – which interestingly enough have crept into Southern English speech of late, as company for the intrusive "r" on vowel endings. But in Scotland the voices of Alastair Sim and Andrew Cruickshank are heard no more, and even debate in the Scottish Parliament can sound like the rowdier exchanges on the Ibrox terracing.

Taking it all in all, I don't seem to approve much in British television, do I? Well, if this has been a diatribe against it, I cannot apologise; it deserves all I have said, and worse, for its degrading of standards and corrupting of values, its often slipshod approach to such diverse things as reporting, grammar, research,* acting, and production, the bland tunnel vision of many interviewers, the growing respect for political correctness, but most of all for its emphasis on the common, the sleazy, the nasty, and the third-rate.

Is it all bad, then? Of course not; there is much that is good and worthy on television, and immensely talented, dedicated, and painstaking people are responsible for it. They do splendid work, far too much to be mentioned here, so I single out only the great State occasions and displays; politics, if you can bear the sorry spectacle of the Commons, the (not invariably) grovelling interviews and evasive responses, and the dreadful boredom of discussions;

* An almost unbelievable example of sloppy research was seen in the teleplay of Evelyn Waugh's *Sword of Honour*, when British officers of the Second World War were shown saluting in the palm-down American or Naval fashion, and *bare-headed*. This was rather like depicting a Bishop in a glengarry instead of a mitre. Were the producers too lazy to *ask* an elderly ex-Serviceman for technical advice, or were they so amateurish that it didn't occur to them?

sport, for those who are interested, and can take the mind-numbing saturation coverage; arts and history, when the presenter knows his stuff (as they sometimes do); the travel programmes which take us to places we can never hope (or want) to visit; the occasional, very occasional, soap or comedy series (but where are you, *Yes, Minister, The Good Life*, and *Fawlty Towers*?) It's all subjective, of course; I've no doubt there are viewers entranced by apparently endless gardening and cookery and those ghastly teams which vandalise people's houses in the name of interior decoration. Personally, I reserve my greatest admiration for the technical wizardry which is little short of magical, and is seen to best advantage in the ads.

But whatever its virtues, the overall effect of television has been disastrous, and if we cannot hold John Logie Baird and Alexander Zworykin directly responsible for the mischief their creations have caused, they still have much to answer for. Whether television is the most evil invention of the twentieth century may be debatable, but what is not is that those who viewed it with misgivings in its early days, Aldous Huxley, C. P. Scott, and T. S. Eliot among them, have had their doubts and fears realised beyond their worst nightmares.

The Perfect Premier

HAVING ALREADY chosen my worst prime ministers, I ought to nominate my best. Obviously it is impossible for anyone of my time to go past Churchill, who was the man for the hour, but I have to confess a liking for the style of Sir Alec Douglas-Home, not because he was on the Right, but because he spent a year in office without, on his own admission, doing a damned thing. This would not commend him to New Labour, who count all time lost when they're not wrecking the country, or to the Tories, who lack Sir Alec's philosophic vision, so similar to that of the wise old eighteenth-century gentleman who looked back on the early 1750s as the happiest time because, he maintained, there were no politics at all.

"Forget Fellini!"

DINO DE LAURENTIIS is a brisk, bright-eyed human dynamo, and no great admirer of Jane Austen – at least, not when there's better stuff available. I was in his suite at Claridge's, waiting to discuss a remake of *20,000 Leagues Under the Sea*, and since his phone calls, in machine-gun-like Italian, were occupying him at length, I was beguiling the time with a pocket edition of *Emma*. He surfaced between calls and barked:

"Eh, George, what you reading?"

I held it up, he frowned, rummaged on his desk, and threw across a script. "Forget it! Read that!" he cried, and started shouting into the phone again.

Red Sonja, said the title on the front, and since the lady promised more excitement than Miss Woodhouse, I was quickly engrossed, and had got to the bit where the Priestesses of the Talisman are being entombed alive under the altar by wicked Queen Gedren, when Dino finally hung up and demanded: "Okay, what you think?"

I said it wasn't bad, in its way, and he nodded decisively and said: "Schwarzenegger, okay. You take it with you, see what you think, work on it maybe." Since we had no deal on *Red Sonja*, I made no sounds of agreement, but I was intrigued, not only because I have a weakness for sword and sorcery but because his mention of Schwarzenegger reminded me that Dino had made a couple of *Conan the Barbarian* films, the second of them with Dick Fleischer and Jack Cardiff, with both of whom I'd be delighted to work again.

In the meantime, he was all enthusiasm for *20,000 Leagues*. Since Fleischer had directed the definitive version for Disney, I supposed he might be called in for the remake, but I was wrong, for Dino had him docketed for *Red Sonja*. Dick Lester, who joined us at Claridge's, declined politely when *20,000 Leagues* was proposed, and when he'd gone Dino cried: "Forget Lester!" and took me flat aback by asking if I could go to Rome to confer with his second choice – Federico Fellini.

I said by all means, but was he sure Fellini was the man for underwater science fiction, which would be rather a change from *La Dolce Vita* and *8½*? Dino waved this aside ("Forget *Dolce Vita*!") He had bumped into Fellini recently, and discovered he was crazy about *20,000 Leagues*; he'd give his right arm to direct it.

It seemed unlikely, but you don't pass up the chance (however slender you suspect it may be) of working with Fellini, so I flew to Rome and was picked up next morning at my hotel by one of Dino's minions, an immaculate hatchet-faced gentleman who was to be my minder and interpreter, and who'd have been perfect casting for a Martin Scorsese movie. We drove to a street near the old city wall, that astonishing red-brick structure which always strikes me as incongruous alongside Rome's marvellous marble, both ancient and modern, but is a reminder that this is indeed the Eternal City, which has everything from the breathtaking ruins of the old Forum to the wonders of the Vatican and that remarkable glittering white extravagance of Mussolini's, whatever it's called.

We arrived at Fellini's office simultaneously with the man himself, burly, balding, cheerful, and I would say quite as disorganised as anyone I've ever met. Fellini defusing a burglar alarm had to be seen to be believed; he produced a massive bunch of keys, shouted instructions to the secretary who accompanied him, and flung himself at his office door at a given signal, undoing locks and muttering in Italian while she pressed buttons and squeaked with alarm when he dropped his keys. A low buzzing noise came from behind the door, Fellini gave a frantic cry, the secretary snatched up his fallen keys, used two of them in lightning succession, shrieked an order at him, thrust him aside when he lunged at what I gathered was the wrong button, and got the door open just as the buzzing was reaching the kind of level that only dogs can hear. The buzzing stopped, Fellini made apologetic ushering gestures, the secretary patiently returned his keys, he dropped them again, and we all had coffee.

He and I sat on a couch in an angle of his office, and I carry a memory of an easy, rather untidy man, amiable but thoughtful, soft-spoken and less demonstrative in manner than Italians usually are. One thing soon emerged: my interpreter was not necessary, for while my Italian begins with "*buon giorno*" and ends with "*ciao*", Fellini's English was far better than I'd been led to expect, not fluent but entirely understandable. I watched him on television years later, feigning incomprehension when interviewed by American journalists, no doubt out of reluctance to answer off the top of his head in a foreign tongue.

What also emerged quickly was that he had no wish to direct *20,000 Leagues Under the Sea*. Dino, he explained, had misunderstood him. "We meet at the airport, he ask what I am doing, I tell him, I ask what he is doing, he say Jules Verne *20,000 Leagues*, and you know how it is . . ." He spread his hands. "I want to say something of nice, so I say, great, Dino, one of my favourite books since I'm a boy." He smiled apologetically. "That is all."

"He hasn't spoken to you about it?"

He shook his head. "He ask that I meet you, I know you write *Three Musketeers*, so I say fine, but we don't talk."

Well, that's show business. It wasn't my hotel bill or first-class air fares, only my time, and Fellini's, and a phone call could have saved much expense and bother. Mind you, I had no regrets; you don't meet one of the great directors every day, especially one as

266

pleasant and courteous and apparently reluctant to end our meeting abruptly. He and my interpreter conversed at some length in Italian, and whether anything he said gave Fellini second thoughts, I don't know, but presently he turned back to me and asked what my ideas were for the screenplay of *20,000 Leagues.*

I said Dino had asked for a straight adaptation of the book, and that was as far as we'd gone. Fellini nodded and then asked with a smile: "What do you *see*?" I said, not much so far, my deal wasn't settled with Dino, but I had a picture in my mind of the *Nautilus,* at some point or other, lying on the sea bed among the ruins of Atlantis, while an enemy on the surface dropped mines which floated slowly down in trails of silvery bubbles and then exploded in dead silence.

"Is not in the book," he said, and I admitted it wasn't, but was just an idea. He nodded and said: "Silent explosions. No noise. Just ... light." I got the impression that he liked the idea as a visual effect, but I don't recall what else he said at that point, for the talk turned to other things, and it was only after about twenty minutes that he broke off to talk to my interpreter again, and then asked me if I could stay in Rome for a few weeks. I said I couldn't, but why did he ask?

I don't pretend to understand what he meant by his reply, which was that we could talk about the *20,000 Leagues* project, and then he added, searching for words: "Maybe it is like a ... you know, like a musical. But, no, no, I don't mean a musical, only ..." He fluttered a hand, but that was all he said, and then the interpreter, who had been busy on the phone, thrust the receiver at him and said: "Dino."

Italian exchanges followed, friendly enough so far as I could judge, and then Fellini handed me the phone, and I heard those remarkable words, uttered in the dismissive bark of a Roman Emperor washing his hands of Gaul.

"Eh, George ... forget Fellini!" He didn't add, "Who needs

him?" but I suspect he was thinking it. "You come home, we get someone else, okay?"

So that was as close as I got to working with one of the twentieth century's great cinema artists. We talked a little longer and went out to a cafe for more coffee, and I took the opportunity to congratulate him on *Roma*, whose opening sequence matches anything I've ever seen in the cinema for sheer beauty and brilliance of observation. Then we parted (he had a powerful handshake), and I have been wondering ever since what might have happened if I'd stayed in Rome and we had talked about *20,000 Leagues* as a-musical-not-a-musical. What did he have in mind – or was he just saying "something of nice"?

20,000 Leagues never happened. I wrote a script, following Verne pretty closely, for one thing I have learned is that trying to improve on a classic is seldom a good idea; yes, you must adapt and shape and perhaps put a different spin on it, but it is well to bear in mind that it isn't a classic for nothing, and the closer you can follow the author, the better. It never ceases to amaze me, the number of writers who think that they know better than the original, and whose attitude is "What a good idea – now stand back and let me do it my way!" The result is usually a godawful mess. Oh, for David O. Selznick, who never permitted *unnecessary* liberties with masterpieces like *David Copperfield, Tale of Two Cities, Gone with the Wind,* and *Prisoner of Zenda*, and made sure above all that their spirit was respected.

That by the way. My script was shelved (I think I have a letter from Dino somewhere suggesting that we should modernise it) because he wanted me to rewrite *Red Sonja* with Fleischer directing.

So Kathy and I flew to Rome, and stayed at one of the most august and restful hotels I've ever been in, the Grand. It isn't the most modern hostelry in the world, it doesn't have the same nostalgic charm as the Raffles, or the convenience of the Hilton and others, but it has an atmosphere that is all its own. It's terribly Roman, and gives you a strange impression that you can't get any higher in the scale of civilisation. The essence of the Grand was encapsulated for me in a brief incident. Kathy and I were descending the broad stairway to the lobby, and a very old, beautifully dressed gentleman with the profile of a Caesar, was coming up. He was a total stranger to us, but as Kathy neared him he stopped, turned, and bowed to her with an old-world elegance that had plainly taken several centuries to perfect. Regarding him, I thought then, and still do, you've either got, or you haven't got, style.

I don't remember why the script of *Red Sonja* needed attention, for it had been done by a very capable pro, but I know I worked hard on it for two weeks at Dino's studio outside the city (and must have been fairly preoccupied, for when Kathy came back one afternoon from visiting the Sistine Chapel, I asked what must have been the dumbest question of 1984: "What was it like?")

The film was to be a fairly normal Schwarzenegger fantasy, about this gorgeous red-haired Amazon (Brigitte Nielsen), who, with the help of big Arnie and a small princeling skilled in unarmed combat, rescues the dreaded Talisman before the evil queen (who has lesbian designs on Sonja) can use it to blow up the world. There was lashings of blood and swordplay, and fine acrobatic work from Miss Nielsen (whom I met only once, while she was having her hair washed in the make-up department) and little Ernie Reyes, a delightful child whose beaming charm belied his lethal ability at kick-boxing and karate.

Schwarzenegger himself was impressive, not only by reason of his extraordinary physique, but because he was a great deal cleverer than a Mr Universe has any right to be, with a degree in economics and a shrewd interest in the part he was to play – it wasn't Hamlet, exactly, but he wanted it to be more than a mere comic-book cut-out, and had clear ideas of how the hero, Prince Calidor (a name I dredged out of the index to Bullfinch's *Mythology*) should come across. He also had an unexpected sense of humour which emerged when we had dinner with Fleischer and Dino.

The dining room of the Grand was undoubtedly hot, and presently Schwarzenegger slipped off his jacket. An anxious conference of waiters took place, and the maître d. approached and, with perfect courtesy, murmured to Arnold that the wearing of jackets was obligatory. Arnold said, reasonably enough, that it was rather warm, and the maître d. acknowledged this but suggested with winning deference that it wasn't really all *that* warm, and with due respect he must insist on the jacket.

Arnold looked at him, and when you have been looked at by Schwarzenegger you cannot help feeling that it is only a matter of time before you are seen to; it is rather like being regarded by a dissatisfied Easter Island head with muscles to match. My admiration for the maître d. increased; his gulp may have been audible in Ostia, but he stood his ground.

"I'll put on my jacket," said Arnold at length, "if you will put on the air conditioning." He turned slowly in his chair to face the maître d. fully, and you could almost hear his biceps being flexed. The maître d. gave a whimpering noise and a ghastly smile.

"The air conditioning is on," he said.

Arnold frowned. "But you are sweating. Look, I can see you are sweating." Which the maître d. was, and small wonder, but he was still game.

"That," he said, "is because I have been hurrying among the tables." And he added: "Please . . . ?"

What he would have done if Arnold had refused, I can't think but it didn't come to that. Arnold smiled, made a little applauding gesture, and slipped on his jacket, and harmony returned to the dining room of the Grand Hotel.

Red Sonja was given the critical raspberry when it opened. Barry Norman was kind enough to say that he suspected the other writer and I had been unlucky in that mice must have got at the script, but in fact it was all our untampered work, give or take a few economy cuts, and I remain perfectly happy with it. Very well, it is not rated above *Casablanca*, but I still get residuals from exotic foreign parts (I suspect the Japanese have got a thing about Brigitte Nielsen) and the reviews when it is shown on television have got kinder with the passing years.

I liked Dino De Laurentiis, and if I think of him as a very professional and practical man, it is probably because of the last head-to-head talk I had with him. While I was working on *Red Sonja* he had been trying to interest me in scripting an unusual movie: a mystery of which the solution would not be shown on screen, it being left to audiences to come up with the answer for a prize of a million dollars, or near it. I wasn't enthusiastic, and at the last studio conference in his office he suddenly ordered everyone else out, clasped his hands on the desk in front of him, stared at me unwinkingly, and said:

"Okay, George. You like to do this movie?"

I said it wasn't really my cup of tea.

"Okay, George. That's fine." He reached across the table to shake hands, smiling. And that was all; no humming and hawing or unnecessary words, but just straight talk, firm decision, and forget Fraser.

This Unsporting Life

SHORTLY AFTER THE WAR, Keith Miller, the Australian all-rounder, playing in a Test, took a diving catch very low down. The batsman was given out until Miller signalled that the ball had touched the ground before he caught it, the umpire rightly reversed his decision, and the batsman stayed.

Many years later, in a World Cup semi-final, an Argentine footballer prevented a certain goal by Poland by handling the ball on the line. Poland missed the resultant penalty, and Argentina went on to win the tie and, subsequently, the World Cup.

That is the difference between then and now in sport. Miller's act was applauded, but taken for granted in an age when sportsmanship and fair play were the rule rather than the exception. Argentina's blatant cheating was likewise taken for granted, as was their gloating delight when Poland missed the penalty. Perhaps the most deplorable aspect of the affair was that only one of the panel of TV commentators expressed disgust at it; the others shrugged it off as part of the modern game.

It may be that among the professional games players of today there are still a number who would behave as Miller did, but it is doubtful if, in an age when winning is all and money rules, they would get much thanks for it, either from their colleagues or their team's supporters. Most modern professional games players (as distinct from sportsmen) would probably think that Miller was off his head; how many cricketers nowadays would not be content to profit by an umpiring error? And from the sorry spectacle which soccer presents on TV (I was going to say every week, but every waking hour would be nearer the mark) it is obvious that sportsmanship is not at the forefront of the modern footballer's mind. The game has degenerated to a point where anything goes, and the "professional foul" is commonplace – and the spectating public abet the dishonesty, by condoning and even approving it when it suits them.

Possibly it has not occurred to the footballers of today that in winning by cheating they are stealing money from their opponents as surely as though they were to go through their pockets in the dressing-room. But if this were pointed out to them, they would probably shrug and say: "That's different, innit?" And in a new millennium where moral standards have sunk to a nadir, they would probably be sincere in thinking that it was, indeed, different; those are the lights by which they have been brought up, God help them.

Nor are cheating and hooliganism confined to football. Cricket Test captains have been seen tampering with balls, reviling umpires, and exchanging insults with opponents; deliberate attempts to maim are not uncommon in rugby, drug-taking in athletics has increased to an alarming extent, and even in such a supposedly genteel game as tennis the lowest kind of foul-mouthed guttersnipe is allowed to bring Wimbledon into disrepute – and the public not only tolerate this, but enjoy it.

It is common to blame professionalism for the decline in standards, and it has been argued that the man who plays for fun has less reason to act dishonestly than the man who plays for a living. But that is not quite fair. There are honourable and decent professionals in all games, and some sports whose participants set a standard which the general public would do well to emulate – snooker, for example, and golf, although the good behaviour of players in the latter does not always extend to the spectators, especially in the United States. And even in soccer there are still, I am sure, players as honest and well-behaved as Stanley Matthews, and that immaculate gentleman of Hearts and Scotland whose sportsmanship was such a byword that it was said that "the dirtiest thing in football is a foul on Tommy Walker". But the Matthewses and Walkers are a much rarer breed today – and I wonder how many modern managers would explode with rage when one of their young players pulled an opponent's jersey, as I saw Bill Shankly do when he was managing Carlisle – and it was only a practice game at that. He played to win, but not at any price. He played clean.*

Paradoxically, it is not professionalism but money that has ruined soccer – not the ridiculous overpayment of the leading players, although that has done nothing to raise standards, but the total transformation of a sport into a commercial racket. The huge lucrative TV deal, the profits of European competition at club and international level, the exorbitant admission fees to games (in which, contrary to the inane euphoric outpourings of sports writers, standards of skill are certainly no higher than they were half a century ago, and entertainment value is considerably less), the disgraceful profiteering of those clubs who change their strips regularly to cash in on the youth market – all these things have combined with lower standards of conduct on the field, and on the terracing, to render ugly and squalid the once-beautiful game.

To be sure, hooliganism on and off the pitch is nothing new. There were persistent cheats and foulers in the old days, but they were a despised minority, held in contempt by players and public. I won't say that "going over the top" or diving were unknown, but they were certainly rarer than they are now, and one seldom saw the deliberate assaults that disfigure the game today, the hooligan

---

* But I have to admit that having delivered his rebuke, he added: "Ye wantin' tae give away a bluidy penalty?"

harassment and filthy language to which referees are subjected, or the contempt shown to the paying public. At worst, the players' conduct is that of a jungle; at best of a demented kindergarten where the scoring of a goal is greeted by a frenzy of congratulation, imbecile gesturing and capering, and slobbering embraces, usually in a heap on the ground. To quote Gussie Fink-Nottle, it alters one's conception of man as Nature's last word.

And it cannot be truthfully said that such uncontrolled idiocy is harmless; lack of restraint in exultation very easily spreads to the play itself, and results in the petulant fouling and vicious assault which are now everyday. And boys, alas, copy their sporting heroes. Even more deplorably, parents at school matches all too often seem to model their behaviour on that of senior supporters.

But while football continues merely to play at discipline, with such nonsense as its red and yellow card system, whereby a player can be banished from the field for a technical offence, or even handling the ball, while the most vicious kind of thuggery can pass unpunished, it will continue to degenerate. The card system, by its automatic nature which implicitly denies judgment and common sense in match officials, has done nothing but harm to the game, while signally failing to raise standards of conduct among players.

Yet the remedy is obvious and simple. The mannerless lout, the persistent fouler, the screamer of insults at the referee, the indescribable low life who bares his bottom in contempt of the crowd, are at present fined or suspended for "bringing the game into disrepute" – a wonderfully silly expression, since it is the offender, not the game, that is disreputable. Slapping him on the wrist is useless; he should be permanently banned from the game which he has disgraced, and never allowed on a football field again. Let this be done, and hooliganism will depart the scene like yesterday's snow. It's easy, the sine die suspension (known in Glasgow as "syne dye") worked fifty years ago; it would work today.

But it will never get the chance, because the football authorities, taking their cue from government, are a spineless lot unwilling to deal effectively with the troublemakers. Think what it would cost the clubs to have their spoiled brats suddenly rendered worthless. What it would cost in terms of European and international failure, in hugely profitable TV deals jeopardised – and what it might well cost, in today's compensation-mad culture, in damages awarded (by the European Court, who else?) to whining malcontents banished from the game.

No, it won't happen. It would take courage and honesty and intelligence far beyond the capacity of football legislators.

On a lighter note . . . and yet it is one which has turned me, and I dare swear many others, away from spectating quite as effectively as what I see on the field. I refer to the much (but insufficiently) maligned television commentators whose inane, uneducated, useless babble destroys any enjoyment one might get from watching sport. Because they are disembodied voices, they are beyond our reach; if one had the dreadful misfortune to find oneself on the terracing alongside such a garrulous ignorant bore who insisted on deafening one with his uninformed, ungrammatical drivel, usually in a street-corner accent, one would be justified in striking him to the ground. But all one can do is turn down the volume, and possibly miss, once in about three hours, a nugget of interest emerging from a morass of turgid, opinionated tripe. Their ghastly efforts have been defended on the ground that sport should be "dramatised", which overlooks the plain fact that if a thing isn't dramatic in itself, no amount of fatuous commentary is going to make it so.

Oh, for Maskell and Arlott and Longhurst, great men in their time who did not labour under the modern conceit that what they said was more important than the game itself. That is the plague of televised sport, the great swatches of time before and after an event given over to interminable panel discussions by professional windbags from whom one would run a mile in pub or club, players equipped neither by God nor their schoolteachers to utter intelligently, or even intelligibly in some cases, and managers of limited vocabulary with nothing sensible to say.

Ah, well, backgammon's not a bad game, uncursed with commentators or interviews . . . oh, dear, why do I tempt providence?

The Ones that Got Away

FOR EVERY FILM that reaches the screen, a dozen don't. Many projects consist of only a phone call asking: "Are you interested?" followed by silence, others expire at the discussion stage, some get as far as synopsis (or treatment, I've never been clear on the difference), and a few, like *Taipan* and *The Lone Ranger*, become screenplays only to vanish into limbo. Producers are the world's greatest optimists. They dream dreams, buy rights, commission scripts, sign up stars, wheel and deal, sometimes spend millions of dollars (occasionally even their own) on pre-production, go crazy . . . and then more often than not the project has to be abandoned for any of a score of reasons – the money runs out, studios or backers get cold feet, the rights revert, negotiations break down, or the thing just dies of natural causes. Which doesn't stop a producer trying again, and again, and so on ad infinitum.

For a writer, stillborn productions are not necessarily unrewarding, at least in financial terms, and I've heard one eminent author say that writing unproduced scripts for which you've been paid is an ideal arrangement. I can't agree, for while I've been well paid for screenplays which never reached production, I have an aversion, probably born of newspaper work, to writing for the spike. I want to see it up there on the screen, if only because it keeps actors and crews off street corners and I can feel I've given the producers their money's worth. I know there is a general callousness towards those who finance and organise pictures, but I hate it when they've paid me and finish up out of pocket. Eccentric, no doubt, and certainly Presbyterian.

There are occasions, to be sure, when you work and don't get paid. This has happened to me more than once, but I shan't name the defaulters because some of them at least tried, and anyway the motion picture industry and the enthusiastic optimists who finance it have rewarded me so generously over the past thirty years that I feel it is I who owe them. All told I'm out only a few thousand bucks, and most film professionals would say: "Think yourself lucky."

So far as I can judge I've also been lucky in the percentage of my scripts which actually got made into movies. I've just said that the number of stillborn projects outnumbers films produced by twelve to one, but that was a random remark, and I'd guess the figure is considerably higher. So my tally of eight films made, out of eighteen screenplays written, is well above average, thanks entirely to my good luck in working for top-drawer producers who were artists as well as *poets d'argent*. At least one of the films I worked on didn't wash its face at the box-office, but the others turned a profit, some of them astronomically, so I can sleep at nights. (It's the same with publishers' advances: I hate them, simply in case I don't earn them.)

How many projects I've been on which didn't get the length of screenplays I can't be sure; you get some weird and wonderful proposals, and if like me you're only a part-time screenwriter, more concerned with books than with movies, some of the wilder turkeys fade from memory. So the following list of pictures written, synopsised, discussed, or just briefly considered, which I haven't dealt with so far, may not be complete. Some I regret losing, others I was glad to be shot of, but most of them were fun while they lasted.

My only television film, *Casanova*, already briefly referred to, was a happy experience with two excellent Hollywood producers,

Frank Konigsberg and Larry Sanitsky, who were among the most professional I've ever worked with. Half of the principal players I'd written for on previous pictures: Richard Chamberlain, who played Casanova, Frank Finlay, Faye Dunaway, Christopher Lee, Roy Kinnear and Jean-Pierre Cassel among them; a fine supporting cast included Ken Colley and Richard Griffiths, and Casanova's ladies were, appropriately, a thoroughly international bevy, including Ornella Muti, Hannah Schygulla, Sylvia Kristel, and Sophie Ward. Simon Langton directed, and the whole thing went like a writer's dream; I had one airport conference with the producers (and since I'd never met them, there I was at Terminal 4 self-consciously carrying a board which read: CASANOVA). We had a couple of three-way phone calls with Chamberlain, and that was it; I must have rewritten some of my first draft, but I don't remember it. Would that all movies were so simple, and so rewarding.

I have seen no reason to name the producers of the following films that never were. Suffice to say that they were good folk who did their level best to get their projects under way.

UNPRODUCED SCREENPLAYS

The General Danced at Dawn. This was a dramatisation of one of my own novels, commissioned by an eccentric Scots-American. It died short of pre-production in 1972.

Prince of Thieves. This was a literary curiosity: Alexandre Dumas' version of Robin Hood, and a spirited piece of work it is, much shorter and more tightly written than the average Dumas, and ideal for an action movie. Kevin Costner's film of 1991 had the same title, but was in no way connected.

Bulldog Drummond. I can't recall that my script bore much resemblance to any of Sapper's novels, since it chiefly concerned

Drummond's feud with a criminal mastermind who had discovered an instantly addictive drug and was preparing to flood the world with it.

Hannah was an adaptation of a massive novel based on the life of Helena Rubinstein. It was to be directed by the late Jack Clayton, but he and I did not see eye to eye, and the project folded.

Thirteen Against the Bank was a lovely true story about a very odd character who had devised a means whereby a team of players could beat the roulette wheel. He recruited his team, a mixture of eccentrics and perfectly ordinary people, by advertising in the papers, and they went to Monte Carlo and actually broke the bank and were barred by the casino authorities. It didn't go beyond first draft.

The Lone Ranger, despite problems with my politically incorrect first draft, already alluded to, would have made a rousing action movie, and John Landis and I had good fun with it so far as it went, which as I recall was to revisions on my third draft. It had every Western character, cliché, and incident imaginable, but it perished when the rights, which I gathered had been the subject of heavy negotiations beforehand, ceased to be available, having run out or reverted or gone walkabouts or something. It's one I regret losing, but not having worked on. Landis and I got on like ham and eggs.

William Tell was a bit of a heartbreaker, because it could have been a blockbuster. Like Robin Hood, he's a semi-mythical figure, but with a firmer place in history, and I was able to use the legendary stuff (with, I think, an entirely new twist on the apple-shooting incident) as well as the facts of the Swiss struggle for independence, including their spectacular victory over the Austrians at Mortgarten in 1315. Yes, given the money and Lester or Fleischer directing, it could have been big.

The Ice People came from a most imaginative novel by a French author, and I suppose could be called sci-fi. Antarctic explorers discover the remnants of a buried civilisation, including a man and woman who are revived from deep freeze, and the story consists in part of a flashback to prehistory showing how the civilisation ended and the two became entombed.

Berry and Co, or it may have been another Dornford Yates title, I can't be sure, was proposed to me by the most unlikely director imaginable, Lindsay Anderson. I'd never read a Yates story, and for those who share my ignorance I should explain that, on my acquaintance with that one book, he struck me as being quite some distance to the right of Bismarck; if you think Buchan, Sapper, and P. C. Wren are the ultimate reactionaries, you haven't met our Dornford. For example, the heroes of the romantic thriller which Anderson wanted to film were excruciatingly upper class, and had their forelock-tugging personal attendants, the social distinctions being rigidly observed even when the party were besieged and under fire. I don't say that a wounded valet ever asked permission to bleed, but there was an air of beg-pardon-sir-for-not-laying-out-your-hacking-jacket-but-I've-been-shot about the thing that seemed totally out of keeping with Anderson's radical Free Cinema reputation.

My first thought, which I voiced when we met, was that he wanted the story and characters sent up or satirised (which heaven knows wouldn't have been difficult), but I was wrong: he wanted it straight-faced, and for two hours or so we discussed blood and thunder – it was rather like having Thomas Carlyle enthusing about *Sergeant Fury and the Howling Commandos*, or so it seemed to me. And yet, why not? It may be that inside every serious radical-intellectual film-maker there is a mad swashbuckler roaring and slashing to get out. But if this was the case with Lindsay Anderson, he fought it down, or perhaps thought better of it, for the project went no further.

Stortebekker was a medieval German pirate, or so I was informed by Wolfgang Petersen when he invited me to Munich to discuss a production based on his blood-soaked career. I felt I was an odd choice as writer, and Petersen, whom I remember as tall, blond, and very Germanic (I see him as Hardy Kruger) may have reached the same conclusion, for although that talk lasted some hours, it was the only one we had. I have no memory of Munich apart from its airport, where I and fellow-passengers discovered that our homeward flight had been overbooked and we were stranded, which provoked from the back of the check-in queue a North Country bellow of "No wonder you lost the bloody war!" All that lingers in mind of Stortebekker himself is that according to legend he continued to run about after being beheaded. I can't say I'm sorry the project died; the only one I can think of that was less attractive was the proposal, to Dick Lester and me, that we should undertake Rabelais's *Gargantua* and *Pantagruel*. We decided that leading men forty or fifty feet tall would be difficult to handle.

Quentin Durward has some claim to being the best adventure story Walter Scott ever wrote, and why the 1955 Robert Taylor–Kay Kend-all version departed so far from the original plot I can't imagine. I thought I was lucky to be given such a brilliantly constructed swashbuckler with such splendid characters, and stuck as close to Scott as I could. The last I heard efforts were being made to get it under way in California, but I'm not optimistic.

20,000 Leagues Under the Sea for Dino De Laurentiis I have already covered; likewise *Taipan*. That was the really big one that got away ... but that's show business.

Along the way I have done treatments (or synopses) for Conan Doyle's *Brigadier Gerard* and *The Lost World* (the latter partly scripted), and have discussed, to varying lengths, such assorted subjects as Dan Dare, Sherlock Holmes, a projected remake of *Quo*

Vadis? (not a good idea, I thought), a sequel to *Tom Jones* (an even worse idea), and a sci-fi extravaganza called *Colossus* for which I still have storyboards, drawings, and someone else's script, but what it was all about has faded from memory.

Another that unfortunately ended at the discussion stage was Richard Dreyfuss's excellent idea for a film based on the premise that the American Revolution never happened, thus enabling the most famous private eye, Sir Samuel Spade, to investigate a modern mystery. And I also regret an American producer's failure to fulfil his ambition to film a Rider Haggard novel; when he asked me if I was familiar with the author I was able to stun him into gratifying silence by saying: "My father buried Alan Quatermain." (This was true. Quatermain was based on the famous white hunter, F. C. Selous, who was killed in East Africa in the First World War, when commanding the Legion of Frontiersmen, to which my father had been attached as medical officer.)

And there was a mysterious phone caller who claimed to have rights in a Hornblower novel, and would I like to write it with Michael Caine in the title role? I'm still waiting for a second call, but doubt if I'll get it, having learned later from Caine himself that he'd never heard of the producer or his project. And that, too, is show business.

It's been an interesting, rewarding, and erratic career in films, and I wouldn't have missed it for anything. It taught me a lot, principally about writing – making a few words or even a silence do the work of a scene (thank you, Steve McQueen), playing to an actor's strength, the importance of seeing it in your mind and hearing it in your ear and knowing how it will play. You'll never master it, or even come close, but at least you learn what to try for. For the rest, get a good agent, hope the fates give you good directors and performers, and get the money up front.

One thing I have not learned: what, precisely, is the British film industry? The films I've worked on, while they've usually had

American directors, and often continental producers, have had largely British casts and crews, and have been made for the most part out of Pinewood and Twickenham. Where the money to make them has come from, I don't know, but I suspect that it has not been raised in the United Kingdom, and that, I rather think, disqualifies them as "British" productions. None of them has had government finance, thank God, for that seems to put the kiss of death on projects with almost unfailing regularity. I suppose movies like the Musketeers and *Octopussy* should be called international productions, but I would like to be put out of my uncertainty and hear an authoritative pronouncement on what is, and is not, a British film.

For the Record

*A*ND THAT, *for the moment at any rate, is that, so far as the film business and my manly rage against the bludgeonings of fate, change, decay, politicians, political correctness, etc., are concerned – at least until some optimist asks me to do another screenplay (unlikely) or some new evil or folly needs to be smitten and scorned (all too probable). Thus far it has been a fairly rambling, eccentric sort of book, no doubt intemperate on occasion, though not without good cause, and I make no apology for it: the polemical stuff needed saying, if only because I'm shot if I'll go silent into that good night, whenever it falls, and I couldn't leave my memoirs of the wonderful, crazy, enchanting world of movies unwritten.*

But it's not the whole story by a long chalk, and it strikes me that if ever there was a convenient space for G.M.F. His Life and Times, this is it. I haven't the inclination or patience (or conceit) for a pukka autobiography, so what follows is just a backward glance at a life which I must not say has so far been happy or lucky, because if I do the Chinese gods will fix my wagon. So I record it without comment.

Unlike P. G. Wodehouse, who confessed to having spent the first five years of his life "just loafing, I suppose", I may well have decided at the age of three to become an author, and taken the first tentative steps in that direction. It seems that at bedtimes I would frequently excuse my parents from telling me a story, and insist on telling them one about myself and a fictional companion, Georgie Henderson. I don't remember this, or any details of the stories themselves, but I have my parents' word for it that I would recount lurid adventures of Georgie and myself; whether this sent them to sleep or not I have no means of knowing.

Perhaps this was something in the blood. My ancestry is entirely Highland Scottish, Celtic-Norman-Viking mostly, and they have always been great story-tellers; my own grandmothers, one a Glencoe MacDonald and the other a Hebridean MacNeill, used to hold me spellbound with their tales; for that matter, everyone in the family told stories, usually of a quite sensational nature, which is right in the Celtic tradition – as witness the names of Scott, Stevenson, Buchan, Ian Fleming, J. M. Barrie, Conan Doyle, and many others. Romance and adventure are at the heart of Scottish literature – or rather, since literature is a pretentious word, at the heart of their storytelling. Anyway, for whatever reason, the bug of the *senachie*, the Highland teller of tales, seems to have bitten me early, and has never let go.

My father was a family doctor, the son of a grocer in the village of Cardross, near Glasgow. Grandpa Fraser had left his people's croft in Sutherland as a boy, walking south to Glasgow to find employment, and sustaining himself on his southern journey with oatmeal and water mixed in his shoe. He prospered, and two of his four children, my father and an uncle, graduated in medicine at Glasgow University, thanks to the "Carnegie money" which Andrew Carnegie provided for young Scots who couldn't afford the tuition fees. At Glasgow Royal Infirmary my father met and married a nursing sister, Anne Struth Donaldson, in 1916, and then went off to war in East Africa where he became Captain William Fraser, Royal Army Medical Corps, serving briefly with the Legion of Frontiersmen, a remarkable group of adventurers too old for normal military service, but enlisted for their irregular experience and knowledge of rough service.

Having come out of the war with a wound a̶ [̶
Despatches, my father, like many another young Sco̶
came south after the war, and settled in Carlisle, the Bord̶
which had been England's northern bulwark in the old days. M̶
sister Ila (named after my Hebridean grandmother's island birth-
place) was born in 1920, and I followed in 1925, on April 2, a
birthdate which I share with Hans Andersen and Casanova, and
that piece of irrelevant information is typical of my talent for
accumulating trivial and utterly useless knowledge which I will share
at the drop of a hat. (What did Claude Rains drop in a wastebasket
at the end of *Casablanca*? Who were the quartermasters on *HMS
Bounty*? What was the name of Tarzan's ape mother? These things
remain, but don't ask me what exegesis means.)

My birth took place in a house built on the site of a medieval
leper colony (my mother claimed that she suffered from a sore
throat all through our occupation), but when I was two we moved
to a house which my father had built on a hill in the suburbs,
where the ancient Britons had had a fort, or *curragh*, hence the
district's name, Currock. And there I had a very happy childhood,
climbing trees, playing football, killing pirates and redskins in the
woods nearby, being chased off railway property by gruff men in
big boots, and running in gangs with like-minded urchins. My
education began in a small private school from which I was once
sent home in disgrace for saying "piss" (female teachers were easily
shocked in 1930) and was continued at Carlisle Grammar School,
a foundation of immense antiquity – officially it was twelfth century,
but it traced its history back six hundred years before that, to the
days when Christianity came to the Border country.

Like the dear old red city itself, the school had survived more
than a thousand years of siege and battle, of invasion by Norse
sea-rovers, medieval Scottish armies, Cromwell's Ironsides, and
Prince Charlie's Highlanders; its boys had helped the townsfolk man
the city walls against Bruce's besiegers after Bannockburn, and played

the entertainment of Mary Queen of
... ...dured those turbulent centuries when
... ...ominated by the terrible armed bands of
... ...border reivers who created a lawless no-
... ...gland and Scotland in Queen Elizabeth's time
... those riding brigands were identical with the
... in my class at school, if not with mine, for I
... ...atman and forroner", and I learned much about
racism ... rivalry, if not about race hatred, in those early
years under the chestnut trees of the old school, with its strange
traditions and catchphrases which Chaucer might have recognised.

It was officially what was called a "public" school, which in
England conjures images of exclusive, privileged education of the
kind provided by Eton and Harrow, from whom it could not have
differed more dramatically. The old grammar schools carried the
cachet of "public" simply because of their age, and Carlisle Grammar School from time immemorial had educated, without social
distinction, the cleverest boys in the city, who entered it annually
after competitive examination. I was not among them; I was one
of the few whose fathers paid the annual £10 fee, and was consequently in danger of being swamped scholastically by the flood of
talent that poured in from the elementary schools each year. I
languished miserably at the bottom of my class in French, Latin,
maths, and the sciences, but perplexed my fellows by coming first
in English and history. Not that that mattered, any more than it
mattered whether you were a fee-payer or a free scholar; the leading
brains with their eyes on Oxford and Cambridge scholarships might
compete with a ferocity worthy of their bandit ancestors, but for
the rest it was games that counted, and I could hold my own at
cricket and rugby, and aspire to championship at fives, that brutal
and ancient fore-runner of squash which left you with red and
swollen palms after an hour of thrashing a hard and tiny ball with
your bare hands.

It was a strange, wonderful education, in much more than book learning. That old school took you in, whoever and whatever you were, and wrapped you up and absorbed you in a tradition that went back almost to the time when King Arthur sat in "Merrie Caerlile" and Childe Roland set off on his mythical pilgrimage. You wore the black and gold jacket and the cap with its odd hollow star as though they were robes of honour (which, of course, they were) and sang the school song, which naturally, unlike any other school anthem, was a blood-thirsty war-chant about the city's desperate past, with an intense but only half-understood pride. Children who grow up in the shadow of Hadrian's Wall, and invade the city museum to sit in its ancient punishment stocks, and scramble over the very chair in which Bonny Prince Charlie slept, and view the graffiti scratched by prisoners of war in the battered old Cathedral where Cromwell stabled his horses, and play on the battlements where Edward I and Richard III once walked – such children tend to take history for granted and give it little thought. Perhaps I was different; outman and forroner though I was, the Border City left its mark on me, and on my voice (for I can slip with perfect ease into that strange snarling dialect that is the Cumbrian speech).

The Grammar School has gone now, a millennium and more of incalculable worth and tradition swept away by socialist reformers to whom competitive examination seems to be anathema; what Bruce couldn't subdue has been destroyed in the name of "progress". It taught me more of life than it did of learning; my education, such as it has been, was founded on ten volumes of Arthur Mee's *Children's Encyclopedia* which my parents bought for my sister and me in a moment which I can only count inspired. Hour after hour I seem to have spent, prone on the carpet on summer afternoons when sunlight fell on the pages, and winter days with the rain lashing the windows, lost in those marvellous volumes.

I went for the stories, at first, the tales and fables of every land on earth, but the genius of Mee's work was that to get from one section of stories to another you had to leaf through pages of poetry and painting and natural history and science-simply-explained – it was just one dam' thing after another: coloured pre-Raphaelite paintings and verses by Shakespeare and Browning and pictures of volcanoes erupting and proverbs and puzzles and How To Make Your Own Telephone With A Tin Can And A Piece Of String (which didn't work) and How To Blow Over A Brick (which did, oddly enough – you use a paper bag) and photographs of Italian statues and French churches and Albanian peasants and snakes and Turkish janissaries and spiders ("Little Many Legs" was the caption to a tarantula, so help me) and illustrations of famous people's autographs from Erasmus to Oliver Wendell Holmes, and stuff about Greek philosophy and Egyptian burial rituals and religion and history and you-name-it, it was all there – and some of it stuck. Haphazard, no doubt, disorganised and random, but if there is a name that I thank God for, it is that of Arthur Mee, whose books influenced me more than any other.

It was, by modern standards, hopelessly reactionary, being thoroughly Christian and British Imperial, preaching values which are now thought outmoded, and inculcating lessons which are no longer taught. It was strong on duty and responsibility and discipline and good manners; it was not, repeat not, politically correct, for it was honest and true. Not that I imagine I came away from it a better and wiser child; I was only there for the information and the pictures and statues and stories and Six Easy Tricks A Boy Can Do With An Empty Matchbox. And I have seen to it that my three sets of grandchildren have the *Children's Encyclopedia*. Who knows, they too may be entranced by the picture of some emperor or other picking up Titian's brush for him, and Michelangelo striking the rock and bringing out Moses, and even Little Many Legs, when their computers and electronic games break down.

But if Arthur Mee was the bedrock, the icing on top were the prizes my father had won at school – books by R. M. Ballantyne and his like, telling tales of high adventure far away, and Hawthorne's *Wonder Book and Tanglewood Tales* (which I know I was reading at the age of five, for it was a Christmas present with the date inscribed), and Norse Legends, and Kingsley's *Heroes*, and the children's writers of the time, Grahame and Milne and, inevitably, *Alice*, and the "tuppenny bloods", those boys' weekly magazines like *Wizard* and *Hotspur*, packed with stories about cowboys and buccaneers and secret agents and defenders of the Empire – no wonder I finished up writing the same kind of stuff. Nor was comedy neglected – that immortal work, *1066 And All That*, had just come out (and I maintain that there is no better starting point for a serious study of history than that book), and when I was eight I encountered a writer who was my humorous hero then and still is: Stephen Leacock. When I borrowed *Nonsense Novels* from the grammar school library a lordly prefect assured me that I wouldn't understand it; the finer nuances may have escaped me, but I laughed myself sick over it nonetheless. No writer surely was ever so funny with so few words.

And then when I was ten the thunderbolt struck. His name was Sabatini, and he opened up the past for me as he has done for millions – many of them writers. His great art was to present history not as a dry chronicle of names and dates and treaties, but as a real drama, an unending adventure story that far outstripped fiction, related in an elegant, sophisticated, half-cynical style that bore the reader effortlessly along. Critical opinion has not been kind to him, probably because he sold in vast quantities and translated easily to the cinema – that was another formative experience, watching open-mouthed as the curtains parted and Erich Wolfgang Korngold's trumpets came thundering out over the credits of *Captain Blood*.

The cinema, to my generation, was what television is today, discouraged by teachers and parents, but caviare to the general. We patrolled the North-West Frontier with Gary Cooper and Victor

McLaglen, went hand in hand through Sherwood and across the Spanish Main with Errol Flynn, sauntered nonchalantly through the dungeons of Zenda and the sands of Algeria with Ronald Colman (and learned much of courtly behaviour and imperturbable style from that hero); mimicked the wisecracks of Cagney, and fell about at Laurel and Hardy. Tom Mix and *Barrack-Room Ballads*; soccer stars and the poems of Henry Newbolt, Alfred Noyes, and Walter de la Mare; Edward G. Robinson and Drake going west; Cecil DeMille and Tchaikovsky's *Chanson Triste* and Mendelssohn's *Spring Song* (scraped out execrably on the violin my parents had insisted on my learning); vague names like Hitler and Mussolini in the background – it was a strange, mixed culture into which algebra and Latin verbs and Archimedes' principle hardly intruded; no wonder my parents, despairing of school reports which included remarks like "A strict neutral in the battle for knowledge", decided I needed a proper education, and a Scottish education at that.

The choice lay between George Watson's in Edinburgh, and Glasgow Academy, both prestigious public schools. Watson's building looked new and energetic, but there was a trail of blood spots on one of its marbled corridors, and I voted for Glasgow Academy, which looked more used and familiar and informal, and the boys were a friendly, slightly raffish lot. I was to be a boarder, and I suspect my father was impressed by the boarding-house master, a bald and commanding ex-Indian Army officer, Captain John Colman Smith, with a cold eye and a parade-ground bark, usually of "What-what?" and "You silly young fool!"

"Coley" was a martinet, and as kind and decent a man as I have ever known. He and his wife ran the house of thirty boys (reduced to four in the first year of the war) fairly and strictly; it was an education you didn't get at home; you made your own bed, polished your shoes, looked after your own clothes and effects, and learned to take care of yourself in a way which was to pay dividends later. Coley was in charge of the Academy's games, coaching the rugby team with fanatical energy, and it did me no harm that I was a competent full back and fast bowler, eventually winning my first team colours at rugby and cricket. But rugby was *the* game, played at a level unknown in Carlisle, and I thanked God I was a back and not a forward as I watched Coley training the heaving, straining pack, belabouring the crouched mass of bodies with his umbrella and bellowing "Get that bottom down!" He was also in charge of the school gymnasium, and during the war was employed by the BBC to keep the nation fit with early-morning broadcasts in which his stentorian commands ran through the length and breadth of the British Isles.

Coley was a great man of the old school, what used to be called an English gentleman, and ruled by personality alone; he never needed to use corporal punishment, which was common in the school itself.

Scholastically, Glasgow Academy was formidable. Its brightest boys won exhibitions and scholarships to the great universities, and for the rest it turned out aspiring doctors, lawyers, accountants, and businessmen for what was then one of the world's great mercantile centres. Among its alumni were the playwrights J. M. Barrie and James Bridie; Lord Reith, founder of the BBC, and the musical comedy star, Jack Buchanan. Its teaching staff in my time was a curious mixture of Scots in the old, sound pedagogic tradition, and Englishmen, most of them young and enthusiastic sportsmen, from Oxford and Cambridge. They gave probably as good an education as was obtainable anywhere on earth, and if I continued on my placid way, first in English and nowhere in any other subject, it was not their fault. And one of them at least was a profound influence on my life, not by his teaching but by his unstinting encouragement: he was the man who convinced me that I was a writer.

His name was Walter Barradell-Smith, head of English, and himself a prolific author of school stories for boys under the name of

Richard Bird. He was small, sturdy, grizzled of hair and crimson of face, which earned him the nickname Beery, apparently irascible in speech and manner but invariably good-humoured and, to me at least, a priceless friend. Until I met him, I hadn't thought of myself as a writer; indeed, I felt that English composition was something I wasn't very good at. Beery never taught me to write; he never even said I might have a talent that way; he simply treated me as though I *was* already a writer at the age of thirteen, marking my essays extravagantly (it seemed to me) whatever the subject, whatever I wrote. Analysis and parsing I knew nothing about, and don't try me even now; I was in my forties before I discovered what an adverb was. Beery didn't seem to care; he simply returned my essays with eighteen or nineteen out of twenty every time, and when I ignored the subject he'd set for composition, and took off on some wild flight of my own, he would smile and nod and say nothing as he appended the inevitable high mark.

Gradually I came to accept that this was something I could do; after all, he was a professional judging by professional standards, so who was I to argue? When I was about sixteen, Coley summoned me to his study, smiling for once, and told me that he had heard Beery enthusing in the common room about some youngster who was going to make a name as a writer, and on inquiry discovered that he was talking about me. That impressed me, and I began to wonder about perhaps being an author some day – heaven knew I wasn't educationally equipped to be anything else, and it was wartime anyway, and the Army would soon beckon, and writing or any other career would have to wait. Beery himself continued to say nothing, just marking me as highly as ever, and I would suggest to any teacher who thinks he has a budding writer on his hands, that he LEAVE HIM ALONE to write whatever he pleases the way he wants to write it. That was what Beery did with me, and however far short I may have fallen of the name he prophesied for me, it is thanks to him I've made a living doing what I like best.

One thing he did teach me, a love for Shakespeare. He took us through *Henry IV*, himself playing Falstaff with a gusto worthy of the Old Vic; then it was *Henry V, Hamlet, Macbeth*, and the comedies, and by some magic he brought it all to life so that the classroom became the Globe and we the players, with himself the star. He even inspired me to take part in a school production of *Hamlet*, but I was demoted from Laertes to Francisco for losing my temper in rehearsing the duel and trying to kill the Prince of Denmark.

Strange, I can remember only one thing Beery said on the subject of writing: "Never say that someone is a bad writer. I once read *Tarzan of the Apes*, and thought it most appallingly written ... until I thought, 'No, this man has caught the imagination of untold millions with his words. How on earth can he be called a bad writer?'"

I left the Academy in the middle of the war, with no academic qualifications whatever, and only two prizes, for English and general knowledge – oh, and a cup for throwing the cricket ball. Whenever my eye falls on the general knowledge prize today (it was *The Savoy Operas*), I'm reminded of a splendid contest once held in the United States to find the champion of sheer trivia and useless information, the winner being presented with a plastic bucket while the assembled competitors sang: "There he goes, think of all the crap he knows." I wish I could have taken part.

My parents' hopes that I would follow my father into medicine had long since dissolved in the face of my abysmal exam results, and Glasgow University wouldn't look at me, to my profound relief, for I had only one thought, and that was to get into the war. The Army agreed, and presently I found myself 14687347, Private Fraser, G.M., in a draughty Nissen hut in the windswept grounds of a castle in County Durham, along with thirty other assorted conscripts, one-third of them gypsies and illiterate. We were taught to march and drill and shoot and stick bayonets into canvas dummies, all of which I knew already, having been in the military cadet force known as the Officers' Training Corps at school. It was assumed that if you'd been to a public school you would become an officer, and while that early martial training gave me an advantage, I'm not sure that what I'd learned as a school boarder about looking after myself and my effects, to say nothing of discipline and prompt obedience, wasn't more valuable still. At least I wasn't as bemused as my fellows in that strange, hostile environment of screaming instructors, iron routine, and mysterious rituals which seemed to have no point but to bewilder and dismay. I'd been there before.

But it was a strange new world just the same. When the North Country Englishman is disoriented he usually gets aggressive, and that barrack-room was no place for the faint-hearted; you could see the embryonic bullies, the keen types who welcomed the imposition of disciplined order, the patient plodders, the misfits and eccentrics, emerging in those first few weeks, and note the odd contrasts: the animal squalor and obscenity of some, the quiet acceptance of others, the hopeless terror of a few, and the bovine stolidity of the massive young farmhand in the bunk next to mine, who knelt to say his prayers every night. A few of the gypsies jeered, and one (nature imitating the art of *Tom Brown's Schooldays*) threw a boot at him, and had to be revived by his associates; the farmhand wasn't as bovine as he looked.

Personally, I kept quiet, not acting too good nor talking too wise (thank you, Kipling), impatient to be done with a regime which had less to do with training than with what the Army called getting us "sorted out". I resisted an attempt by the authorities to send me to the Signal Corps because I knew Morse; the infantry, and nothing but the infantry, was what I wanted, and with a real regiment. There were many irritants about primary training – being taught what I knew already; sleeping in coarse blankets (no sheets then) in my shirt, for while I had a pair of pyjamas in my kitbag, wearing them in that company would have been like passing port

298

to the right; getting a raw neck from damp chafing serge on rain-swept parade grounds; having no nocturnal toilet facilities except a large iron bucket outside the hut in the icy darkness, but worst of all, having to wear the plastic badge of the General Service Corps which somehow made me feel only half a soldier, and a pretty scruffy one at that.

All that changed when I was posted to a young soldiers' unit for potential officers at Derby. There we were all eager teenagers, the non-com instructors had been hand-picked, the training was far harder but considerably more advanced, standards of dress, drill, deportment and performance were immeasurably higher – and we knew that at the end of two months we would be sent to selection boards to see if we were fit for officer training. That was the Holy Grail – a commission, and being young and keen and ambitious we drilled and marched and shot and hurled ourselves over assault courses and hung on the lips of lecturers as though nothing else in life mattered – which it didn't, then. We knew the Army was taking us seriously (and vice versa), and if ever we were in danger of forgetting it there was the awe-inspiring figure of Regimental Sergeant-Major Charlie Bradley of the Coldstream Guards to remind us. He was one of those legendary Guards RSMs, like Freddy Archer and Paddy Flynn, but even more celebrated, a tall, spare immaculate terror of a man with a piercing eye and a word of command that would have petrified Napoleon. The sight of him coming on parade, straight as a lance, pace-stick and peaked cap at the exact angle, crashing to a perfect halt, and sweeping the ranks with that dreadful glare (Gerald Kersh the novelist swore that Bradley could detect a missing trifle of equipment in a full battalion) was truly frightening; when that fearsome shriek of command struck your ear you could be in no doubt that you were in the Army now.

I met him at close range only once, as a trembling member of a guard being inspected, and it was a revelation. I knew I was as smart as several hours of frantic scrubbing and polishing could make me, but when that cold eye was turned on me I knew real panic. Then he spoke, very softly: "Easy, lad. You'll do," and passed on his magisterial way. Not surprisingly, I have a high regard for RSM Charlie Bradley.

Three things could happen to you at a selection board – you could be passed, graded NY ("not yet"), or failed outright. I was one of the quarter or so who failed, and couldn't believe it. In a book called *The General Danced at Dawn*, many years later, I have described the eccentricities of selection boards, whose decisions no man could fathom, but I think I failed because during one especially fatuous test, I muttered a contemptuous complaint. Or perhaps I just wasn't good enough. Anyway, I was posted, nursing my wounded vanity, to the ranks of the 5th Battalion of the Border Regiment, was thrice promoted lance-corporal and thrice demoted, and eventually was sent to India, and into action in Burma with the Borders' 9th Battalion.

Fighting the Japanese, frequently at close quarters, is an important experience. It was very primitive, old-fashioned warfare, but since I have recounted it in some detail in *Quartered Safe Out Here*, published nearly half a century later, I need say no more than that I learned much about soldiering and myself and about that matchless fighting man, the British infantryman, and his Indian and Gurkha comrades – yes, and the Japanese. And having led a section in action, I was not worried about going again before a selection board, which I passed this time, and found myself an officer cadet at the Officer Training School, Bangalore.

That, in its way, was just as influential as Burma. The British Raj was going down beneath the horizon, and the old Indian Army with it (for us, if not for the Indian cadets). But we saw the end of Empire, the very last of Kipling's India – the cool whitewashed interiors of the two-man rooms, one of which I shared with a Punjabi princeling, the soft-footed bearers fetching and carrying, the twinkling lance-points of the Mysore Lancers, gorgeous in their blue and gold and long-tailed puggarees as they rode from their barracks next door, the vast, dusty parade where the young Winston Churchill had exercised his horse, the great cadets' dining mess with the young Briton rising at the end of the table to propose "Mr Vice, the King!" and the stalwart Sikh rising at the other end to reply: "Gentlemen, the King-Emperor!" echoed by two hundred young men from the home country and all the warrior races of the sub-continent: Maharattas, Dogras, Sikhs, Afghans, Pathans, Gurkhas, Bengalis, and some from as far as Burma, Iran, and Nigeria. It was the end of an old and glorious song, and I was lucky to be part of it.

Not that I always thought so, for in memory it matches Burma and the two days' stevedoring I once did in Port Said as the most physically gruelling experience of my life. Pampered brutes we may have seemed with bearers bringing tea and picking up our clothing where we dropped it, but we couldn't have survived without them. The endless succession of parades, field exercises, lectures, marches, assault courses, physical training, and firing-range work, would have been impossible without their valeting; if you weren't sweating across the plain you were being instructed in Urdu by patient *munshis*, or ploughing your way through tomes on Indian military law, or learning to ride a motorbike, or swinging on ropes or climbing walls, or prowling the night playing war games, or trying to stand still on a sun-baked parade – and somehow still managing to play three sets of tennis in the midday sun and a game of football in the evening before riding in a tonga (man-drawn rickshaw) into town to a restaurant or club or cinema – unless conscience intervened and you stayed in with your law books and Urdu grammars and military manuals while the big moths fluttered round the light and the lizards played on the white walls. For the thought of failure was never far away, and the prospect of being returned ignominiously to your unit. Indeed, you never felt safe until you paraded for the last time, with your second lieutenant's stars beneath your white cadet epaulettes, and marched off a cadet no longer but His Majesty's trusted and well beloved friend.

In those days you were an officer of two regiments, one British, one Indian, and could choose to serve with one or the other. The young cadets just out from England mostly opted for Indian units, on the assumption that sepoys would be easier to command than ornery British swaddies who couldn't wait to get out of the Army. Those of us who had been in the ranks had different priorities; I'd seen enough of India, and opted for my British regiment, the Gordons, with whom my great-uncle had served on Roberts' march to Kandahar in 1879; he's buried somewhere in Afghanistan. So out of India I went, first to Cairo, and then to Tripoli, North Africa, where the Gordons' second battalion, the famous "Ninety-second" of Waterloo and elsewhere, were stationed in the very barracks which the US Air Force later bombed in reprisal against Colonel Gadaffi.

Tripoli was a happy time. Highland regiments are different from others, terribly military and tradition-conscious, yet marvellously friendly and informal. Gordons' officers were a mixture of Sandhurst regulars, some of them English, and Scots of varying degrees; the lordly drawl mingled with the broad sing-song of Aberdeenshire in complete harmony. They were a family, and far closer to their men than officers usually were, even in that democratic time. But that is a very Highland thing with its roots in clanship, and comfortable though I'd been in the Border Regiment, among the Cumbrians with whom I'd grown up, in the Gordons I felt that at last I'd come home. I've written one book about my time in the Borders, but three about the Gordons, recounting my adventures (fiction mingled with a great deal of fact) with my *bête noire* Private McAuslan, the Dirtiest Soldier in the World. I've been told that he had his counterparts among the military misfits of other regiments, British and American and Commonwealth, but I can hardly believe they were as slovenly, disorderly, well-meaning and accident-prone, or tried their commanders more sorely than he tried me. God bless him, wherever he is.

Service with the Gordons was punctuated by an unpleasantly nerve-racking period in Palestine, where the state of Israel was being born in a welter of terrorist bombings, ambushes, gunfire, reprisal, and mutual mistrust, with Jew and Arab at each other's throats and the much-maligned British holding the ring, reaping the bitter harvest of our own sowing, and wishing we were well out of it. I was on Haifa beach, stood security on the Mount of Olives on Armistice Day, and for my sins commanded the Cairo–Jerusalem night train. In a way it was worse than Burma, where at least you knew who the enemy was; it is no fun having to take your revolver into the shower, or sleep in a room whose window has to be covered with barbed wire. Everyone has his own view, of course; mine is that of a British subaltern, who wanted only to be a soldier, not a referee or a policeman.

Yet curiously enough when I left the Army in 1947 I toyed with the idea of joining the Palestine Police (£10 a week, not bad money then) because I suspected that civilian life would be dull. Fortunately, through my father's influence, I got a job as a trainee reporter on a weekly paper in Carlisle, and entered on the trade which cynical journalists describe as better than working and which (writing books and movies excepted) is the best job I know, or was in those days, before the rot set in – but I've already said my piece about that, and am well aware that I'm a fogey who will never get hot-metal newspapers out of his system, or forget the excitement of being a young reporter on the make in the typewriter age.

I'd been in newspapers only a few months when the most important thing in my life happened. I met, fell hopelessly in love with, and proposed to a glamorous reporter on another paper, Kathleen Margarette Hetherington, who was well ahead of me in the journalistic stakes, having worked on one of the big evening papers. To my delight she said "yes" . . . and here we are, thank God, more than half a century later, with Simon a sheriff (judge) in Scotland; Caroline, who has somehow managed to combine being a barrister with writing nine novels and raising four of our eight grandchildren; and Nicholas, running his own company in London, staging shows and events which range from theatrical productions to installing dinosaurs in the Natural History Museum.

The children all arrived in the 1950s, after we had come home from a year spent working as reporters on a daily paper in Canada. That had been our independent fling, but now life got serious. It was a time of heavy work, shortage of money, and great happiness, with Kathy carrying the major burden of running the home and rearing the family while I was in succession a reporter, sub-editor, foreign news editor, leader writer, features editor, and finally deputy editor of the oldest continuously-published daily newspaper in the world, the *Glasgow Herald*. Working on a daily means that you are something of an absentee father, out of circulation evening, night, and morning, and seeing the children at weekends, and how their wives cope is something that daily newspapermen can never quite understand. What made it worse in my case was that I spent much free time moonlighting on an evening paper, covering rugby matches, and writing bits and pieces for my own paper to boost our tight budget, but we got by; we were quite a team, Kathy and I, and our reward is that when the children get together and reminisce, they seem to be looking back on a time of laughter and happiness.

By the mid-fifties, I had the newspaperman's dream of writing a best-seller, and had produced one historical novel which no one would publish. Meanwhile I ploughed ahead with the bits and pieces aforesaid, earning a few extra quid a week with the wonderful bonus of hearing Kathy laughing in the next room at what I'd written – for humour paid best and came most easily to me; I knew by then I was a "light" writer or nothing.

How the idea of Flashman came into my head I do not know.

I had read *Tom Brown's Schooldays* as a boy, and recognised the bullying rotter as the most interesting character in the book, and at some point in 1966 I must have asked myself (not for the first time) what could have happened to him after he was expelled from Rugby in drunken disgrace. Two things combined to make me look for the answer. One, I had just spent two weeks in Borneo and Malaya (my only "foreign" journalism) during the anti-terrorist campaign, and got the smell of the Orient and soldiering again. Two, I had just spent three months as acting editor before reverting again to deputy, and the prospect of twenty years in the job was not inviting. Kathy tells me that I said: "I'm going to write us out of this."

I wrote *Flashman* in nightly bursts after coming home from work; in all it took ninety hours, no advance plotting, no revisions, just tea and toast and cigarettes at the kitchen table. Halfway through I broke my arm and couldn't type, and had put the book from my mind when Kathy asked if she could read what I'd done. When she did, her reaction was to quote a line from *The Treasure of the Sierra Madre*: "Boy, you don't know the riches you're standing on!" She is the best judge I know, indeed, the only one, so I finished it, and for two years publisher after publisher in Britain and the US turned it down – one eminent agent wouldn't even handle it – until I was ready to give up. Not Kathy; she *knew* it was going to succeed, so off went the battered manuscript yet again, this time to an agency who had tried valiantly with my first novel, and whose fine old Highland name appealed to me, John Farquharson. That king of literary agents, George Greenfield, tried five more houses unsuccessfully, and struck oil with the sixth, the small firm of Herbert Jenkins, publishers of Wodehouse and little other fiction. They enthused, Christopher MacLehose especially, and published *Flashman* just as I wrote it.

The result was remarkable, and instructive. It wasn't a best-seller – none of my books has been – but it got splendid reviews, the film rights were sold, and various foreign language rights, starting with Finland of all places, but what took me flat aback was the reception to the American edition. I'd written the book in the first person, as the memoir of Sir Harry Flashman, VC, admired military hero (he having concealed his perfidy and cowardice successfully for sixty years), and had appended a spoof introduction about the manuscript being discovered in a saleroom, plus footnotes. This was done for fun, not to deceive. My publishers had agreed that no one would take it for a genuine memoir for a moment, and indeed, no British reviewer did (although one seemed to be hedging his bets), but in the States *one-third* of about fifty reviews hailed it as the real thing. Since some of the reviewers were academics, this was alarming; one even described it as the most important literary discovery since the Boswell Papers. The *New York Times* rather mischievously rounded up all the reviews which had taken it as genuine, and I reflected that there were some universities from whom I could never expect an honorary degree.

I cannot be a hypocrite and say that I wasn't amused, but I do sympathise genuinely with those who were deceived. I'm as gullible as the next man, and there are works of whose authenticity I have honest doubts – Louis Le Golif's *Memoirs of a Buccaneer*, for example, and a script I was once shown of an allegedly true memoir of a nineteenth-century slave-trader. It depends on the mood in which you approach a book, how it strikes you at first glance, and whether you *want* to believe it. Readers still ask me whether Flashman was real or not, plainly hoping that he was. Others, alas, are in no doubt, like the students who occasionally write to request a sight of the original manuscript, and wonder why he is missing from the Dictionary of National Biography.

The Flashman series, of which there have been eleven so far, are all dedicated to Kath, and always will be. But for her that first manuscript would be mouldering in the attic, and if one thing made and has sustained me as a professional author it was her absolute certainty, from the very first, that it was going to happen. That kind of confidence is the ultimate encouragement, and it was essential in the early years when, with one novel published and the sequel under way, I took a deep breath, quit newspapers, and decided with considerable misgivings to try my luck as a full-time writer.

Making a living from books alone is not easy, except for those who produce the big blockbusters, and I don't know how I'd have done if it hadn't been for a massive stroke of luck at the end of 1972. In three years' free-lancing I had produced three Flashmans, the first volume of short stories about McAuslan and the Gordons, a history of the Anglo-Scottish Border reivers, *The Steel Bonnets*, which Kathy and I researched together, wading through State Papers, Tudor correspondence, and Privy Council records at Trinity College, Dublin, amassing great heaps of material which I then reduced to some sort of order in a tome of about 200,000 words.

Then around Christmas 1972 Richard Lester and the Musketeers came over the horizon, and the world changed, as I've described in earlier chapters. Looking back on it, on the elations and disappointments, the triumphs and disasters, I am struck by how much kindness and sheer good fellowship and enthusiasm I encountered in the film world. I like film people, and their crazy trade. It is great fun, and rewarding not only in money, for as I've said it wafted Kathy and me to Hollywood and Budapest and Paris and Rome and Madrid and Yugoslavia and the Riviera and elsewhere, courtesy of prodigal producers.

Flashman has sent us abroad, too, to Samarkand's Golden Road and Custer's last battlefield on Little Big Horn and the Number 10 saloon where Wild Bill Hickok died and the Black Hills and the snowbound road from Fort Laramie; to the jungle rivers of Borneo and the South China Sea and Hong Kong and the Pearl River at Canton; to the salt-mines of the Salzkammergut and the cotton-wood banks of the Rio Grande and the Gila Forest where the

Apaches rode their warpaths; to the Valley of the Kings and the wonderful bergs and glaciers of Alaska; across the Pacific and to the olive-groves above Delphi; on the Orient Express and through the back streets of Venice (which beat the canals, for my money); to Bent's Fort and Singapore and Kit Carson's house and Gattemalatta's statue and the Windward Passage and the Suez Canal and Panama and the black sands of Tahiti . . . it has been quite a trip, and if I haven't covered all Flashman's tracks there have been the memoirs of old travellers to fill in the places I've missed.

One likes what one knows, as Vincent Price wisely remarked, and alternating Flashman and various other books with movie scripts has been, for me, an ideal writing schedule. The big difference is that a film has to be written to satisfy not only the writer, but the producers and director, and ultimately the actors who are going to have to bring the thing to life. It is *their* movie, and you must write to suit them, especially the producers, who are paying you. It is a matter of compromise and fighting your corner when you're right and giving way when you're wrong, and if you're lucky you'll have wonderful casts and great crews and directors as brilliant and experienced as Lester and Fleischer and Hamilton to guide you, encourage you, put up with you and make it all work on the screen.

With a novel you're on your own, writing for yourself, with no one to satisfy except the reader at the end of the day. I am, and always have been, a secretive writer; I won't talk about a book when I'm doing it, or even let my publishers know what it's about until I've finished – when I read of writers (and Stevenson was one of them) who actually read their stuff aloud to friends as they go along, I'm baffled, for my toes curl under at the thought. I've never written a synopsis for a book, which I believe is quite common nowadays, to get the okay from a publisher in advance; I want what I write to be a surprise (to me, for one; I may know vaguely where I'm going when I start a book, but how I'll get there I leave to chance as I go along, with, in the case of a Flashman, history providing the milestones). Nor have I ever written a second draft; I revise as I write, and when I'm done, that's it. When Kathy has read it and given the thumbs up, which she has done unfailingly for more than thirty years, I'm not really worried about other opinions, although obviously the approval of agents and publishers is eagerly awaited.

If Kathy makes a suggestion, I think hard about it. Once in the middle of a Flashman I was unhappy about the way it was going, and took the unprecedented step of asking her to read the story so far and tell me what she thought; she agreed that the thing had gone off the rails at such-and-such a point, and then said: "You're good at court-rooms; suppose there was a trial somewhere." I thought about that; there didn't seem to be an immediate opening for a trial, but it might be a good thing to plot *towards* one at the end. Inspiration struck when I was having a shower, I redirected the plot . . . and *Flash for Freedom!* ends in a court-room.

Again, in the first book, when Flashman hurled a herculean dwarf into a snake-pit by sheer main strength, she thought he should do it by some appropriately crafty trick . . . and so he does. She will have forgotten these things, but I remember gratefully, possibly because I am not normally receptive to suggestions, which I suppose makes me an editor's nightmare. I make no apology for this; they're my books, and while I'm grateful to have mistakes or inconsistencies and repetitions pointed out (I've just been grateful twice in the same paragraph, to show what I mean) I permit no other editorial interference. It goes into print as I've written it, without so much as a comma altered, and if any changes seem advisable, I'll make them myself.

Possibly I'm an egomaniac – and unusual, for I gather that many authors allow, and even encourage, editors to help them write their books. I don't, because I'm not aware that anyone else is fit or qualified to make Stradivarius's violins for him, and have no evidence that an editorial hand would benefit work that I have thought hard about and written with as much care as I can command. I know what I want to say; it may be tripe, but it's *my* tripe, no one else's. I sat open-mouthed hearing Angus Wilson confess that "young editors" had rewritten some of his work, adding mournfully that he supposed they knew best. I couldn't credit it – some vain oaf, no doubt with a degree in creative punctuation from the University of Peebles and probably not a book to his name, had dared to "edit" *Angus Wilson*? I've also heard a horror story about some vandal who "edited" Wodehouse, even. If words fail me . . . well, they're going to be my words.

Nor am I impressed when I hear that Hemingway felt indebted to the editor who cut his million words by three-quarters. For all I or Hemingway or anyone else knows, that book, uncut, may have been a masterpiece; we have only the word of an editor that it wasn't. In my youthful ignorance I once told a Dickens addict that the great man could have done with a stern sub-editing; he silenced me properly by replying: "But I don't want him subbed. I want him all."

My resistance to editorial interference was recognised early in our acquaintance by Christopher MacLehose, who published most of my books. He let me alone, and his successors have done likewise, with the exception of an American who changed my punctuation throughout a book – and had to change it back. Once I refused to make substantial changes in a book, and took it to another publisher, who accepted it as it stood. I say this not in triumph but for the record (and perhaps to encourage other authors to ask themselves, when faced with an editor's opinion: "Does this person really know better than I do?")

Another reason why I'm probably the Editor's Curse is that I simply can't be bothered to think about a book once I've finished it; my only interest then is to see that it gets into print untampered. Which prompts the frequently-asked questions: do I never get tired of Flashman? Yes, invariably. Having completed a volume of his

Papers, I never want to see or think about the brute again (not for a few years anyway). It is a relief to turn to something else, preferably a subject I haven't tried before. This thirst for variety probably stems from journalism, where you might turn from covering a schools' rugby match to writing a light piece about your children's visit to Santa Claus, sub-edit a travel article on the Horn of Africa, and round off the evening's work with a leading article on unrest in Chile (thank God for the *Economist* and *Herald Tribune*) or the state of the Glasgow underground.

Perhaps that explains why, in the intervals of eleven historical picaresques, three volumes of short stories, and about twenty film scripts, I have been only too glad to write one straight history, a burlesque fantasy on every swashbuckler I ever read or saw (*The Pyrates*), a rather dark morality tale – at least I meant it to have a moral – in what I hope was a reasonable imitation of Elizabethan English (*The Candlemass Road*), a couple of radio plays for the BBC, an immensely long novel (conventional for once) about a Western gunfighter in Edwardian England (*Mr American*), an illustrated comparison of historical movies with the real events and characters they set out to portray (*The Hollywood History of the World*), and a couple of books to which I have already referred, *Black Ajax*, and my recollections of infantry soldiering in Burma with XIVth Army, *Quartered Safe Out Here*.

CONCLUSION

That is the story so far, or as much of it as I have room for. There were many topics that I'd have liked to touch on, but I'd have needed a second volume: something of my parental family, an ordinary doctor's house seen through the eyes of childhood in those far-off years "before the war"; more about our children and *their* childhood – and that astonishing unexpected bonus that you get at the end of the day if you're lucky ... grandchildren; adventures in the newspaper trade on both sides of the Atlantic; my brief career as an encyclopedia salesman in Toronto (three days knocking on doors and not a set sold, not even to the distraught householder who erupted from his cellar covered in foam, demanding: "Do your goddam books tell how to fix a washing machine?"); my views on arts and letters and all that (as if you'd care); observations on the rise and fall of Carlisle United and the eccentricities of the Partick Thistle – and a bizarre episode which has just come back to me from the closing days of the Burma war, when I suspect, but can't be sure, that I may have been duped into helping to run guns into China. It may have been a legitimate operation, but I very much doubt it, and can only plead my gormless trusting youth, my fatal habit of doing what my elders told me, and the fact that there were some damned odd characters floating about the Far East in 1945.

And I can only mention memories of enchanted evenings at the theatre: *Carmen* outdoors in Budapest, *Fledermaus* in Bad Ischil, *Lohengrin* in Leningrad (well, the first act); little Julie Andrews' debut in *Starlight Roof* in 1948; Leonard "Mr Spock" Nimoy as Sherlock Holmes in Century City: the buxom blondes bouncing in the Leningrad Music Hall, a display which left me wondering how Kruschev had the nerve to protest at the can-can as performed in Hollywood; Gielgud in *Hamlet* and *Blithe Spirit* on alternate nights in Bangalore; Laurel and Hardy resplendent in full fig of kilt and bowler hats; Andy Stewart knocking them dead in the Gaiety, Isle of Man, and the finest stand-up comedian I have ever seen, a true jester in the old tradition, the inimitable Ken Dodd.

All that by the way. Since it has been such a mixed bag of a book, the following anecdote may fit in well enough, and indeed may not be a bad note to end on, for it points up one of the themes I've belaboured, the difference between then and now. Anyway, I have to tell it, because twenty-odd years ago I promised my old Colonel, the late great Reggie Lees of the 2nd Battalion, Gordon Highlanders, that I would set it down, and it's about time. It is the true story of one Wee Wullie, a Scottish soldier and hero, which I fictionalised in a story in one of my earliest books, *The General Danced at Dawn*, and Reggie, who had soldiered with him since the first war, was concerned that I should set the record straight some day.

The story as I wrote it was about this Herculean roughneck whose regimental life was one long brawl with the military police and provost staff, a wild man and a nuisance out of the line but worth two in the day of battle, who performed an amazing solo march through the Western Desert in '42 without food or water, and carrying a captured German; he was out on his feet when a patrol came upon him, the German was dead, but Wee Wullie was still marching, refusing to give up. His rescuers had to stop him in his tracks forcibly; one of them said he thought he could have gone on forever.

Now that actually happened in the desert war, but not to Wee Wullie; I never discovered who the real man was, but I borrowed his story and ascribed it to Wee Wullie (no matter why) whose heroism was of a different nature, but no less worthy in its self-sacrifice and sheer unconquerable courage. It happened when he and the Colonel were prisoners of the Japanese on the infamous Siam railway (they were among those who built the celebrated Kwai bridge). You know what that was like; you've seen the pictures of those half-starved emaciated scarecrows whom those dirty little yellow bastards set to slave labour in appalling conditions. Many of them died; among the survivors were a few that my battalion picked up as we came south towards Rangoon, and they were like wasted ghosts. If you'd seen them you'd have thought twice about buying a Honda or a Toyota (but I know that's unreasonable after fifty years; I can't help the way I feel about those people, that's all).

The story of the Colonel and Wee Wullie in the Jap prison camp, as I was told it, is as follows:

Some big metal files went missing, and the Jap commander went berserk. The Colonel, who knew nothing about the files, was interrogated, and limped for the rest of his life. "They set about me with a crowbar at first, and then by the grace of God they changed it for a pick handle." They might have beaten him to death, who knows, but then Wee Wullie came forward and said he'd taken the files. He hadn't, so of course he couldn't tell the Japs where they were, but they stopped hammering the Colonel and turned their attention to the regimental hard man, and when they had finished they decided to make an example of him in a most unpleasant, most Japanese way.

They got a bundle of files like the missing ones, great two-foot iron bars, and made Wullie stand on the parade ground holding them before him. It was about 100 degrees in the shade, and just standing at attention would have been horrible enough, but carrying that cruel weight it must have been torture, without water or shade or even the relief of movement. What sanction or threat the Japs used to make him do it, I never learned; my informant (not the Colonel, who had been in no fit state to know what was happening) said threats would have been useless anyway; Wee Wullie took it as a challenge, himself against the Japs.

So he stood in the sun. He stood all day, holding the files, swaying a little now and then, the sweat streaming down his face beneath the balmoral bonnet which was his only shield. The Japanese sentry who had been set to guard him actually passed out in the awful heat, but Wullie went on standing.

Night came, and his comrades in the huts could barely see the huge figure in the dark, but when day broke he was still on his feet. When the sun came up and turned the parade into a furnace, he seemed to waver a little, and they wondered if he would fall. His eyes were closed, and they wondered if he was still conscious. He opened his eyes, but didn't speak, just stood with the files before him, his elbows in his sides.

Just after noon, when he had been standing for more than twenty-four hours, the Jap commandant, who had been watching from his veranda, marched up to him and barked at him to fall out. Wullie stood for a few seconds, as though gathering himself, and then, plainly struggling to keep his balance, bent down and laid the files on the ground. Then he straightened up, very slowly squared his enormous shoulders, threw the commandant a salute, took one careful step forward and then another, until he was quick marching, none too steadily, but marching until he reached a hut, and there he fell full length on a cot and lay like one dead. "I swear to God he couldn't see, or hear hardly, or know what the hell was happening, but he wasn't going to fall down in front of the Japs. We had to pour a drink into him, into his mouth all cracked and swollen black, and we wondered if he would go west, but next morning he was up and about again." Thus my informant, and that is all I know, for twenty years later all the Colonel said about my fiction was: "You'll have to tell the true story some day, you know." So I have.

Why do I say it's a good note to end on? Because it's a fine story about a fine man, but also because, as I've said already, it enables me to make the comparison between then and now. I am not complaining or criticising, because I've no right to; I am not sound-ing off (says he, who could make Schopenhauer sound like Tommy Cooper), I am simply looking here, upon this picture, and on this, and feeling sorry for today. And I'm aware that I'm repeating myself, but it's worth saying once more: when I read of policemen being given hundreds of thousands of pounds because they were upset by doing what policemen used to do as a matter of course, or firemen being counselled and compensated after a disaster which would once have been regarded as an unpleasant day's work, and people being "traumatised" by hardship or harrowing experience which their grandparents would have taken in their stride, and children being taught the "grieving process" of weeping and laying flowers . . . well, while I know Wee Wullie would be the last man on earth to imagine himself being used to read a lesson or point a moral, I can't help thinking of him and what, in every sense of the word, he stood for.

Next time I roll paper into my machine it will, I hope, be to write some fiction, on what subject I don't know yet. Flashy still has a few trails to flee along, and there are other ideas I might like to tackle, vague trains of thought that always remind me of Robert Service's poem about his own favourite literary creation, which ends:

> Ah, how I love each word of it,
> The little book I never wrote.

I suppose I ought to wind up with some profound thoughts on writing, but mine are all too simple. *Cacoethes scribendi*: I tell stories because they aren't there, and no doubt to air my views in the process, and it's all one whether I'm at my typewriter today (word processors are not for an old newspaper hand who can make any-thing electronic break down just by looking at it) or sitting on my children's beds years ago, the aim is the same: to entertain, to amuse if possible, to tell it honestly, to pass on what I think is worth knowing about life, but always to remember Charles Reade's advice: "Make 'em laugh, make 'em cry, make 'em wait."

It's a serious business in which you must never take yourself too seriously. It's a trade, a craft, like any other, and when people ask earnestly: "How do you get your ideas?" I can only reply: "By thinking, sometimes for months." Inspiration takes a lot of thought, with glue on the writer's chair, as Trollope knew. Scott and Dickens didn't produce all that work by waiting for lightning to strike; they put their heads down and went at it, and it's the only way I know.

The silliest thing I ever heard about writing was Cyril Connolly's dictum in *The Unquiet Grave* that the writer's only function is to produce a masterpiece, suggesting that when he knows he is not, he should put it aside. At that rate no one would ever finish anything, for I doubt if anyone consciously produced a masterpiece yet. I am sure that when Shakespeare wrote "Go, bid the soldiers shoot" he was entirely unaware that he had just completed the greatest play ever written – it may well have been his sixteenth shot at a snappy ending, and being a professional he probably thought: "Well, thank God that's finished. Denmark, forget it! It'll do, with any luck." And then wondered, as I do now: Right, what's next?

INDEX

Aberdeen, Lord xxi
Act of Settlement 80
Addington, Henry xxi
Afghanistan 17, 19, 20, 22, 73, 89, 92, 185, 193, 195, 302
Africa 20, 114, 117
African Queen, The 56fn.
Agate, James 254
Agincourt 122
Alaska 308
American Graffiti 139
American Revolution 20fn.
Amin, Idi 159
Amis, Kingsley 94–97
Amis, Martin 94, 95
Amritsar 118
Andersen, Hans 289
Anderson, Lindsay 282
Andress, Ursula 56
Andrews, Harry 29–31, 59, 63
Andrews, Julie 313
angling 25
animal rights 24, 25
Apaches 118
Archer, Freddy 299
Arlott, John 276
Armada, the 122
armed forces 180–193
Armstrong, Rev. Henry 225
Ashanti 205, 206, 242
Ashe, Arthur 214
asylum seekers 229–232
Attlee, Clement 88
Austen, Jane 264

BBC xvii, 150, 217, 218, 228, 295, 311
Bach, Barbara 131, 137, 141
Badel, Alan 131, 137, 139, 140, 201, 208
Bader, Douglas 188
Bad Ischl 313

Baer, Max 57fn.
Baird, John Logie 262
Baker, Nicholas 236
Ballantyne, R.M. 292
Bangalore 176, 300, 301, 314
Barabbas 27
Barbosa, Arthur 30 & fn.
Barrack-room Ballads 294
Barradell-Smith, Walter 295, 296
Barrie, J.M. 122, 288, 295
Barry, B.H. 32, 37, 38
Barrymores, the 245
Bates, Alan 83
Batt, Bert 131, 134
Bautzer, Greg 240
Beatles, the 1, 3
Beckenbauer, Franz 75
"Becket, Samuel" 135
Bedi, Kebir 205, 206, 242
Beethoven, Ludwig 75, 77
Begelman, David 235, 236
Belsen xvii, 74, 77
Benton, Robert 55, 56, 60, 61
Bent's Fort 308
Berlin 18
Berlin Wall 78
Best, Willie 225
Beverly Hillbillies, The 102
Bickford, Charles 173
Bill of Rights 74
Bin Laden, Osama 17, 19, 20 & fn.
Birmingham Post 251
Bismarck, Otto von 75
Black Ajax 111, 112, 311
"Black Cat" Division 21
Blackcock's Feather 128
Black Hills, the 307
Blair, Tony xxii, 17–22, 25, 49, 72, 73, 89 & fns., 116, 117, 144, 185, 193, 195, 251, 252
Blencathra Hunt 25

Blithe Spirit 314
Blitz, the 122
Blucher, Marshal 75
Bolt, Robert 208
Bond, James 234–244
Border Regiment 21, 190, 300, 302
Borgnine, Ernest 27, 35, 40, 160
Borneo 305, 307
Boston Strangler, The 27
Bounty, The 207, 208
Bracknell, Lady 233
Bradley, R.S.M. Charley 187, 299, 300
Brady, Ian 142, 146, 149
Brando, Marlon 57–59, 63, 87
Braveheart 114, 157
Brecht, Bertolt 70
Bremner, Rory 14
Bridie, James 295
British Empire 157–9, 190, 227
Broadcasting Standards Commission 217
Broccoli, Albert ("Cubby") 234–238, 241, 242, 244
Bronson, Charles 56
Brown, Gordon 88
Bruce, Robert 31, 186, 289, 291
Brute Force 173
Buchan, John 288
Buchanan, Jack 295
Budapest 32 passim, 313
bullying 153, 154, 189
Burke, Edmund 48, 49
Burma 21, 97, 184, 225, 300, 301, 313
Burnet, Alastair 248
Burns, Robert 124
Burroughs, Edgar Rice 97fn, 199
Bush, George W. 17–22, 195

Cagney, James 245, 294
Caine, Michael 205, 284
Cairo-Jerusalem train 303
Canada 101, 194
Candlemass Road, The 311
Cannes Film Festival 204, 205
Canterbury, Archbishop of 106, 117, 118
Canton 307
capital punishment 143–147, 155
Captain Blood 208
Cardiff, Jack 28, 31, 36, 37, 40, 41, 86, 265
Carlisle 98, 100, 186, 225, 289, 291
Carlisle Grammar School 289–291
Carlisle Journal 99, 303
Carlisle United 99, 274, 313

Carlyle, Thomas xix, 282
Carmen 313
Carnegie, Andrew 288
Casanova 113, 279, 280
Casanova, Giacomo 289
Cash, Johnnie 97
Cassel, Jean-Pierre 10, 12, 280
Cattrall, Kim 12, 16
Cawnpore 118
Ceylon 18
Chamberlain, Richard 3, 6, 10, 12, 113, 280
Chaplin, Charlie 97
Chaplin, Geraldine 6
Charles I 11–13, 66fn.
Chase, James Hadley 97 & fn.
Chatham, Earl of 68
Chatterley case 258
Chaucer, Geoffrey 290
Chesterton, G.K. 122
Chiang Kai-shek, Madam 236
Children's Encyclopedia 291, 292
Churchill, Winston 18, 68, 190, 263, 301
Cincinnatus 51
Citizen Kane 16
Clair, Rene 55 & fn.
Clarke, Alan 26, 45
Clavel, James 199–202
Clayton, Jack 281
Clift, Montgomery 171 & fn.
Clinton, William 91, 104
Clydebank 77
Coburn, James 35
Cohn, Harry 144
Colley, Ken 280
Colman, Ronald 294
Colman Smith, John 294–296
Commission for Racial Equality 217, 220
Conan Doyle, Arthur 199, 288
Conan the Barbarian (comic) 54, 264
Conan the Destroyer 27
Connery, Sean 201, 203, 204, 244
Connolly, Billy 13, 86
Connolly, Cyril 318
Connors, Jimmy 214
Conrad, Joseph 54
Cook, Robin 91fn.
Cooke, Alistair 249
Cooper, Gary 293
Cooper, Henry 57fn., 83 & fn.
Cooper, Tommy 317
Corbett, James J. 57fn.
Cording, Harry 28

corporal punishment 143, 149, 152–155
Cravat, Nick 166, 167, 172
Cribb, Tom 111
Crimean War 20fn.
Crimson Pirate, The 38, 160, 161, 168
Cromwell, Oliver xx, 11, 12, 66fn., 69, 118, 289, 291
Cromwell, Richard 88
Cronin, A.J. 96
Cronyn, Hume 173
Crosby, Bing 37fn.
Crossed Swords (see *The Prince and the Pauper*)
Cruickshank, Andrew 261
Culloden 125
Culver, Roland 30
Curtis, Tony 182fn.
Curtiz, Michael 29
Custer, George Armstrong 307

Dachau xvii, 74
Dad's Army 74
Daniell, Henry 139
Darien Scheme 123
David Copperfield 268
Davis, Bette 245
Davis, Sammy 222
Dawson, Les 9
Dean, Felicity 35
Declaration of Arbroath 74
de la Billiere, Peter 191
de la Mare, Walter 294
De Laurentiis, Dino 60, 264 passim, 283
Delphi 308
Deluca, Rande 243, 244
DeMille, Cecil B. 294
Devil's Disciple, The 162
Dickens, Charles 250, 310, 318
Die Fledermaus 313
Dieterle, William 140
Dietrich, Marlene 75, 188
Djablak, see Zhablak
Dr Dolittle 27
Dodd, Ken 314
Donner, Richard 59, 60
Douglas, Kirk 173, 174, 198
Douglas, Sarah 56
Douglas-Home, Alec 263
Drake, Francis 294
Dresden 116, 117
Dreyfuss, Richard 284
Drogheda 118

Dublin 18
Dumas, Alexandre 3, 9, 11, 12, 16, 237
Dunaway, Faye 6, 7, 9, 10, 87, 280
Durham Light Infantry 189, 190
Durning, Charles 208
Dyke, Greg 219fn.

Eastwood, Clint 204
Ebsen, Buddy 101–103
Economist, The 311
Eddison, E.R. 54
Edward I 31, 291
Edward VI 27
8½ 265
Eisenhower, Dwight 21
Ekland, Britt 83
Eliot, T.S. 262
Elizabeth I 68, 290
Elizabeth II xvii, 65, 66fn., 89fn., 116, 117, 195, 217, 218, 251
Ellington, Duke 225
Emma 264
Empire Windrush 225
Enemy of the People, An 208
England and the English xvi, 121, 122, 123 & fn., 215
Enniskillen 18, 116
Equal Opportunities Commission 184fn.
Ethelred the Unready 88
European Court 67
European Union 50, 66–79

Fairbanks, Douglas, jnr 94
Fairbanks, Douglas, snr 82, 94, 168
Falklands campaign 20, 21, 190
Fantastic Voyage 27
Farnol, Jeffrey 37, 86, 161, 165, 166
Farquharson, John 305
Fawlty Towers 262
Fellini, Federico xxiii, 264–267
Field of Shirts 128
Finland 306
Finlay, Frank 6, 9, 10, 12, 86, 280
Finlayson, Jimmy 98
Fischer, Joe 241, 242
Flame and the Arrow, The 161
Flashman 1, 2, 96, 109–111, 154fn., 161, 172, 304, 305–311
Flashman and the Angel of the Lord 96
Flashman at the Charge 30fn., 96
Flashman and the Redskins 28, 96
Flash for Freedom! 309

Fleischer, Max 27
Fleischer, Mickey 26, 139, 240
Fleischer, Richard 5, 26, 28, 31, 33, 35–41,
  57, 59, 60, 82, 84, 85, 139, 160fn., 165,
  199, 201–206, 208, 210, 211, 240, 264,
  265, 268, 269, 281, 308
Fleming, Ian 199, 244, 288
"Flower of Scotland" 121
Flynn, Errol 27, 82, 85fn., 168, 171fn., 210,
  245, 294
Flynn, Paddy 299
Fonda, Henry 173
Force Ten from Navarone 57, 62, 131–141,
  201, 202
Ford, Harrison 130, 131, 136–139, 141
Foreman, Carl 131, 132, 141, 202, 203
Fort Laramie 307
Fort Venango 118
Fort William Henry 118, 119
Four Musketeers, The 8, 9–11
Fowlie, Eddie 12, 32, 41, 207
Fox, Edward 81, 130, 131, 135–137, 139–141,
  201, 208
Fra Diavolo 98
Franco, Francisco 69
Frasers, clan 125, 128, 216
Fraser, Hugh 94
Fraser, William 116, 126–128, 284, 288,
  289
Frasier, TV 162
Frederick the Great 75
French Revolution 68
French Without Tears 30
Fresh Prince of Bel Air 222
Froebe, Gert 75, 243
From Here to Eternity 171

Gable, Clark 245
Gaiety Theatre, I.O.M. 314
Galento, Tony 57fn.
Gamester, The 120
Gardes Ecossaies 190
Gattemalatta, statue 308
Gaunt, John of xxiii, 165
General Danced at Dawn, The 280, 300,
  314
George Watson's College 294
Germany 74–79, 190, 193, 215
Gibbon, Edward xviiifn.
Gielgud, John 140, 201, 314
Gila Forest 307
Gilbert, W.S. 108, 184fn.

Glasgow Academy 294, 295, 297
Glasgow Herald, The 53, 120, 251, 304
Glen, John 237
Glenbuck Cherrypickers 99
Glencoe 129
Goebbels, Josef 108, 150
Goethe, Johann 75
Goldfinger 56fn.
Gone With the Wind 211, 268
Good Life, The 262
Gordon Highlanders 190, 302, 303, 314
Gordon, John 254
Gothard, Michael 10
Gover, Alf 86
Grand Hotel, Rome 268–270
Grandarse 98
Granger, Stewart 206
Grant, Cary 27, 242
Gray, Thomas 122
Graziano, Rocky 57fn.
Great Escape, The 201
Great Race, The 182fn.
Greene, Graham 250
Greenfield, George 96, 305
Griffiths, Richard 280
Guardian xviii, 172, 251
Guinness, Alec 26, 260
Guns of Navarone, The 131

H.M.S. Pinafore 102
Hackman, Gene 55, 61–64
Hague, William 231
Haider, Jorge 69
Haifa 303
Haley, Jack 103
Halliwell, Leslie 40fn.
Hamilton, Guy xxiii, 5, 15, 55 & fn., 56,
  57, 59, 63, 65, 131–133, 135–138, 308
Hamlet 297, 314
Hardy, Oliver 98, 99, 294, 314
Hardy, Thomas 250
Harrison, Rex xxii, 27–31, 35, 38–42, 87,
  168, 198, 205, 208
Hayward, Louis 242
Hayworth, Rita 140, 163
Hazlitt, William 112
Heath, Edward xxii, 66, 72, 88
Hecht, Harold 38, 161–164, 167, 169, 170,
  174
Hemingway, Ernest 310
Hemmings, David 27, 36
Henry IV 297

Henry V 297
Henry VI 88
Henry VIII 27, 29–31, 40, 80
Hepburn, Katherine 245
Herald-Tribune, The 311
Herbert, A.P. 255
Heroes, The 293
Heston, Charlton 6, 8, 10, 27–31, 35, 40, 81, 87, 97, 208
Hetherington, Alastair 248
Hickok, Wild Bill 307
Hill, James 103, 161–163, 167, 169, 170
Hindley, Myra 142, 146, 149
Hitchcock, Alfred 27
Hitler, Adolf 19, 69–71, 75–78, 213, 294
Hitler Youth 78
Hobbit, The 53
Hobbs, William 12
Hobson, Valerie 260
Holden, William 198, 205
Hollywood History of the World, The 311
Holocaust, the 67, 69, 76, 253
Hong Kong 200, 203, 207
Hoon, Geoffrey 128, 184
Horn of Africa 311
Horne, Lena 225
Hoskins, Bob 83
House of Lords 89, 90
Howard, Alan 12
Howard, Trevor 30, 59, 63
Howell, C. Thomas 12
Hoyt, John 173
Huckleberry Finn 112, 173
Hughes, Thomas 109
human rights 67, 72
hunting 24, 25
Hussein, Saddam 193
Huston, John 56fn., 131
Huxley, Aldous 262

Ice People, The 64
India 225, 226, 242, 300–302
Indian Mutiny 118
Ink Spots, the 225
Inquisition, the 67
I.R.A. xvii, 17, 118
Irish Famine 116, 117
Irish Republic 17
Islam 20
Island of Dr Moreau, The 168
Isle of Man xiii, xvi, 125, 149, 150, 206
Israel 186, 303

Jade of Destiny, The 37, 86
James II 88
James, Sid 187
Japan 18, 118, 190
Japanese 21, 184, 300, 315, 316
Jardine Matheson 200
Jason, David 83
Jefferson, Thomas 51, 68
Jenkins, Herbert 305
Jesus 115fn., 141
Jhansi 118
Johnson, Beverly 206
Johnson, Samuel xxii, 123
Jourdan, Louis 244
Julius Caesar 173
Jurado, Katy 168

Kabul 18, 22
Kaiser Wilhelm 75
Kandahar 302
Kendall, Kay 283
Kennedy, Edward 104
Kerima 55
Kerr, Deborah 171
Kersh, Gerald 299
Kidnapped 128
Kiel, Richard 133, 136
Kiev 176, 178
Killiecrankie 127
King, Dennis 98
Kinnear, Roy 6, 8, 12–14, 82, 280
Kipling, Rudyard 68, 93, 249, 298, 300
Knox, John 128
Konigsberg, Frank 280
Korngold, Erich Wolfgang 40, 208, 293
Kosovo 89–93
Kray twins 142
Kristel, Sylvie 280
Kruschev, Nikita 314
Kwai bridge 315

La Dolce Vita 265
Lancaster, Burt xxiii, 38 & fn., 97, 103, 160, 162–174
Landis, John 113, 281
Langton, Simon 280
Laughton, Charles 140
Laurel, Stan 98, 294, 314
Lawrence, Stephen 222
Leacock, Stephen 97, 293
Lean, David 207, 208

Lee, Christopher 5–7, 9, 10, 12, 14–16, 56, 87, 168, 208, 280
Lees, Lt-Col R.G. 314–316
Legion of Frontiersmen 284, 288
Legrand, Michel 6, 39
Legree, Simon 213
Lemper, Ute 75
Lenin, V.I. 71, 178
Leningrad 176, 178, 179
Leningrad Music Hall 314
Leopard, The 172, 173
Lester, Mark 27, 29, 31–37, 40, 41
Lester, Richard 1–16, 57, 59, 60, 63, 64, 82, 83, 265, 281, 283, 307, 308
Lettow-Vorbeck, von 75
Liberal Democrats xviii, 51, 52
Lidice 77
Lincoln, Abraham 47, 68
Little Big Horn 307
Liverpool Echo 251
Lohengrin 313
Lombard, Carole 245
Lone Ranger, The 113, 278, 281
Longford, Lord 145
Longhurst, Henry 276
Lord Chancellor's office 105,106
Lord of the Rings, The 53
Loss, Joe 9
Louis XIV 69
Louis, Joe 98, 225
Loy, Myrna 245

Metro-Goldwyn-Mayer 235, 236, 245, 246
Maastricht Treaty 71
Macaulay, Lord 122, 205
McAuslan, Private 302, 303
Macbeth 297
McCullogh, Willie 124
MacDonalds, clan 128, 288
MacDonald, Donald (great-uncle) 302
MacDonald, George 53
MacDonald, Janet (grandmother) 125, 127, 288
McDowell, Malcolm 83, 208
MacGregor, Rob Roy 127
MacInnes, Angus 62
MacKay, Ian 254
McLaglen, Victor 294
MacLaine, Shirley 201
MacLehose, Christopher 305, 310
Macmillan Film Encyclopedia 55fn.
MacMillan, Maurice 94

MacNeill, Isabella (grandmother) 288
MacPherson, Lord 145, 215
McQueen, Steve xiii, xiv, xxiii, 58, 84, 85, 204, 207–211, 284
Magna Carta 74
Maibaum, Richard 237
Mainwaring, Captain 74, 75
Malaya 305
Mandelson, Peter 92
Man with the Golden Gun, The 15
Marks and Spencer 233
Marshall, E.G. 63
Marty 160fn., 162
Marvin, Lee 211
Marx, Mr 221
Mary Queen of Scots 290
Maskell, Dan 214, 276
Matter of Life and Death, A 59
Matthau, Walter 238
Matthews, Stanley 123, 274
Mayer, Louis B. 103, 245
Mazarin, Cardinal 12
Mee, Arthur 291, 292
Meerut 118
Memoirs of a Buccaneer 306
Mencken, H.L. 196, 197
Mendelssohn, Felix 294
Meredith, Burgess 227, 228
Mexico 194
Middleton, Guy 30
Miller, Alice Duer 197
Miller, Keith 272
Milligan, Spike 6, 9
Milosovic, Slobodan 90, 91 & fn.
Mr American 311
Mix, Tom 294
Molineaux, Tom 111, 112
Montaigne, Michel de 255
Montand, Yves 205
Montgomery, Bernard 181fn.
Moore, Roger 208, 211, 234, 235, 237
More, Thomas 128
Moscow 176, 177, 179, 313
Mugabe, Robert 159
Mount of Olives 303
Muggeridge, Malcolm 256
Muhammad Ali xxiii, 15, 57, 226
Mussolini, Benito 69, 294
Muti, Ornella 280

N.A.A.C.P. 214
Napoleon 69, 188

Narrow Margin, The 27
National Front 219
"Native Americans" 113, 116, 118, 119
Nelson, Horatio 188
Nero, Franco 131, 136–138
Never Say Never Again 244
New Labour xxi, 18, 52, 88–93, 114
Newbolt, Henry 294
Newman, David 55, 56, 60–62, 64, 65
Newman, Leslie 55, 56, 60–62, 64, 65
Newman, Paul 57, 138, 204, 236
New Yorker, The 111
New York Times 306
News of the World 255
Nielsen, Brigitte 269, 271
Nimoy, Leonard 313
Niven, David 201
No Orchids for Miss Blandish 97fn.
Noiret, Philippe 12
Norman, Barry 270
North, Lord xxiii, 88
Northern Ireland 23
Noyes, Alfred 294

Octopussy 84, 212, 235–245, 285
OTS Bangalore 300, 301
O'Halloran, Jack 56
Old Testament 115
Oliver! 27
Oliver Twist 112
Olivier, Laurence 140, 173
Olympic Games 157, 227
Omagh 18
Oradour 77
Orchard, Julian 31
Orient Express 308
Orwell, George xxi, 97fn.
Outcast of the Islands 55

Palestine 22, 303
Palestine Police 303
Palmerston, Lord 20 & fn.
Panama Canal 308
Parliament 19, 44–52, 66fn. (see also
  Westminster)
Parkinson, Michael (show) 82, 211
Parrish, Bob 97
Partick Thistle 313
Paterson, Bill 12, 13
Patriot, The 157
Peacock, Thomas Love 249
Peake, Mervyn 161

Peel, Robert 117
Peninsular Hotel 233
Penshurst Place 28
Perrine, Valerie 62
Petersen, Wolfgang 283
Phillips, Leslie 187
Pink Turtle cafe 221
Pinochet, Augusto 89, 92, 93
Pocohontas 157
political correctness (p.c.) xv, xviii, xxi,
  24, 104–119, 151, 155, 181 & fn., 188, 214,
  221, 222, 224, 292
Pope, Alexander 229fn.
Pope John Paul 116–118, 252
Pope Pius XI 117
Pope Pius XII 117
Powell, William 245
Power, Tyrone 168, 171fn.
Price, Vincent 308
Prince and the Pauper, The 26–43, 57, 84,
  85fn., 199, 207
Prince Charles Edward 289, 292
Prince of Wales 244
Princess and Curdie, The 53
Princess and the Goblin, The 53
Princess Diana 115, 195, 244, 251
Prisoner of Zenda, The 268
proportional representation 51, 52
Proust, Marcel 97
Punch 20fn.
Puritanism 119
Puzo, Mario 56, 64
Pyrates, The 168, 311

Quartered Safe Out Here 300, 311
Queen Mother 8, 9
Quentin Durward 283
Quinn, Anthony 35, 201

Rabelais, Francois 283
race relations 213–229
Radio City Music Hall 42
Rae, Douglas 174, 199, 237
Raft, George 245
"Rapid Reaction Force" 193
Rathbone, Basil 168
Ravel, Maurice 208
Reade, Charles 318
Redford, Robert 57
Redgrave, Michael 140
Red Beret, The 31
Red Circle School 126

Red Sonja 27, 60, 264, 268–271
Reed, Carol 56fn.
Reed, Oliver xxiii, 6, 10, 12, 13, 27, 33–38, 40, 41, 81–87, 210
Reeve, Christopher 57, 62
Reform Club 20fn.
Reith, Lord 295
Return of the Musketeers, The 11–16, 85, 87
Reyes, Ernie 269
Richard III 291
Rio Grande 307
Ritt, Martin 236
Robertson, Lord 108, 184
Robeson, Paul 225
Robin Hood 122
Robinson, Edward G. 245, 294
Rochester, comedian 225
Rodeo Drive 238
Roma 268
Roman Catholic Church 80, 112, 113, 116, 119
Rooney, Mickey 56, 173
Roosevelt, Theodore 113fn.
Roots 227
Rosenbloom, Maxie 57fn.
Royal Flash 11, 57, 83
Rubinstein, Helena 281
Ruman, Sig 75
Rumsfeld, Donald 20fn.
Runymede Trust 223
Russell, Lord John 117
Russell, Ken 83
Russia 88, 176–179, 193

Sabatini, Rafael 120, 293
Sabu 37, 225
Salkind, Alex xxiii, 3, 7, 11, 26, 27, 34, 35, 39, 57–79, 60, 63
Salkind, Bertha 9, 34
Salkind, Ilya 2, 6, 11, 34, 39, 42, 55, 57, 60, 63
Salome 140
Saltzkammergut 76, 307
Saltzman, Harry 244
Samarkand 176, 177, 179, 307
Sand Creek 118
Sanders, George 168
Sandhurst 189
Sanitsky, Larry 280
Savalas, Telly 198, 201
Savoy Operas, The 297

Sawyer, Tom 173
Schiller, Johann 75
Schopenhauer, Arthur 317
Schulberg, Budd 111
Schwarzenegger, Arnold xxii, 60, 264, 269, 270
Schygulla, Hannah 280
Scofield, Paul 173
Scotland xvi, 89, 120–129, 209, 215
Scotsman, The 251
Scott, C.P. 262
Scott, George C. 27, 35, 40, 41, 81, 87, 165, 201, 203
Scott, Walter 124, 250, 288, 318
Sea Hawk, The 208, 209
Second World War xvii, xix, 19
Selous, F.C. 284
Selznick, David O. 268
Separate Tables 162
Service, Robert 317
Shakespeare, William 122, 195, 196, 297, 318
Shankly, Bill 99–101, 121, 274 & fn.
Sharif, Omar 205, 206
Shaw, George Bernard 163, 249
Shaw, Robert 131, 133, 136–138, 141, 201
Sheridan, Ann 245
Shewing Up of Blanco Posnet, The 163
Siam Railway 315
Sierra Leone 92, 190
Sim, Alastair 83, 261
Sinatra, Frank 171
633 Squadron 201
Slaughter, Tod 32
slave trade 114, 117, 118, 227
Slim, William 21, 97, 98, 181fn.
Smith, Chris 109
Solzhenitsyn, Alexander 148
Somers, Will 31
Soo, Frank 224
Sopron 33, 36
Soylent Green 27
Spain 18
Spector, Maud 201
Spengler, Pierre 6, 11–14, 27, 34–36, 39, 55, 57, 63, 64, 86
Spielberg, Steven 182
Springer, Jerry 79
sport 272–277
Squire Western 122
Stalin, Josef 69, 92
Stamp, Terence 56

Stark, Graham 29, 31
Starlight Roof 313
Star Wars 138
Steel Bonnets, The 101, 307
Steiger, Rod 201
Stephenson, Pamela 86
Stevenson, R.L. 96, 288, 308
Stewart, Andy 314
Stewart, James 173
Stilwell, Joseph 236
Sting, The 138
Sting II 84
Straw, Jack 222, 224
Suez Canal 308
Suez campaign 21
Sullivan, John L. 57fn.
Sun, newspaper 255
Superman films xxiii, 3, 11, 55, 57–65, 131, 132
Surtees, R.S. 24
Swaffer, Hannen 254
Sweet Smell of Success 162
Sword of Honour 261fn.
Synthetic Men of Mars 97

Tahiti 308
Taipan 58, 84, 199–212, 235, 278, 283
Tale of Two Cities, A 268
Taliban 17, 20
Tanglewood Tales 293
Tarzan of the Apes 97fn., 297
Tashkent 176–179
Taylor, Robert 283
Tchaikowsky, Piotr 294
Teal, Ray 28
television xvii, 255–262, 274, 278
10 Rillington Place 27
1066 And All That 293
Thalberg, Irving 245
Thatcher, Margaret 45
Thief of Bagdad, The 37
Third Man, The 56fn.
Thirty Years War 75
Thomson, D.C. 249
Three Musketeers, The 1–11, 81, 166, 266
Time, magazine 8, 11
Times, The 250
Tito, Josip Broz 131
Todd, Bob 5, 83
Tolkien, J.R.R. 53, 54
Tom Brown's Schooldays 154fn., 298, 305
Tora! Tora! Tora! 27

Toronto 313
To Sir, With Love 201
Tourist Trophy (T.T.) xiii, xiv, 242, 243
Tracy, Spencer 245
Train, The 173
Trajan 194
Treasure of the Sierra Madre, The 305
Trinity College, Dublin 307
Trollope, Anthony 24, 250, 318
Twain, Mark 26, 27, 42
20,000 Leagues Under the Sea 27, 264, 265–268, 283
Twenty Years After 11–16
Tynan, Kenneth 258

Unknown Soldier, The 68
United States 18–22, 73, 194–197
unproduced screenplays 278–285
Unquiet Grave, The 318
Updike, John 177
Ustinov, Peter 205, 206

Valdez is Coming 173
Veidt, Conrad 75
Verne, Jules 266
Venice 308
Venice Boulevard 240
Vera Cruz 162
Vikings, The 27
Vuille, Georges-Alain 198, 199, 201, 203–208, 210, 211
Vuille, John 205, 206

Wagner, Richard 75
Wakibi 216
Walcott, Jersey Joe 57fn.
Wales 89
Walker, Tommy 274
Wallace, William 68
Ward, Lalla 35, 40–42
Ward, Simon 6, 9
Ward, Sophie 280
Washington, George 68
Waterloo Cup 24
Waugh, Evelyn 261fn.
Wayne, John 14, 184
Weathers, Carl 131, 136, 137
"Wee Wullie" 314–317
Weill, Kurt 75
Welch, Raquel 6, 9, 27, 34, 36, 37, 40, 41
Wessex, Countess of 251
West, Mae 188

West, Timothy 236
Western Mail 251
West Point 189
Westminster xvi, 44–49, 51, 52, 120, 123fn., 149 (see also Parliament)
Wheatley, Dennis 22
Wilder, Billy 3
Williams, Charlie 222
Wilson, Angus 310
Wilson, A.N. 74–79
Wilson, Michael G. 237, 238
Windward Passage 308
Wizard of Oz, The 101, 103
Wodehouse, P.G. 51, 97, 287, 310
Wolf of Kabul 97 & fn., 126
Women in Love 83
Wood, Natalie 182fn.
Wooll, Nigel 32, 36
World Cup 69
Worm Ouroboros, The 54
Wounded Knee 118

World Trade Centre 17
Worsthorne, Peregrine 248
Worth, B.J. 243, 244
Wyndham, Dennis 28

XIVth Army 22

Yates, Dornford 282
Yes, Minister 262
York, Archbishop of 106
York, Duke and Duchess of 15
York, Michael 6, 7, 9–12, 86, 168, 208
York, Susannah 63
Yorkshire Post 252
Yugoslavia 132, 133, 141

Zagreb 132, 141
Zhablak 130, 131, 133, 134
Zimbabwe 92
Zuleika Dobson 86
Zworykin, Alexander 262